A.U.A. Language Center
Thai Course

Book 2

Prepared by

J. Marvin Brown

Published by

Cornell University Southeast Asia Program

Ithaca, N.Y.

1992

© 1974 by Adrian S. Palmer

Originally published by the American University Alumni Association Language Center, Bangkok, Thailand.

Reprinted with permission by the Cornell Southeast Asia Program, 1992

ISBN 0-87727-507-6

The. A.U.A. Thai Course

Thai Book 1
Thai Book 2
Thai Book 3
Thai Book A (Small Talk)
Thai Book B (Getting Help)
Thai Book R (Reading)
Thai Book W (Writing)

A.U.A. Thai Course Books can be ordered from:

> SEAP Publications
> Cornell University
> East Hill Plaza
> Ithaca, NY 14850
>
> (607) 255-8038

Tapes are available for Books 1, 2, 3, A, and B. Order from:

> Tape Sales
> DMLL, 009 Morrill Hall
> Cornell University
> Ithaca, NY 14853
>
> (607) 255-7394

For a master set of A.U.A. tapes, institutions should order directly from A.U.A. Language Center, 179 Rajadamri Road, Bangkok 10330, Thailand.

PREFACE

This edition of Book 2 of the AUA Language Center Thai Course is a direct continuation of the 1967 edition of Book 1 and should be used only by students who have studied from that book; for without Book 1 as a background, even students whose vocabulary and sentence patterns go far beyond it might often find themselves in tonal difficulties. In any case a student of Book 2 should also have a copy of Book 1 for its introduction (which applies in every detail to Book 2 as well), its explanation of the transcription symbols used, and the numerous notes and drills in it that are referred to in Book 2.

The present edition is a major revision of the earlier course and has benefited greatly from suggestions made by the following teachers who taught that course: Matana Chutrakul, Niphapharn Chutrakul, Nitaya Amaraket, Saengthong Beokhaimook, Srim Nolrajsuwaj, Khomsan Hathaidharm, and Preecha Ratanodom. These same teachers also read the revision and made corrections, as did Peter J. Bee of the London School of Oriental and African Studies. But with all the changes that have been made, most of the dialogs are still basically those written several years ago by Churee Indaniyom. My own contributions have been made with the constant assistance of Preecha Ratanodom.

J. M. B.

Bangkok, Thailand

February 1968

CONTENTS

viii

ix

As in Book 1, the regular text appears on the right-hand pages only. On the pages facing from the left, all Thai words and sentences are printed in normal Thai writing.

บทที่ ๒๑

๒๑.๑ คำศัพท์

ว่าง	ก่อน
ไม	ยัง
ทำไม	หิว
ทาน	หิวข้าว
ประทาน	หิวน้ำ
รับ	เตือน
รับประทาน	ทัก
ด้วย	แก้ว
กัน	ขวด
ด้วยกัน	ช้อน
ลา	ถัง
เว	ชาม
เวลา	ป้า
เร็ว	โมง
เร็วเร็ว	ครึ่ง
ข้าว	
ทานข้าว	

LESSON 21

21.1 Vocabulary and expansions.

wâaŋ	To be unoccupied, free.
may thammay	Why.
thaan	Short for *rápprathaan*.
prathaan ráp rápprathaan	To eat (formal).
dûay	In addition.
kan	Each other.
dûaykan	Together.
laa wee weelaa	Time.
rew	Fast (expressing a fact).
rewrew	Fast (expressing a judgement).
khâaw	Rice. (With modifiers this refers to other grains as well.)
thaan khâaw	To eat a meal.
kɔ̀ɔn	Before. This word is often used like the English *first* (before me) or *separately* (before and hence without me).
yaŋ	Still, yet. This is used as the negative answer to a question with *lέεw*. The following example explains this. The parenthesized words are omitted.

khun thaan khâaw lέεw rɯ́ yaŋ (mây dây thaan).	You have eaten already or not yet?
thaan lέεw.	Already have eaten.
yaŋ (mây dây thaan).	Not yet.

hǐw	To hunger or thirst for.
hǐw khâaw	To be hungry.
hǐw náam	To be thirsty.
tɯan	To remind, warn.
thák	To greet, say hello to.
kε̂εw	Glass, a glass.
khùat	A bottle.
chɔ́ɔn	A spoon.
thǎŋ	A bucket.
chaam	A bowl.
pâa	Father or mother's older sister, aunt.
mooŋ	O'clock (daytime hours).
khrɯ̂ŋ	Half.

3

๒๑.๒ โครงสร้างของประโยค

คุณว่างไหม

โทรศัพท์ว่างไหม

ห้องน้ำว่างไหม

เวลาว่าง

ห้องว่าง

บ้านว่าง

โต๊ะว่าง

จะไปหาอะไรทาน

จะไปหาอะไรอ่าน

จะไปหาอะไรเช็ดโต๊ะ

ไปด้วยกัน

อยู่ด้วยกัน

ทำงานด้วยกัน

เรียนด้วยกัน

กลับบ้านด้วยกัน

พูดเร็วเร็ว

เดินช้าช้า

กินมากมาก

อยู่ใกล้ใกล้

เขียนดีดี

อยู่ว่างว่าง

เวลาทานข้าว

เวลาคุณพูดเร็วเร็ว

เวลาคุณทำงาน

เวลาเขาลืมเอาบุหรี่มา

เวลาฉันกินข้าว

คุณทานแล้วหรือ

เขาปิดไฟแล้วหรือ

คุณพบเขาแล้วหรือ

๒๑.๓ บทสนทนา

ก. คุณว่างไหม

    ข. ว่าง, ทำไม

ก. ผมจะไปหาอะไรทาน, ไปด้วยกันไหม

    ข. พูดช้าช้าหน่อยได้ไหม, เวลาคุณ
       พูดเร็วเร็วผมไม่เข้าใจเลย

ก. ไปทานข้าวกันไหม

    ข. ไม่ไป, เชิญคุณไปทานก่อน

ก. ทำไม, คุณทานแล้วหรือ

    ข. ยัง, แต่ผมไม่หิวเลย

21.2 Patterns.

khun wâaŋ máy.	Are you free?
thoorasàp wâaŋ máy.	Is the telephone free?
hôŋ náam wâaŋ máy.	Is the bathroom free?
weelaa wâaŋ.	Free time.
hôŋ wâaŋ.	An unoccupied room.
bâan wâaŋ.	A vacant house.
tóʔ wâaŋ.	A table that is not being used.
ca pay hǎa ʔaray thaan.	I'm going to go look for something to eat.
ca pay hǎa ʔaray ʔàan.	I'm going to go look for something to read.
ca pay hǎa ʔaray chét tóʔ.	I'm going to go look for something to wipe the table with.
pay dûaykan.	To go together.
yùu dûaykan.	To live together.
tham ŋaan dûaykan.	To work together.
rian dûaykan.	To study together.
klàp bâan dûaykan.	To go home together.
phûut rewrew.	To speak fast.
dəən chácháa.	To walk slowly.
kin mâkmâak.	To eat a lot.
yùu klâyklây.	To live nearby.
khǐan didii.	To write well.
yùu wâŋwâaŋ.	To have nothing to do.
weelaa thaan khâaw.	Eating time. When you're eating.
weelaa khun phûut rewrew.	When you speak fast.
weelaa khun tham ŋaan.	While you're working.
weelaa kháw luum ʔaw burìi maa.	When he forgets to bring cigarets.
weelaa chán kin khâaw.	While I'm eating.
khun thaan léɛw lǒə.	You've already eaten?
kháw pìt fay léɛw lǒə.	He has already turned the light off?
khun phóp kháw léɛw lǒə.	You've already seen him?

21.3 Dialog.

A. khun wâaŋ máy.	Are you free?
B. wâaŋ. thammay.	Yes. Why?
A. phǒm ca pay hǎa ʔaray thaan. pay dûaykan máy.	I'm going to go get something to eat. Do you want to come along?
B. phûut chácháa nɔ̀y, dây máy. weelaa khun phûut rewrew phǒm mây khâwcay ləəy.	Can you speak a little slower? When you speak fast I don't understand at all.
A. pay thaan khâaw kan máy.	Do you want to go eat with me?
B. mây pay. chəən khun pay thaan kɔ̀ɔn.	No. You'd better go without me.
A. thammay. khun thaan léɛw lǒə.	Why? Have you already eaten?
B. yaŋ. tɛ̀ɛ phǒm mây hǐw ləəy.	No. But I'm not hungry at all.

5

๒๑.๔ แบบฝึกหัดการฟังและการออกเสียงสูงต่ำ

ก.

ตกลง   ลูกหิน   แซนวิช   เปปซี่   ขอนแก่น

ข.

บอกแดงหรือเปล่า   เตือนแดงหรือเปล่า
    บอก   เตือน
แล้วทำไมไม่ได้บอกดำล่ะ   แล้วทำไมไม่ได้เตือนดำล่ะ
    บอก   เตือน

ถามแดงหรือเปล่า   ทักแดงหรือเปล่า
    ถาม   ทัก
แล้วทำไมไม่ได้ถามดำล่ะ   แล้วทำไมไม่ได้ทักดำล่ะ
    ถาม   ทัก

พูดกับแดงหรือเปล่า
    พูด
แล้วทำไมไม่ได้พูดกับดำล่ะ
    พูด

6

21.4 Tone identification and production.

a. Identify the tones and record the number of repetitions required for each.

To decide.	tokloŋ	....	....
A marble.	luuk hin	....	....
A sandwich.	sɛɛnwit	....	....
Pepsi Cola.	pepsii	....	....
Khon Kaen.	khɔɔnkɛn	....	....

b. Response drill. (Notice especially how stress affects the tones.)

bɔ̀ɔk dɛɛŋ rɯ́ plàaw, bɔ̀ɔk.	Did you tell Daeng? Yes.
lɛ́ɛw thammay mây dây bɔ̀ɔk dam lâ. *bɔ̀ɔk.*	Then why didn't you tell Dam? *I did.*
thǎam dɛɛŋ rɯ́ plàaw. thǎam.	Did you ask Daeng? Yes.
lɛ́ɛw thammay mây dây thǎam dam lâ. *thǎam.*	Then why didn't you ask Dam? *I did.*
phûut kàp dɛɛŋ rɯ́ plàaw. phûut.	Did you speak to Daeng? Yes.
lɛ́ɛw thammay mây dây phûut kàp dam lâ. *phûut.*	Then why didn't you speak to Dam? *I did.*
tɯan dɛɛŋ rɯ́ plàaw. tɯan.	Did you remind Daeng? Yes.
lɛ́ɛw thammay mây dây tɯan dam lâ. *tɯan.*	Then why didn't you remind Dam? *I did.*
thák dɛɛŋ rɯ́ plàaw. thák.	Did you say hello to Daeng? Yes.
lɛ́ɛw thammay mây dây thák dam lâ. *thák.*	Then why didn't you say hello to Dam? *I did.*

๒๑.๕ แบบฝึกหัดการสลับเสียงสูงต่ำ

ก.

น้ำสองขวด	(สี่)	น้ำพันถัง	(ชาม)
น้ำสี่ขวด	(แก้ว)	น้ำพันชาม	(ร้อย)
น้ำสี่แก้ว	(ห้า)	น้ำร้อยชาม	(ถัง)
น้ำห้าแก้ว	(ช้อน)	น้ำร้อยถัง	(ห้า)
น้ำห้าช้อน	(ร้อย)	น้ำห้าถัง	(หก)
น้ำร้อยช้อน	(แก้ว)	น้ำหกถัง	(ช้อน)
น้ำร้อยแก้ว	(ขวด)	น้ำหกช้อน	(สอง)
น้ำร้อยขวด	(ห้า)	น้ำสองช้อน	(แก้ว)
น้ำห้าขวด	(ชาม)	น้ำสองแก้ว	(พัน)
น้ำห้าชาม	(แปด)	น้ำพันแก้ว	(ขวด)
น้ำแปดชาม	(สาม)	น้ำพันขวด	(ช้อน)
น้ำสามชาม	(ถัง)	น้ำพันช้อน	
น้ำสามถัง	(พัน)		

๒๑.๖ แบบฝึกหัดการออกเสียงสระและพยัญชนะ

ก.

หัด	หัก	หัน	คั้น	มั่น
หาด	หาก	หาน	ค้าน	ม่าน

ข.

ผ้าพี่	(ป้า)	บ้านพี่	(ปืน)
ผ้าป้า	(บิ๋ม)	ปืนพี่	(ป้า)
ผ้าบิ๋ม	(บ้าน)	ปืนป้า	(บิ๋ม)
บ้านบิ๋ม	(ป้า)	ปืนบิ๋ม	
บ้านป้า	(พี่)		

8

21.5 Tone manipulation.

a. Substitution drill.

náam sɔ̌ɔŋ khùat. (sìi)	Two bottles of water. (4)
náam sìi khùat. (kɛ̂ɛw)	Four bottles of water. (glass)
náam sìi kɛ̂ɛw. (hâa)	Four glasses of water. (5)
náam hâa kɛ̂ɛw. (chɔ́ɔn)	Five glasses of water. (spoon)
náam hâa chɔ́ɔn. (rɔ́ɔy)	Five spoonfuls of water. (100)
náam rɔ́ɔy chɔ́ɔn. (kɛ̂ɛw)	A hundred spoonfuls of water. (glass)
náam rɔ́ɔy kɛ̂ɛw. (khùat)	A hundred glasses of water. (bottle)
náam rɔ́ɔy khùat. (hâa)	A hundred bottles of water. (5)
náam hâa khùat. (chaam)	Five bottles of water. (bowl)
náam hâa chaam. (pɛ̀ɛt)	Five bowls of water. (8)
náam pɛ̀ɛt chaam. (sǎam)	Eight bowls of water. (3)
náam sǎam chaam. (thǎŋ)	Three bowls of water. (bucket)
náam sǎam thǎŋ. (phan)	Three buckets of water. (1,000)
náam phan thǎŋ. (chaam)	A thousand buckets of water. (bowl)
náam phan chaam. (rɔ́ɔy)	A thousand bowls of water. (100)
náam rɔ́ɔy chaam. (thǎŋ)	A hundred bowls of water. (bucket)
náam rɔ́ɔy thǎŋ. (hâa)	A hundred buckets of water. (5)
náam hâa thǎŋ. (hòk)	Five buckets of water. (6)
náam hòk thǎŋ. (chɔ́ɔn)	Six buckets of water. (spoon)
náam hòk chɔ́ɔn. (sɔ̌ɔŋ)	Six spoonfuls of water. (2)
náam sɔ̌ɔŋ chɔ́ɔn. (kɛ̂ɛw)	Two spoonfuls of water. (glass)
náam sɔ̌ɔŋ kɛ̂ɛw. (phan)	Two glasses of water. (1,000)
náam phan kɛ̂ɛw. (khùat)	A thousand glasses of water. (bottle)
náam phan khùat. (chɔ́ɔn)	A thousand bottles of water. (spoon)
náam phan chɔ́ɔn.	A thousand spoonfuls of water.

21.6 Vowel and consonant drills.

a. a-aa contrast drill.

hàt	hàk	hǎn	khán	mân
hàat	hàak	hǎan	kháan	mâan

b. Substitution drill. (ph, p, and b).

phâa phǐi. (pâa)	Older One's cloth. (Auntie)
phâa pâa. (bǐm)	Auntie's cloth. (Bim)
phâa bǐm. (bâan)	Bim's cloth. (house)
bâan bǐm. (pâa)	Bim's house. (Auntie)
bâan pâa. (phǐi)	Auntie's house. (Older One)
bâan phǐi. (pʉʉn)	Older One's house. (gun)
pʉʉn phǐi. (pâa)	Older One's gun. (Auntie)
pʉʉn pâa. (bǐm)	Auntie's gun. (Bim)
pʉʉn bǐm.	Bim's gun.

9

๒๑.๗ แบบฝึกหัดไวยากรณ์

ก.

เชิญคุณไปทานก่อน
(ทำงาน)

เชิญคุณไปทำงานก่อน
(เรียน)

เชิญคุณไปเรียนก่อน
(พูดกับคุณยัง)

เชิญคุณไปพูดกับคุณยังก่อน
(หาคุณประสงค์)

เชิญคุณไปหาคุณประสงค์ก่อน

ข.

ทำไม, คุณไม่ทานหรือ
(ทำงาน)

ทำไม, คุณไม่ทำงานหรือ
(เรียน)

ทำไม, คุณไม่เรียนหรือ
(พูดกับเขา)

ทำไม, คุณไม่พูดกับเขาหรือ
(ไปหาเขา)

ทำไม, คุณไม่ไปหาเขาหรือ

ค.

เชิญคุณไปทานก่อน
    ทำไม, คุณไม่ทานหรือ

เชิญคุณไปทำงานก่อน
    ทำไม, คุณไม่ทำงานหรือ

เชิญคุณไปหาคุณประสงค์ก่อน
    ทำไม, คุณไม่ไปหาเขาหรือ

เชิญคุณไปพูดกับคุณยังก่อน
    ทำไม, คุณไม่ไปพูดกับเขาหรือ

21.7 Grammar drills.

a. Substitution drill.

chəən khun pay thaan kɔ̀ɔn.	Please go and eat without me.
(tham ŋaan)	(work)
chəən khun pay tham ŋaan kɔ̀ɔn.	Please go on to work without me.
(rian)	(study)
chəən khun pay rian kɔ̀ɔn.	Please go study without me.
(phûut ka khun yaŋ)	(speak to Mr. Young)
chəən khun pay phûut ka khun yaŋ kɔ̀ɔn.	Please go speak to Mr. Young without me.
(hǎa khun prasǒŋ)	(call on Khun Prasong)
chəən khun pay hǎa khun prasǒŋ kɔ̀ɔn.	Please go call on Khun Prasong without me.

b. Substitution drill.

thammay. khun mây thaan lɔ̌ə.	Why? Aren't you going to eat?
(tham ŋaan)	(work)
thammay. khun mây thaɪn ŋaan lɔ̌ə.	Why? Aren't you going to work?
(rian)	(study)
thammay. khun mây rian lɔ̌ə.	Why? Aren't you going to study?
(phûut ka kháw)	(talk to him)
thammay. khun mây phûut ka kháw lɔ̌ə.	Why? Aren't you going to talk to him?
(pay hǎa kháw)	(go call on him)
thammay. khun mây pay hǎa kháw lɔ̌ə.	Why? Aren't you going to go call on him?

c. Response drill.

chəən khun pay thaan kɔ̀ɔn. thammay. khun mây thaan lɔ̌ə.	Please go eat without me. Why? Aren't you going to eat?
chəən khun pay tham ŋaan kɔ̀ɔn. thammay. khun mây tham ŋaan lɔ̌ə.	Please go on to work without me. Why? Aren't you going to work?
chəən khun pay hǎa khun prasǒŋ kɔ̀ɔn. thammay. khun mây pay hǎa kháw lɔ̌ə.	Please go call on Khun Prasong without me. Why? Aren't you going to call on him?
chəən khun pay phûut ka khun yaŋ kɔ̀ɔn. thammay. khun mây pay phûut ka kháw lɔ̌ə.	Please go speak to Mr. Young without me. Why? Aren't you going to go speak to him?

11

ง.

ฉันจะไปทานข้าว, ไปด้วยกันไหม
   ไม่ไป, เชิญคุณไปทานก่อน

ฉันจะไปเรียนภาษาไทย, ไปด้วยกันไหม
   ไม่ไป, เชิญคุณไปเรียนก่อน

ฉันจะไปพูดกับคุณยัง, ไปด้วยกันไหม
   ไม่ไป, เชิญคุณไปพูดกับเขาก่อน

ฉันจะไปหาคุณประสงค์, ไปด้วยกันไหม
   ไม่ไป, เชิญคุณไปหาเขาก่อน

จ.

คุณประสงค์ไปแล้วหรือยัง
   ไปแล้ว
แล้วคุณสวัสดิ์ล่ะ, ไปแล้วหรือยัง
   ยัง

พบแดงแล้วหรือยัง
   พบแล้ว
แล้วดำล่ะ, พบเขาแล้วหรือยัง
   ยัง

สั่งเบียร์แล้วหรือยัง
   สั่งแล้ว
แล้วอาหารล่ะ, สั่งแล้วหรือยัง
   ยัง

๒๑.๘ เวลา

บ่ายโมง	(บ่าย) สี่โมง
บ่ายโมงครึ่ง	สี่โมง (เย็น)
(บ่าย) สองโมง	ห้าโมง (เย็น)
(บ่าย) สองโมงครึ่ง	ห้าโมงครึ่ง (ตอนเย็น)
(บ่าย) สามโมง	หกโมง (เย็น)

d. Response drill.

chán ca pay thaan khâaw.	I'm going to go eat.
pay dûaykan máy.	Want to come along?
mây pay.	No.
chəən khun pay thaan kɔɔn.	You go eat without me.
chán ca pay rian phasǎa thay.	I'm going to go study Thai.
pay dûaykan máy.	Want to come along?
mây pay.	No.
chəən khun pay rian kɔɔn.	You go study without me.
chán ca pay phûut ka khun yaŋ.	I'm going to go talk to Mr. Young.
pay dûaykan máy.	Want to come along?
mây pay.	No.
chəən khun pay phûut ka kháw kɔɔn.	You go talk to him without me.
chán ca pay hǎa khun prasǒŋ.	I'm going to go see Khun Prasong.
pay dûaykan máy.	Want to come along?
mây pay.	No.
chəən khun pay hǎa kháw kɔɔn.	You go see him without me.

e. Response drill.

khun prasǒŋ pay lɛ́ɛw rú yaŋ.	Has Prasong gone yet?
pay lɛ́ɛw.	Yes.
lɛ́ɛw khun sawàt lâ. pay lɛ́ɛw rú yaŋ.	And Sawat? Has he gone yet?
yaŋ.	No.
phóp dɛɛŋ lɛ́ɛw rú yaŋ.	Have you see Daeng yet?
phóp lɛ́ɛw.	Yes.
lɛ́ɛw dam lâ. phóp kháw lɛ́ɛw rú yaŋ.	And Dam? Have you seen him yet?
yaŋ.	No.
sàŋ bia lɛ́ɛw rú yaŋ.	Have you ordered the beer yet?
sàŋ lɛ́ɛw.	Yes.
lɛ́ɛw ʔaahǎan lâ. sàŋ lɛ́ɛw rú yaŋ.	And the food? Have you ordered it yet?
yaŋ.	No.

21.8 Time of day.

1:00 p.m.	bàay mooŋ	4:00 p.m.	(bàay) sìi mooŋ
1:30 p.m.	bàay mooŋ khrɯ̂ŋ	4:00 p.m.	sìi mooŋ (yen)
2:00 p.m.	(bàay) sɔ̌ɔŋ mooŋ	5:00 p.m.	hâa mooŋ (yen)
2:30 p.m.	(bàay) sɔ̌ɔŋ mooŋ khrɯ̂ŋ	5:30 p.m.	hâa mooŋ khrɯ̂ŋ (tɔɔn yen)
3:00 p.m.	(bàay) sǎam mooŋ	6:00 p.m.	hòk mooŋ (yen)

Practice reading the following times without the parenthesized parts. Try to get the time under 30 seconds.

6:00 p.m.	3:30 p.m.	6:30 p.m.	1:00 p.m.	4:00 p.m.
1:30 p.m.	2:00 p.m.	5:00 p.m.	2:30 p.m.	3:00 p.m.
4:00 p.m.	4:30 p.m.	5:30 p.m.	5:00 p.m.	6:30 p.m.
5:00 p.m.	1:00 p.m.	1:30 p.m.	3:30 p.m.	1:30 p.m.
2:30 p.m.	3:00 p.m.	4:30 p.m.	5:30 p.m.	6:00 p.m.

21.9 Conversation.

The teacher should read the narrative of lesson 5 (Book 1) to the class and ask questions about it. The sentences following the narrative can be used as a source of ideas for the questions.

๒๑.๑๐ การเขียน

มือ	มืด	แสน	แสด	แดง	แดค
	แปน		แขน		มืด
	แปด		แขก		มือ
	มาง		ปืน		ถือ
	มาก		ปืด		จือ
	สือ		ลืม		จืด
	สืบ		ลืบ		ชืด
	บอง		หมาก		ผืด
	บอก		มาก		ผือ
	ขืม		ขอบ		คือ
	ขืด		กอบ		คืบ

14

21.10 Writing.

มือ	มืด	แสน	แสด	แดง	แดด
mɰɰ	mɰ̂ɰt	sɛ̌ɛn	sɛ̀ɛt	dɛɛŋ	dɛ̀ɛt
Hand.	Dark.	100,000.	Orange.	Red.	Sunshine.

When ɰɰ is not followed by a consonant, the symbol for the vowel ɔɔ must be added.

Syllables that end abruptly (p, t, k, or ʔ) have different tones when written with no tonal marker from those that don't (m, n, ŋ, y, w, or no final consonant). The tone with low initials is falling. That with mid and high initials is low. The names of the three classes (low, mid, high) have no connection with the tones. They are merely meaningless names.

แปน	pɛɛn	แขน	*khɛ̌ɛn	มืด	*mɰ̂ɰt
แปด	*pɛ̀ɛt	แขก	khɛ̀ɛk	มือ	*mɰɰ
มาง	maaŋ	บืน	*pɰɰn	ถือ	thɰ̌ɰ
มาก	*mâak	บืด	pɰ̀ɰt	จือ	cɰɰ
สือ	sɰ̌ɰ	ลืม	*lɰɰm	จืด	cɰ̀ɰt
สืบ	sɰ̀ɰp	ลืบ	lɰ̀ɰp	ชืด	chɰ̂ɰt
บอง	bɔɔŋ	หมาก	màak	ผืด	fɰ̀ɰt
บอก	*bɔ̀ɔk	มาก	*mâak	ผือ	fɰ̌ɰ
ยืม	*yɰɰm	ขอบ	khɔ̀ɔp	คือ	khɰɰ
ยืด	yɰ̀ɰt	คอบ	khɔ̂ɔp	คืบ	khɰ̂ɰp

15

บทที่ ๒๒

๒๒.๑ คำศัพท์

ไปกัน	ผัด
พูดกัน	ข้าวผัด
	แล้วก็
เหมือน	มะนาว
เหมือนกัน	น้ำมะนาว
เหมือนกัน	
	เที่ยว
เสร็จ	ไปเที่ยว
เสร็จแล้ว	
ทำเสร็จแล้ว	ของ
	ซื้อของ
ยังงั้น	
ถ้ายังงั้น	ทราย
	เม็ด
รอ	
	เส้น
ตกลง	
	แผ่น
เดี๋ยว	
	ใบ
ตาม	
	ลูก
จาน	หิน
จานหนึ่ง	ลูกหิน

LESSON 22

22.1 Vocabulary and expansions.

pay kan	To go together.
phûut kan	To speak to each other.
mŭan	To be similar.
mŭankan	Likewise.
múankan	Likewise.
sèt	To finish, be finished.
sèt léɛw	To have finished.
tham sèt léɛw	To have finished doing it.
yaŋŋán	Like that.
thâa yaŋŋán	In that case.
rɔɔ	To wait for.
tòkloŋ	To come to an agreement, decide.
dĭaw	In a moment. This is especially convenient in delayed imperatives where it implies 'Go ahead and finish what you are doing, but as soon as you are free ......'.
taam	To follow.
caan	A plate.
caan nɯŋ	A plate of something.
phàt	To stir fry.
khâaw phàt	Fried rice.
léɛw kɔ̂	And, and then.
manaaw	Limes.
nám manaaw	Limeade.
thîaw	To go from place to place.
pay thîaw	To go out. To go somewhere for pleasure as opposed to business.
khɔ̌ɔŋ	Things.
sɯ́ɯ khɔ̌ɔŋ	To buy things.
saay	Sand.
mét	A seed. A 'kernel' of something. A classifier* for 'kernel' like things.
sên	A line. A 'string' of something. A classifier for 'string' like things.
phɛ̀n	A 'sheet' of something. A classifier for 'sheet' like things.
bay	A leaf. A classifier for containers (dishes, glasses, etc.).
lûuk	A 'ball' of something. A classifier for 'ball' like things.
hĭn	Rock, stone.
lûuk hĭn	A marble.

๒๒.๒ โครงสร้างของประโยค

ไปกินข้าวกันไหม

ไปเที่ยวกันไหม

ไปซื้อของกันไหม

ฉันหิวแล้วเหมือนกัน

ฉันว่างเหมือนกัน

ฉันไม่เข้าใจเหมือนกัน

ฉันอยู่ที่ซอยหกเหมือนกัน

ทำงานไม่เสร็จ

กินข้าวไม่เสร็จ

ทำงานไม่ได้

ไปเที่ยวไม่ได้

ยังทำงานไม่เสร็จ

ยังไม่ว่าง

ยังไม่หิว

ยังไม่ได้ถามเขา

*Classifiers. There are three different ways of counting things in English.

	Unit	Substance
1.	a day	(of time)
2.	a bottle	of beer
3.	a (rod	of) pencil

In the first type, the unit implies the 'substance' (a day doesn't measure anything besides time), and the substance isn't mentioned.

In the second type, both unit and substance must be mentioned since, for example, a bottle measures things other than beer, and beer can come in units other than bottles.

In the third type, the word for the substance implies the unit. Iron can come in sheets, rods, balls, etc., but pencils only in 'rods'. The unit isn't mentioned. -There are, however, a few words in English that are like type three in meaning but type two in form: a head of lettuce, a head of cattle, a sheet of paper, a stick of dynamite, a pair of scissors.

Thai has only types one and two. When counting things in Thai, the unit (classifier) must always be mentioned: 2 rods of pencil, 2 rolls of cigarette, 2 bodies of dog.

The following dialogue might help illustrate the function of classifiers. An English speaker ends up grasping for a classifier that doesn't exist.

> How much is lettuce?
>> Five dollars a case.
> How much a head?
>> We don't sell them by the head.
> And how much are cigarettes?
>> Thirty cents a pack.
> And how much apiece?
>> We don't sell them by the (?).

22.2 Patterns.

pay kin khâaw kan máy.	Shall' we go eat together?
pay thîaw kan máy.	Shall we go out (on the town) together?
pay súu khɔ̌ɔŋ kan máy.	Shall we go shopping together?
chán hǐw lɛ́ɛw mɯ̆ankan.	I'm hungry, too.
chán wâaŋ mɯ̆ankan.	I'm free, too.
chán mây khâwcay mɯ̆ankan.	I don't understand, either.
chán yùu thîi sɔ̌ɔy hòk mɯ̆ankan.	I live on Soi 6, too.
tham ŋaan mây sèt.	I haven't finished working.
kin khâaw mây sèt.	I haven't finished eating.
tham ŋaan mây dây.	I can't work.
pay thîaw mây dây.	I can't go out.
yaŋ tham ŋaan mây sèt.	I haven't finished working yet.
yaŋ mây wâaŋ.	I'm not free yet.
yaŋ mây hǐw.	I'm not hungry yet.
yaŋ mây dây thǎam kháw.	I haven't asked him yet.

(More.)   19

เดี๋ยวฉันจะตามไป   ข้าวจานหนึ่ง

เดี๋ยวเขาจะมา   ข้าวผัดจานหนึ่ง

เดี๋ยวคุณจะพบเขา   น้ำแก้วหนึ่ง

เดี๋ยวไปเที่ยวกันนะ   น้ำมะนาวแก้วหนึ่ง

เดี๋ยวเลี้ยวซ้ายนะ

เดี๋ยวพูดกันนะ   ข้าวผัดหนึ่งจาน

เดี๋ยวเอากาแฟมานะ   ข้าวผัดสองจาน

                        ข้าวผัดห้าจาน

ฉันจะสั่งให้

ฉันจะทำให้

ฉันจะเปิดประตูให้

ฉันจะส่งให้

๒๒.๓ บทสนทนา

ก. ผมหิวแล้ว, ไปกินข้าวกันไหม

    ข. ผมหิวแล้วเหมือนกัน, แต่ยังทำงานไม่เสร็จ

ก. ถ้ายังงั้น, ผมจะไปรอที่ร้านอาหารนะ

    ข. ตกลง, เดี๋ยวผมจะตามไป

ก. คุณจะกินอะไรบ้าง, ผมจะสั่งให้

    ข. เอาข้าวผัดจานหนึ่ง, แล้วก็น้ำมะนาวแก้วหนึ่ง

๒๒.๔ แบบฝึกหัดการฟังและการออกเสียงสูงต่ำ

ก.   เนยแข็ง   เปรียบเทียบ   น้อยหน่า   ต้นไม้   สาธร

dǐaw chán ca taam pay.	I'll follow you in a moment.
dǐaw kháw ca maa.	He'll come shortly.
dǐaw khun ca phóp kháw.	You'll meet him in a few minutes.
dǐaw pay thîaw kan ná.	Let's go out in a little while.
dǐaw líaw sáay ná.	Turn left (at the next corner).
dǐaw phûut kan ná.	Let's have a talk when we get a chance.
dǐaw ʔaw kaafɛɛ maa ná.	Bring me some coffee when you get around to it.
chán ca sàŋ hây.	I'll order for you.
chán ca tham hây.	I'll do it for you.
chán ca pə̀ət pratuu hây.	I'll open the gate for you.
chán ca sòŋ hây.	I'll send it to you.
khâaw caan nɯŋ.	A plate of rice.
khâaw phàt caan nɯŋ.	A plate of fried rice.
náam kɛ̂ɛw nɯŋ.	A glass of water.
nám manaaw kɛ̂ɛw nɯŋ.	A glass of limeade.
khâaw phàt nɯ̀ŋ caan.	One plate of fried rice.
khâaw phàt sɔ̌ɔŋ caan.	Two plates of fried rice.
khâaw phàt hâa caan.	Five plates of fried rice.

22.3 Dialog.

A. phǒm hǐw lɛ́ɛw.	I'm hungry.
pay kin khâaw kan máy.	Shall we go eat (together)?
B. phǒm hǐw lɛ́ɛw mɯ̌ankan.	I'm hungry, too.
tɛ̀ɛ yaŋ tham ŋaan mây sèt.	But I haven't finished work yet.
A. thâa yaŋŋán	In that case,
phǒm ca pay rɔɔ thîi ráan ʔaahǎan ná.	I'll go wait for you at the restaurant.
B. tòkloŋ.	Okay.
dǐaw phǒm ca taam pay.	I'll join you in a few minutes.
A. khun ca kin ʔaray bâaŋ.	What do you want to eat?
phǒm ca sàŋ hây.	I'll order for you.
B. ʔaw khâaw phàt caan nɯŋ,	I'll have a plate of fried rice,
lɛ́ɛw kɔ̂ nám manaaw kɛ̂ɛw nɯŋ.	and a glass of limeade.

22.4 Tone identification and production.

a. Identify the tones and record the number of repetitions required for each.

Cheese.	nəəy khɛŋ	....	....
To compare.	priap thiap	....	....
Custard apple.	nɔɔynaa	....	....
Trees.	ton maay	....	....
Sathorn.	saathɔɔn	....	....

21

ข.

ดีไหม	ร้อนไหม
ดี	ร้อน
ไม่ดีหรือ	ไม่ร้อนหรือ
ดี, ทำไมจะไม่ดี	ร้อน, ทำไมจะไม่ร้อน

อยู่ไหม	สวยไหม
อยู่	สวย
ไม่อยู่หรือ	ไม่สวยหรือ
อยู่, ทำไมจะไม่อยู่	สวย, ทำไมจะไม่สวย

ได้ไหม
ได้
ไม่ได้หรือ
ได้, ทำไมจะไม่ได้

๒๒.๕ แบบฝึกหัดการสลับเสียงสูงต่ำ

ก.

เห็นทรายกี่เม็ด	เห็นแก้วกี่ใบ
เห็นทรายหกเม็ด	เห็นแก้วหกใบ

เห็นผมกี่เส้น	เห็นลูกหินกี่ลูก
เห็นผมหกเส้น	เห็นลูกหินหกลูก

เห็นกระดาษกี่แผ่น
เห็นกระดาษหกแผ่น

b.   Response drill.   (Notice especially how stress affects the tones.)

dii máy.	Is it good?
dii.	Yes.
mây dii lšə.	It's no good, huh?
dii.	Sure it is.
thammay ca mây dii.	What makes you think it isn't?
yùu máy.	Is he here?
yùu.	Yes.
mây yùu lšə.	He's not here, huh?
yùu.	Sure he is.
thammay ca mây yùu.	What makes you think he isn't?
dây máy.	Can you do it?
dây.	Yes.
mây dây lšə.	You can't do it, huh?
dây.	Sure I can.
thammay ca mây dây.	What makes you think I can't?
róɔn máy.	Is it hot?
róɔn.	Yes.
mây róɔn lšə.	It's not hot, huh?
róɔn.	Sure it is.
thammay ca mây róɔn.	What makes you think it isn't?
sǔay máy.	Is she pretty?
sǔay.	Yes.
mây sǔay lšə.	She's not pretty, huh?
sǔay.	Sure she is.
thammay ca mây sǔay.	What makes you think she isn't?

22.5   Tone manipulation.

a.   Response drill.

hěn saay kìi mét.	How many grains of sand do you see?
hěn saay hòk mét.	I see six grains of sand.
hěn phǒm kìi sên.	How many hairs do you see?
hěn phǒm hòk sên.	I see six hairs.
hěn kradàat kìi phὲn.	How many sheets of paper do you see?
hěn kradàat hòk phὲn	I see six sheets of paper.
hěn kɛ̂ɛw kìi bay.	How many glasses do you see?
hěn kɛ̂ɛw hòk bay.	I see six glasses.
hěn lûuk hǐn kìi lûuk.	How many marbles do you see?
hěn lûuk hǐn hòk lûuk.	I see six marbles.

b.   Response drill.   Do the above drill with   the answer 'two'.

c.   Response drill.   Do the above drill with the   answer 'five'.

๒๒.๖ แบบฝึกหัดการออกเสียงสระและพยัญชนะ

ก.

ใส   สาย   เขา   ขาว

ข.

ถุงทอม	(ต้อย)	ด้ายแดง	(ต้อย)	เตียงทอม	(ต้อย)
ถุงต้อย	(แดง)	ด้ายต้อย	(ทอม)	เตียงต้อย	(แดง)
ถุงแดง	(ด้าย)	ด้ายทอม	(เตียง)	เตียงแดง	

๒๒.๗ แบบฝึกหัดไวยากรณ์

ก.	ข.
หิวแล้ว (รู้จัก)	ยังทำงานไม่เสร็จ (กินข้าว)
รู้จักแล้ว (เข้าใจ)	ยังกินข้าวไม่เสร็จ (พูดโทรศัพท์)
เข้าใจแล้ว (เรียน)	ยังพูดโทรศัพท์ไม่เสร็จ (เรียนภาษาไทย)
เรียนแล้ว (พูด)	ยังเรียนภาษาไทยไม่เสร็จ (พูดกับเขา)
พูดแล้ว (ลืม)	ยังพูดกับเขาไม่เสร็จ (ซื้อของ)
ลืมแล้ว (ไป)	ยังซื้อของไม่เสร็จ
ไปแล้ว	

22.6 Vowel and consonant drills.

a. ay-aay and aw-aaw contrast drills.

    săy   khăw

    săay   khăaw

b. Substitution drill.

thŭŋ thɔɔm. (tôy)	Tom's sack. (Toy)
thŭŋ tôy. (dɛɛŋ)	Toy's sack. (Daeng)
thŭŋ dɛɛŋ. (dâay)	Daeng's sack. (thread)
dâay dɛɛŋ. (tôy)	Daeng's thread. (Toy)
dâay tôy. (thɔɔm)	Toy's thread. (Tom)
dâay thɔɔm. (tiaŋ)	Tom's thread. (bed)
tiaŋ thɔɔm. (tôy)	Tom's bed. (Toy)
tiaŋ tôy. (dɛɛŋ)	Toy's bed. (Daeng)
tiaŋ dɛɛŋ.	Daeng's bed.

22.7 Grammar drills.

a. Substitution drill.

hĭw léɛw. (rúucàk)	I'm already hungry. (know)
rúucàk léɛw. (khâwcay)	I already know him. (understand)
khâwcay léɛw. (rian)	I already understand. (study)
rian léɛw. (phûut)	I've already studied it. (speak)
phûut léɛw. (lʉʉm)	I've already spoken. (forget)
lʉʉm léɛw. (pay)	I've already forgotten. (go)
pay léɛw.	He's gone.

b. Substitution drill.

yaŋ tham ŋaan mây sèt. (kin khâaw)	I haven't finished work yet. (eat)
yaŋ kin khâaw mây sèt. (phûut thoorasàp)	I haven't finished eating yet. (phone)
yaŋ phûut thoorasàp mây sèt. (rian phasăa thay)	I haven't finished phoning yet. (study Thai)
yaŋ rian phasăa thay mây sèt. (phûut kàp kháw)	I haven't finished studying Thai yet. (speak to him)
yaŋ phûut kàp kháw mây sèt. (sʉʉ khɔ̌ɔŋ)	I haven't finished speaking to him yet. (buy things)
yaŋ sʉʉ khɔ̌ɔŋ mây sèt.	I haven't finished shopping yet.

25

ก.

ไปกินข้าวกันไหม (ทำงาน)
   ไม่ไป, ยังทำงานไม่เสร็จ

ไปทำงานกันไหม (กินข้าว)
   ไม่ไป, ยังกินข้าวไม่เสร็จ

ไปเรียนภาษาไทยกันไหม (พูดกับเขา)
   ไม่ไป, ยังพูดกับเขาไม่เสร็จ

ไปพูดกับเขากันไหม (เรียนภาษาไทย)
   ไม่ไป, ยังเรียนภาษาไทยไม่เสร็จ

ไปซื้อของกันไหม (พูดโทรศัพท์)
   ไม่ไป, ยังพูดโทรศัพท์ไม่เสร็จ

ง.

จะไปรอที่ร้านอาหาร (สถานทูต)

จะไปรอที่สถานทูต (บ้านคุณยัง)

จะไปรอที่บ้านคุณยัง (โรงเรียน)

จะไปรอที่โรงเรียน (ที่ทำงาน)

จะไปรอที่ที่ทำงาน (โรงแรมเอราวัณ)

จะไปรอที่โรงแรมเอราวัณ

จ.

จะกินอะไรบ้าง (ทำ)

จะทำอะไรบ้าง (พูด)

จะพูดอะไรบ้าง (ขอ)

จะขออะไรบ้าง (ถาม)

จะถามอะไรบ้าง (ช่วย)

จะช่วยอะไรบ้าง (ซื้อ)

จะซื้ออะไรบ้าง

c. Response drill.

pay kin khâaw kan máy.
(tham ŋaan)
    mây pay.
    yaŋ tham ŋaan mây sèt.

    Shall we go eat?
    (work)
        No.
        I haven't finished work yet.

pay tham ŋaan kan máy.
(kin khâaw)
    mây pay.
    yaŋ kin khâaw mây sèt.

    Shall we go to work?
    (eat)
        No.
        I haven't finished eating yet.

pay rian phasǎa thay kan máy.
(phûut kàp kháw)
    mây pay.
    yaŋ phûut kàp kháw mây sèt.

    Shall we go study Thai?
    (talk to him)
        No.
        I haven't finished talking to him yet.

pay phûut kàp kháw kan máy.
(rian phasǎa thay)
    mây pay.
    yaŋ rian phasǎa thay mây sèt.

    Shall we go talk to him?
    (study Thai)
        No.
        I haven't finished studying Thai yet.

pay súu khǒoŋ kan máy.
(phûut thoorasàp)
    mây pay.
    yaŋ phûut thoorasàp mây sèt.

    Shall we go shopping?
    (make a phone call)
        No.
        I haven't finished phoning yet.

d. Substitution drill.

ca pay rɔɔ thîi ráan ʔaahǎan.
(sathǎanthûut)

    I'll go wait at the restaurant.
    (Embassy)

ca pay rɔɔ thîi sathǎanthûut.
(bâan khun yaŋ)

    I'll go wait at the Embassy.
    (Mr. Young's house)

ca pay rɔɔ thîi bâan khun yaŋ.
(rooŋrian)

    I'll go wait at Mr. Young's house.
    (school)

ca pay rɔɔ thîi rooŋrian.
(thîi tham ŋaan)

    I'll go wait at the school.
    (the office)

ca pay rɔɔ thîi thîi tham ŋaan.
(rooŋrɛɛm ʔeerawan)

    I'll go wait at the office.
    (the Erawan Hotel)

ca pay rɔɔ thîi rooŋrɛɛm ʔeerawan.

    I'll go wait at the Erawan Hotel.

e. Substitution drill.

ca kin ʔaray bâaŋ. (tham)
ca tham ʔaray bâaŋ. (phûut)
ca phûut ʔaray bâaŋ. (khǒo)
ca khǒo ʔaray bâaŋ. (thǎam)
ca thǎam ʔaray bâaŋ. (chûay)
ca chûay ʔaray bâaŋ. (súu)
ca súu ʔaray bâaŋ.

    What all do you want to eat? (do)
    What are you going to do? (say)
    What are you going to say? (ask for)
    What are you going to ask for? (ask)
    What are you going to ask? (help)
    What are you going to help me do? (buy)
    What are you going to buy?

๒๒.๘ เวลา

หกโมง (เช้า)   สามโมง (เช้า)
หกโมงครึ่ง (ตอนเช้า)   สามโมงสิบนาที (ตอนเช้า)
โมงเช้า   สี่โมง (เช้า)
โมงสิบห้านาที (ตอนเช้า)   ห้าโมง (เช้า)
สองโมง (เช้า)   เที่ยง
สองโมงยี่สิบนาที (ตอนเช้า)   เที่ยงครึ่ง

๒๒.๑๐ การเขียน

เหลอ   เลย   เดิน   เกิด

22.8 Time of day.

6:00 a.m.	hòk mooŋ (cháaw)
6:30 a.m.	hòk mooŋ khrɵ̂ŋ (tɔɔn cháaw)
7:00 a.m.	mooŋ cháaw
7:15 a.m.	mooŋ sìp hâa naathii (tɔɔn cháaw)
8:00 a.m.	sɔ̌ɔŋ mooŋ (cháaw)
8:20 a.m.	sɔ̌ɔŋ mooŋ yîi sìp naathii (tɔɔn cháaw)
9:00 a.m.	sǎam mooŋ (cháaw)
9:10 a.m.	sǎam mooŋ sìp naathii (tɔɔn cháaw)
10:00 a.m.	sìi mooŋ (cháaw)
11:00 a.m.	hâa mooŋ (cháaw)
12:00 noon	thîaŋ
12:30 p.m.	thîaŋ khrɵ̂ŋ

Practice reading the following times without the parenthesized parts. Try to get the time under 50 seconds.

12:15 p.m.	10:20 a.m.	11:00 a.m.	6:15 a.m.	7:00 a.m.
9:00 a.m.	8:00 a.m.	8:20 a.m.	12:20 p.m.	10:00 a.m.
6:10 a.m.	9:10 a.m.	6:00 a.m.	7:10 a.m.	9:15 a.m.
11:20 a.m.	12:00 noon	10:15 a.m.	8:30 a.m.	11:30 a.m.
7:00 a.m.	7:15 a.m.	9:30 a.m.	11:00 a.m.	6:20 a.m.

22.9 Conversation.

The teacher should read the narrative of lesson 10 (Book 1) to the students and ask them the questions.

22.10 Writing.

เหลอ	เลย	เดิน	เกิด
lɔ̌ə	ləəy	dəən	kəət
?	... at all.	To walk.	To be born.

There are three ways of writing the vowel əə depending on whether it has no final, y, or any other final.

(More.)

เกิด	ชอบ	เหลอ
เกิน	ฉอบ	เลอ
สิบ	หลูก	เลิก
สิง	ลูก	เบิก
ชอบ	ขาด	เบิน
ชอม	คาด	เขิน
เปิด	นวด	เขย
เบิน	หนวด	เลย
หก	ฝาด	ลาย
หง	ฟาด	ลาด
เพลิด	แวก	หลาด
เพลิน	แหวก	พลาด

เกิด	kə̀ət	ชอบ	*chɔ̂ɔp	เหลอ	*lə̌ə
เกิน	kəən	ฉอบ	chɔ̀ɔp	เลอ	ləə
สิบ	*sìp	หลูก	lùuk	เลิก	lə̂ək
สิง	sǐŋ	ลูก	*lûuk	เบิก	bə̀ək
ชอบ	*chɔ̂ɔp	ขาด	khàat	เบิน	bəən
ชอม	chɔɔm	คาด	khâat	เขิน	khə̌ən
เบิ๊ด	*pə̀ət	นวด	nûat	เขย	khə̌əy
เบิ๊น	pəən	หนวด	nùat	เลย	*ləəy
หก	*hòk	ฝาด	fàat	ลาย	laay
หง	hǒŋ	ฟาด	fâat	ลาด	lâat
เพลิด	phlə̂ət	แวก	wɛ̂ɛk	หลาด	làat
เพลิน	phləən	แหวก	wɛ̀ɛk	พลาด	phlâat

31

บทที่ ๒๓

๒๓.๑ คำศัพท์

ก๊วย	เบียร์
เตี๋ยว	เย็นเย็น
ก๊วยเตี๋ยว	เบียร์เย็นเย็น
เป็นยังไง	แข็ง
เป็นยังไงบ้าง	น้ำแข็ง
อร่อย	ขนม
อร่อยดี	ปัง
	ขนมปัง
เพราะ	
	พริก
หอม	พริกไทย
พอ	เกลือ
อิ่ม	นม
ชา	ตาน
น้ำชา	
	น้ำตาล
กาแฟ	
กาแฟเย็น	ถ้วย
	ทุ่ม

LESSON 23

23.1 Vocabulary and expansions.

kúay	
tĺaw	
kúaytĺaw	Noodles.
pen yaŋŋay	How is it? How are you?
pen yaŋŋay bâaŋ	How are its various aspects? (If asking about food, for example, 'How is its saltiness, sourness, hotness, etc.?')
ʔarɔ̀y	To taste good.
ʔarɔ̀y dii	To taste good.
phrɔ́ʔ	To sound good.
hɔ̌ɔm	To smell good, fragrant.
phɔɔ	Enough.
ʔìm	To have eaten enough, to be full.
chaa	Tea (the product or the drink).
nám chaa	Tea (the drink).
kaafɛɛ	Coffee.
kaafɛɛ yen	Iced coffee.
bia	Beer.
yenyen	To be judged cold.
bia yenyen	Cold beer. Compare this with *kaafɛɛ yen*, 'iced coffee'. The reduplicated adjective involves the speaker's feelings. With *kaafɛɛ yen*, he is using *yen* to identify one of two kinds of coffee. But with the beer it is another matter: his judgement of the temperature continuum is involved. If the iced coffee isn't cold enough for him, however, he can make his feelings known by saying 'ʔaw yenyen nɔ̀y. nîi mây yen lǝǝy.'
khɛ̌ŋ	To be hard.
nám khɛ̌ŋ	Ice.
khanǒm	Pastry, sweets, dessert.
paŋ	
khanǒmpaŋ	Bread.
phrík	Peppers, chilies.
phrík thay	Pepper.
klʉa	Salt.
nom	Milk, cream.
taan	
námtaan	Sugar.
thûay	A cup.
thûm	O'clock (used only with hours from evening to midnight).

๒๓.๒ โครงสร้างของประโยค

อร่อยดี

สบายดี

สวยดี

หอมดี

เพราะดี

ดีแล้ว

พอแล้ว

อิ่มแล้ว

ถูกแล้ว

กาแฟร้อน

กาแฟเย็น

กาแฟดำร้อน

กาแฟดำเย็น

ชาร้อน

ชาเย็น

ชาดำร้อน

ชาดำเย็น

น้ำแข็งใส่น้ำชา

น้ำแข็ง (เปล่า)

น้ำแข็งเปล่าไม่ใส่น้ำ

น้ำเย็น

๒๓.๓ บทสนทนา

ก. ก๋วยเตี๋ยวเป็นยังไงบ้าง

    ข. อร่อยดี

ก. เอาอีกไหม

    ข. พอแล้ว, อิ่มแล้ว คุณล่ะ, เอาอะไรอีกไหม

ก. เอาเบียร์เย็นเย็นอีกขวดหนึ่ง คุณไม่เอาน้ำชาหรือกาแฟบ้างหรือ

    ข. ไม่เอา, ขอน้ำแข็งอีกแก้วหนึ่งเท่านั้น

23.2 Patterns.

ʔarɔ̀y dii.	Good tasting. Delicious.
sabaay dii.	Good feeling. Comfortable.
sŭay dii.	Good looking. Beautiful.
hɔ̌ɔm dii. ·	Good smelling. Fragrant.
phrɔ́ʔ dii.	Good sounding.
dii lɛ́ɛw.	To have reached the point of being good.
phɔɔ lɛ́ɛw.	To have reached the point of sufficiency.
ʔim lɛ́ɛw.	To have reached the point of being full.
thùuk lɛ́ɛw.	To have reached the point of being correct.
kaafɛɛ rɔ́ɔn.	Hot coffee with sugar and cream.
kaafɛɛ yen.	Iced coffee with sugar and cream.
kaafɛɛ dam rɔ́ɔn.	Hot coffee with sugar but no cream.
kaafɛɛ dam yen.	Iced coffee with sugar but no cream.
	(The last two are more often called by the Chinese: *ʔooyúaʔ* and *ʔoolíaŋ*.)
chaa rɔ́ɔn.	Hot tea with sugar and cream.
chaa yen.	Iced tea with sugar and cream.
chaa dam rɔ́ɔn.	Hot tea with sugar but no cream.
chaa dam yen.	Iced tea with sugar but no cream.
	(For the corresponding eight drinks without sugar, add *mây sày námtaan*.)
nám khɛ̌ŋ sày nám chaa.	Very weak tea with ice.
nám khɛ̌ŋ (plàaw).	Either weak tea or plain water with ice.
nám khɛ̌ŋ plàaw mây sày náam.	Plain ice in a glass.
nám yen.	Cold water without ice.

23.3 Dialog.

A. kúaytǐaw pen yaŋŋay bâaŋ.	How are the noodles?
B. ʔarɔ̀y dii.	Good.
A. ʔaw ʔìik máy.	Do you want some more?
B. phɔɔ lɛ́ɛw. ʔim lɛ́ɛw. khun lâ. ʔaw ʔaray ʔìik máy.	This is enough. I'm full. How about you? Do you want anything else?
A. ʔaw bia yenyen ʔìik khùat nʉ̀ŋ. khun mây ʔaw nám chaa rʉ́ kaafɛɛ bâaŋ lɔ̌ɔ.	I'll have another bottle of cold beer. Don't you want some tea or coffee?
B. mây ʔaw. khɔ̌ɔ nám khɛ̌ŋ ʔìik kɛ̂ɛw nʉ̀ŋ thâwnán.	No. May I have just another glass of ice water?

35

๒๓.๔ แบบฝึกหัดการฟังและการออกเสียงสูงต่ำ

ก.

ถอยรถ   โซดา   มุ้งลวด   จิ้งจก   จดหมาย

ข.

ใครบอก	ใครเตือน
หน่อยบอก	แดงเตือน
หน่อยบอกใคร	แดงเตือนใคร
หน่อยบอกปู่	แดงเตือนลุง
ใครถาม	ใครทัก
ศรีถาม	แอ๊ดทัก
ศรีถามใคร	แอ๊ดทักใคร
ศรีถามป้า	แอ๊ดทักน้อง
ใครพูด	
ต้อยพูด	
ต้อยพูดกับใคร	
ต้อยพูดกับพี่	

๒๓.๕ แบบฝึกหัดการสลับเสียงสูงต่ำ

ก.

กระดาษ	ลูกหิน
กระดาษแผ่นหนึ่ง	ลูกหินลูกหนึ่ง
ผม	ทราย
ผมเส้นหนึ่ง	ทรายเม็ดหนึ่ง
แก้ว	
แก้วใบหนึ่ง	

23.4 Tone identification and production.

a. Identify the tones and record the number of repetitions required for each.

To back up a car.	thɔɔy rot	....	....
Soda water.	soodaa	....	....
Wire screen.	muŋ luat	....	....
House lizard.	ciŋcok	....	....
A letter.	cotmaay	....	....

b. Response drill.

khray bɔ̀ɔk.	Who told?
nɔ̀y bɔ̀ɔk.	Noy told.
nɔ̀y bɔ̀ɔk khray.	Who did Noy tell?
nɔ̀y bɔ̀ɔk pùu.	Noy told Grandpa.
khray thǎam.	Who asked?
sǐi thǎam.	Sri asked.
sǐi thǎam khray.	Who did Sri ask?
sǐi thǎam pǎa.	Sri asked Papa.
khray phûut.	Who spoke?
tɔ̂y phûut.	Toy spoke.
tɔ̂y phûut kàp khray.	Who did Toy speak to?
tɔ̂y phûut kàp phîi.	Toy spoke to Older One.
khray tʉan.	Who warned?
dɛɛŋ tʉan.	Daeng warned.
dɛɛŋ tʉan khray.	Who did Daeng warn?
dɛɛŋ tʉan luŋ.	Daeng warned Uncle.
khray thák.	Who greeted?
ʔéɛt thák.	At greeted.
ʔéɛt thák khray.	Who did At greet?
ʔéɛt thák nɔ́ɔŋ.	At greeted Younger One.

23.5 Tone manipulation.

a. Response drill.

kradàat.	Paper.
kradàat phɛ̀n nʉŋ.	A sheet of paper.
phǒm.	Hair.
phǒm sên nʉŋ.	A hair.
kɛ̂ɛw.	Glass.
kɛ̂ɛw bay nʉŋ.	A glass.
lûuk hǐn.	Marble.
lûuk hǐn lûuk nʉŋ.	A marble.
saay.	Sand.
saay mét nʉŋ.	A grain of sand.

37

ข.

กระดาษ   ลูกหิน
   กระดาษสองแผ่น   ลูกหินสองลูก
ผม   ทราย
   ผมสองเส้น   ทรายสองเม็ด
แก้ว
   แก้วสองใบ

๒๓.๖ แบบฝึกหัดการออกเสียงสระและพยัญชนะ

ก.

ไข้	เข้า	ไซ้	เร้า
ค่าย	ข้าว	ซ้าย	ร้าว

ข.

ช้อนชม	(แจ๋ว)	ขวดแขก	(เกียรติ)
ช้อนแจ๋ว	(จาน)	ขวดเกียรติ	(เกือก)
จานแจ๋ว	(ชม)	เกือกเกียรติ	(แขก)
จานชม	(ช้อน)	เกือกแขก	(ขวด)

๒๓.๗ แบบฝึกหัดไวยากรณ์

ก.

ใส่นมไหม   (น้ำตาล)   ใส่น้ำแข็งไหม (มะนาว)
ใส่น้ำตาลไหม (เกลือ)   ใส่มะนาวไหม (น้ำ)
ใส่เกลือไหม   (พริกไทย)   ใส่น้ำไหม
ใส่พริกไทยไหม(น้ำแข็ง)

b. Response drill.

kradàat.	Paper.
kradàat sɔ̌ɔŋ phèn.	Two sheets of paper.
phǒm.	Hair.
phǒm sɔ̌ɔŋ sên.	Two hairs.
kɛ̂ɛw.	Glass.
kɛ̂ɛw sɔ̌ɔŋ bay.	Two glasses.
lûuk hǐn.	Marble.
lûuk hǐn sɔ̌ɔŋ lûuk.	Two marbles.
saay.	Sand.
saay sɔ̌ɔŋ mét.	Two grains of sand.

c. Response drill. Same as above but answer with 'four'.

d. Response drill. Same as above but answer with 'five'.

23.6 Vowel and consonant drills.

a. ay-aay and aw-aaw contrast drills.

khây	khâw	sáy	ráw
khâay	khâaw	sáay	ráaw

b. Substitution drills. (c, ch, and k, kh).

chɔ́ɔn chom.	(cɛ̌w)	Chom's spoon.	(Jaeo)
chɔ́ɔn cɛ̌w.	(caan)	Jaeo's spoon.	(plate)
caan cɛ̌w.	(chom)	Jaeo's plate.	(Chom)
caan chom.	(chɔ́ɔn)	Chom's plate.	(spoon)

khùat khɛ̀ɛk.	(kìat)	Kaek's bottle.	(Kiat)
khùat kìat.	(kùak)	Kiat's bottle.	(shoes)
kùak kìat.	(khɛ̀ɛk)	Kiat's shoes.	(Kaek)
kùak khɛ̀ɛk.	(khùat)	Kaek's shoes.	(bottle)

23.7 Grammar drills.

a. Substitution drill.

sày nom máy.	(námtaan)	Shall I put some cream in it?	(sugar)
sày námtaan máy.	(klʉa)	Shall I put some sugar in it?	(salt)
sày klʉa máy.	(phrík thay)	Shall I put some salt in it?	(pepper)
sày phrík thay máy.	(nám khɛ̌ŋ)	Shall I put some pepper in it?	(ice)
sày nám khɛ̌ŋ máy.	(manaaw)	Shall I put some ice in it?	(lime)
sày manaaw máy.	(náam)	Shall I put some lime in it?	(water)
sày náam máy.		Shall I put some water in it?	

39

ข.

ช่วยส่งน้ำตาลให้ด้วย   (นม)
ช่วยส่งนมให้ด้วย   (เกลือ)
ช่วยส่งเกลือให้ด้วย   (พริกไทย)
ช่วยส่งพริกไทยให้ด้วย   (ข้าว)
ช่วยส่งข้าวให้ด้วย   (ขนมปัง)
ช่วยส่งขนมปังให้ด้วย

ค.

เอาอะไรอีกไหม   (กาแฟ)
เอากาแฟอีกไหม   (เบียร์)
เอาเบียร์อีกไหม   (น้ำตาล)
เอาน้ำตาลอีกไหม   (น้ำแข็ง)
เอาน้ำแข็งอีกไหม   (แก้ว)
เอาแก้วอีกไหม

ง.

ไม่เอากาแฟบ้างหรือ   (น้ำชา)
ไม่เอาน้ำชาบ้างหรือ   (น้ำแข็ง)
ไม่เอาน้ำแข็งบ้างหรือ   (ถ้วย)
ไม่เอาถ้วยบ้างหรือ   (โอเลี้ยง)

ไม่เอาโอเลี้ยงบ้างหรือ   (โอยั๊วะ)
ไม่เอาโอยั๊วะบ้างหรือ   (เบียร์)
ไม่เอาเบียร์บ้างหรือ

b. Substitution drill.

chûay sòŋ námtaan hây dûay.
(nom)

Please pass the sugar.
(cream)

chûay sòŋ nom hây dûay.
(klʉa)

Please pass the cream.
(salt)

chûay sòŋ klʉa hây dûay.
(phrík thay)

Please pass the salt.
(pepper)

chûay sòŋ phrík thay hây dûay.
(khâaw)

Please pass the pepper.
(rice)

chûay sòŋ khâaw hây dûay.
(khanǒmpaŋ)

Please pass the rice.
(bread)

chûay sòŋ khanǒmpaŋ hây dûay.

Please pass the bread.

c. Substitution drill.

ʔaw ʔaray ʔìik máy.
(kaafɛɛ)

Do you want anything else?
(coffee)

ʔaw kaafɛɛ ʔìik máy.
(bia)

Do you want some more coffee?
(beer)

ʔaw bia ʔìik máy.
(námtaan)

Do you want some more beer?
(sugar)

ʔaw námtaan ʔìik máy.
(nám khɛ̌ŋ)

Do you some more sugar?
(ice)

ʔaw nám khɛ̌ŋ ʔìik máy.
(kɛ̂ɛw)

Do you want some more ice?
(glass)

ʔaw kɛ̂ɛw ʔìik máy

Do you want another glass?

d. Substitution drill.

mây ʔaw kaafɛɛ bâaŋ lɔ̌ə.
(nám chaa)

Don't you want some coffee, too?
(tea)

mây ʔaw nám chaa bâaŋ lɔ̌ə.
(nám khɛ̌ŋ)

Don't you want some tea, too?
(ice)

mây ʔaw nám khɛ̌ŋ bâaŋ lɔ̌ə.
(thûay)

Don't you want some ice?
(cups)

mây ʔaw thûay bâaŋ lɔ̌ə.
(ʔoolíaŋ)

Don't you want some cups?
(sweet, black, iced coffee)

mây ʔaw ʔoolíaŋ bâaŋ lɔ̌ə.
(ʔooyúaʔ)

Don't you want some iced coffee?
(sweet, black, hot coffee)

mây ʔaw ʔooyúaʔ bâaŋ lɔ̌ə.
(bia)

Don't you want some hot black coffee?
(beer)

mây ʔaw bia bâaŋ lɔ̌ə.

Don't you want some beer, too?

41

จ.

ขอน้ำแข็งอีกแก้วหนึ่งเท่านั้น (โอเลี้ยง) ขอแก้วอีกใบหนึ่งเท่านั้น (เบียร์)
ขอโอเลี้ยงอีกแก้วหนึ่งเท่านั้น (ข้าว) ขอเบียร์อีกขวดหนึ่งเท่านั้น
ขอข้าวอีกจานหนึ่งเท่านั้น (แก้ว)

ฉ.

ไม่เอาเบียร์บ้างหรือ (น้ำแข็ง)
ไม่เอา, ขอน้ำแข็งอีกแก้วหนึ่งเท่านั้น

ไม่เอาข้าวบ้างหรือ (เบียร์)
ไม่เอา, ขอเบียร์อีกขวดหนึ่งเท่านั้น

ไม่เอาแก้วบ้างหรือ (ถ้วย)
ไม่เอา, ขอถ้วยอีกใบหนึ่งเท่านั้น

ไม่เอาข้าวผัดบ้างหรือ (กาแฟ)
ไม่เอา, ขอกาแฟอีกถ้วยหนึ่งเท่านั้น

๒๓.๘ เวลา

ทุ่มหนึ่ง	อีกสิบนาทีสี่ทุ่ม
ทุ่มสิบนาที	สี่ทุ่มครึ่ง
อีกสิบห้านาทีสองทุ่ม	อีกห้านาทีสองยาม
สองทุ่ม	สองยาม
อีกยี่สิบห้านาทีสามทุ่ม	สองยามครึ่ง
สามทุ่ม	

e. Substitution drill.

khɔ̌ɔ nám khɛ̌ŋ ʔiik kɛ̂ɛw nɯŋ thâwnán.
(ʔoolíaŋ)

Just bring me another glass of ice water.
(iced coffee)

khɔ̌ɔ ʔoolíaŋ ʔiik kɛ̂ɛw nɯŋ thâwnán.
(khâaw)

Just bring me another glass of iced coffee.
(rice)

khɔ̌ɔ khâaw ʔiik caan nɯŋ thâwnán.
(kɛ̂ɛw)

Just bring me another plate of rice.
(glass)

khɔ̌ɔ kɛ̂ɛw ʔiik bay nɯŋ thâwnán.
(bia)

Just bring me another glass.
(beer)

khɔ̌ɔ bia ʔiik khùat nɯŋ thâwnán.

Just bring me another bottle of beer.

f. Response drill.

mây ʔaw bia bâaŋ lɔ̌ɔ. (nám khɛ̌ŋ)
mây ʔaw. khɔ̌ɔ nám khɛ̌ŋ
ʔiik kɛ̂ɛw nɯŋ thâwnán.

Don't you want some beer? (ice water)
No. Just bring me another glass
of ice water.

mây ʔaw khâaw bâaŋ lɔ̌ɔ. (bia)
mây ʔaw. khɔ̌ɔ bia
ʔiik khùat nɯŋ thâwnán.

Don't you want some rice? (beer)
No. Just bring me another
bottle of beer.

mây ʔaw kɛ̂ɛw bâaŋ lɔ̌ɔ. (thûay)
mây ʔaw. khɔ̌ɔ thûay
ʔiik bay nɯŋ thâwnán.

Don't you want some glasses? (cup)
No. Just bring me
another cup.

mây ʔaw khâaw phàt bâaŋ lɔ̌ɔ. (kaafɛɛ)
mây ʔaw. khɔ̌ɔ kaafɛɛ
ʔiik thûay nɯŋ thâwnán.

Don't you want some fried rice? (coffee)
No. Just bring me
another cup of coffee.

23.8 Time of day.

7:00 p.m.	thûm nɯŋ
7:10 p.m.	thûm sìp naathii
7:45 p.m.	ʔiik sìp hâa naathii sɔ̌ɔŋ thûm
8:00 p.m.	sɔ̌ɔŋ thûm
8:35 p.m.	ʔiik yîi sìp hâa naathii sǎam thûm
9:00 p.m.	sǎam thûm
9:50 p.m.	ʔiik sìp naathii sìi thûm
10:30 p.m.	sìi thûm khrɯ̂ŋ
11:55 p.m.	ʔiik hâa naathii sɔ̌ɔŋ yaam
12:00 mid.	sɔ̌ɔŋ yaam
12:30 a.m.	sɔ̌ɔŋ yaam khrɯ̂ŋ

Practice reading the following times. Try to get the time under 1 minute.

7:15 p.m.	12:00 p.m.	8:40 p.m.	10:05 p.m.	12:10 a.m
11:00 p.m.	7:45 p.m.	10:30 p.m.	8:00 p.m.	9:55 p.m.
6:45 p.m.	9:00 p.m.	11:50 p.m.	7:00 p.m.	10:00 p.m.
10:35 p.m.	8:30 p.m.	9:25 p.m.	11:20 p.m.	6:35 p.m.
8:20 p.m.	12:30 a.m.	7:05 p.m.	9:30 p.m.	12:20 a.m.

23.9 Conversation.

The teacher should read the narrative of lesson 15 (Book 1) to the students and ask them the questions.

๒๓.๑๐ การเขียน

วงเวียน	เขียว	เปรียบเทียบ
เขี่ยน	เยี่ยบ	เสี่ย
เขี่ยด	เหยี่ยบ	เสี่ยบ
เที่ยบ	ขวบ	เรี่ยบ
เที่ยม	ควบ	เรี่ยน
เบี่ยด	หรี่ด	เขี่ยน
เบี่ยน	รี่ด	เจี่ยน
รวบ	แทบ	เจี่ยด
รวม	แถบ	เครี่ยด

23.10 Writing.

วงเวียน
woŋwian
Traffic circle.

เขียว
khĭaw
Green.

เปรียบเทียบ
prìap thîap
To compare.

เขียน	*khĭan	เยียบ	yîap	เสีย	sĭa
เขียด	khìat	เหยียบ	yìap	เสียบ	sìap
เทียบ	*thîap	ขวบ	khùap	เรียบ	rîap
เทียม	thiam	ควบ	khûap	เรียน	*rian
เบียด	bìat	หรีด	rìit	เขียน	*khĭan
เบียน	bian	รีด	rîit	เจียน	cian
รวบ	rûap	แทบ	thɛ̂ɛp	เจียด	cìat
รวม	ruam	แถบ	thɛ̀ɛp	เครียด	khrîat

บทที่ ๒๔

๒๔.๑ คำศัพท์

อาหารเย็น	โทร
อาหารเย็นเย็น	จะโทรมาบอก
วันนี้	แปล
	แปลว่าอะไร
	แปลว่าจะไป
เรา	
	ซุบ
นอก	ซุบไก่
ข้างนอก	
	แซนวิช
กลาง	เนย
กลางวัน	เนยแข็ง
อาหารกลางวัน	แซนวิชเนยแข็ง
แน่	
ยังไม่แน่	

LESSON 24

24.1 Vocabulary and expansions.

ʔaahǎan yen	The evening meal, dinner.
ʔaahǎan yenyen	Cold food.
wan níi	Today.
raw	We, I, you. *raw* is used for 'we' regardless of class relationship, but it is used for 'I' or 'you' only when speaking to a social inferior (a taxi driver or bartender, for example). The student will probably never need to use it for 'I' (he can use *chán* instead). But very often what he intends as a classless 'we' will be understood as a superior 'I' and thus result in an unintentional insult. This arises from the different ways that English and Thai handle meaning category number 2 shown below.

Meaning	English	Thai	Examples
1. Me and only me.	I	phǒm (etc.)	*I* was born in 1925. *My* name is.........
2. Me (among) others.	we		*We* came here in 1966. *Our* house is on Soi 6.
3. Me and others.		raw	*We*'ve known each other for a long time.
4. Me and you.			Where shall *we* meet?

Beware of meaning 2 — especially if you are married. Include your husband, wife, or family only when the meaning specifically demands it.

nɔ̂ɔk	Outside of.
khâŋ nɔ̂ɔk	Outside.
klaaŋ	Center, middle, in the middle of.
klaaŋ wan	Midday.
ʔaahǎan klaaŋ wan	Lunch.
nɛ̂ɛ	To be certain.
yaŋ mây nɛ̂ɛ	I'm not sure yet.
thoo	Short form of *thoorasàp*.
ca thoo maa bɔ̀ɔk	Will phone (the call *coming* to the present location) tell. I'll phone and tell you.
plɛɛ	To mean, to translate.
plɛɛ wâa ʔaray	What does it mean?
plɛɛ wâa ca pay	It means I'll go.
súp	Soup.
súp kày	Chicken soup.
sɛɛnwít	Sandwich.
nəəy	Butter.
nəəy khěŋ	Cheese.
sɛɛnwít nəəy khěŋ	Cheese sandwich.
(More.)	

ชั้น
ไข่
ไข่ไก่
ต้ม
ไข่ต้ม
ไข่ต้มลูกหนึ่ง

ละม้าย
ผล
ผลไม้

เมื่อ
เมื่อไหร่

ฝรั่ง
มัน
มันฝรั่ง
มันทอด

เผ็ด

จืด

๒๔.๒ โครงสร้างของประโยค

วันนี้
วันก่อน
วันหลัง

ยังไม่แน่
ยังไม่ว่าง
ยังไม่พอ

อาหารเช้า
อาหารกลางวัน
อาหารเย็น

แปลว่าจะกลับมากิน
แปลว่าไม่ไป
แปลว่ายังไม่แน่

ข้างนอก
ข้างใน

อะไรก็ได้
ที่ไหนก็ได้
เท่าไหร่ก็ได้
เมื่อไหร่ก็ได้
ใครก็ได้
กี่คนก็ได้

กินที่บ้าน
กินข้างนอก

ฉันโทรไปบอกเขาแล้ว
เขาโทรมาบอกฉันแล้ว

chín	A piece of something.
khày	Eggs.
khày kày	Chicken eggs.
tôm	To boil something.
khày tôm	Hard-boiled eggs.
khày tôm lûuk nɯ̀ŋ	A hard-boiled egg.
faràŋ	European, American, Australian, etc. Occidental.
man	Potatoes, yams, etc.
man faràŋ	Potatoes.
man thɔ̀ɔt	Fried potatoes, potato chips.
lamáay	
phǒn	
phǒnlamáay	Fruit.
mɯ̂a	When.........
mɯ̂arày	When?
phèt	To be hot (peppery).
cɯ̀ɯt	To be tasteless.

24.2 Patterns.

wan níi.	Today.
wan kɔ̀ɔn.	The other day.
wan lǎŋ.	Another day (a later day).
ʔaahǎan cháaw.	Breakfast.
ʔaahǎan klaaŋwan.	Lunch.
ʔaahǎan yen.	Dinner.
khâŋ nɔ̂ɔk.	Outside.
khâŋ nay.	Inside.
kin thîi bâan.	Eat at home.
kin khâŋ nɔ̂ɔk.	Eat out.
chán thoo pay bɔ̀ɔk kháw lɛ́ɛw.	I've phoned and told him already.
kháw thoo maa bɔ̀ɔk chán lɛ́ɛw.	He has phoned and told me already.
yaŋ mây nɛ̂ɛ.	I'm not sure yet.
yaŋ mây wâaŋ.	I'm not free yet.
yaŋ mây phɔɔ.	There isn't enough yet.
plɛɛ wâa ca klàp maa kin.	It means I'll come back to eat.
plɛɛ wâa mây pay.	It means I won't go.
plɛɛ wâa yaŋ mây nɛ̂ɛ.	It means I'm still not sure.
ʔaray kɔ̂ dây.	Anything will do.
thîi nǎy kɔ̂ dây.	Anywhere.
thâwrày kɔ̂ dây.	Any amount.
mɯ̂arày kɔ̂ dây.	Any time.
khray kɔ̂ dây.	Anyone.
kìi khon kɔ̂ dây.	Any number of people.

49

๒๔.๓ บทสนทนา

ก. วันนี้ไม่ต้องทำอาหารเย็น, เราจะไปกินข้างนอก

    ข. อาหารกลางวันล่ะคะ, จะมาทานไหม

ก. ยังไม่แน่, ถ้ามาไม่ได้จะโทรศัพท์มาบอก
แต่ถ้าไม่โทรมา แปลว่าจะกลับมากิน

    ข. คุณจะทานอะไรบ้างคะ

ก. เอาซุบไก่, แซนวิชเนยแข็งสองสามชิ้น,
ไข่ต้มสองลูก, มันทอด แล้วก็ผลไม้

    ข. ผลไม้อะไรคะ

ก. อะไรก็ได้

๒๔.๔ แบบฝึกหัดการฟังและการออกเสียงสูงต่ำ

ก.

ตำรวจ   แท็กซี่   สงขลา   เต้นรำ   ปากน้ำ

ข.

หน่อยไม่ได้บอกปู่หรือ   แดงไม่ได้เตือนลุงหรือ
  บอก, หน่อยบอกปู่ตอนบ่าย   เตือน, แดงเตือนลุงตอนเย็น

ศรีไม่ได้ถามป้าหรือ   แอ๊ดไม่ได้ทักน้องหรือ
  ถาม, ศรีถามป้าตอนสาย   ทัก, แอ๊ดทักน้องตอนเช้า

ต้อยไม่ได้พูดกับพี่หรือ
  พูด, ต้อยพูดกับพี่ตอนเที่ยง

24.3 Dialog.

A. wanníi mây tôŋ tham ʔaahǎan yen.   You don't have to prepare dinner today.
   raw ca pay kin khâŋ nɔ̂ɔk.   We're going to eat out.

B. ʔaahǎan klaaŋwan la khá.   How about lunch?
  ca maa thaan máy.   Are you coming to eat?

A. yaŋ mây nɛ̂ɛ.   I'm not sure yet.
   thâa maa mây dây,   If we can't come,
   ca thoorasàp maa bɔ̀ɔk.   I'll phone and tell you.
   tɛ̀ɛ thâa mây thoo maa,   But if I don't phone,
   plɛɛ wâa ca klàp maa kin.   it'll mean we're coming back to eat.

B. khun ca thaan ʔaray bâaŋ khá.   What do you want to eat?

A. ʔaw súp kày,   Chicken soup,
   sɛɛnwít nɔɔykhɛ̌ŋ sɔ̌ɔŋ sǎam chín, two or three cheese sandwiches,
   khày tôm sɔ̌ɔŋ lûuk,   two hard-boiled eggs,
   man thɔ̂ɔt,   potato chips,
   lɛ́ɛw kɔ̂ phǒnlamáay.   and some fruit.

B. phǒnlamáay ʔaray khá.   What kind of fruit?

A. ʔaray kɔ̂ dây.   Any kind.

24.4 Tone identification and production.

a. Identify the tones and record the number of repetitions required.

Policeman.	tamruat	....
Taxi.	thɛksii	....
Songkhla.	soŋkhlaa	....
To dance.	tenram	....
Paknam.	paaknaam	....

b. Response drill.

nɔ̀y mây dây bɔ̀ɔk pùu lɔ̌ɔ.   Noy didn't tell Grandpa, huh?
   bɔ̀ɔk.   Yes she did.
   nɔ̀y bɔ̀ɔk pùu tɔɔn bàay.   Noy told Grandpa in the afternoon.

sǐi mây dây thǎam pǎa lɔ̌ɔ.   Sri didn't ask Papa, huh?
   thǎam.   Yes she did.
   sǐi thǎam pǎa tɔɔn sǎay.   Sri asked Papa in the late morning.

tɔ̌y mây dây phûut kàp phîi lɔ̌ɔ. Toy didn't speak to Older One, huh?
   phûut.   Yes she did.
   tɔ̌y phûut kap phîi tɔɔn thîaŋ. Toy spoke to Older One at noon.

dɛɛŋ mây dây tʉan luŋ lɔ̌ɔ.   Daeng didn't remind Uncle, huh?
   tʉan.   Yes she did.
   dɛɛŋ tʉan luŋ tɔɔn yen.   Daeng reminded Uncle in the evening.

ʔɛ́ɛt mây dây thák nɔ́ɔŋ lɔ̌ɔ.   At didn't greet Younger One, huh?
   thák.   Yes she did.
   ʔɛ́ɛt thák nɔ́ɔŋ tɔɔn cháaw.   At greeted Younger One in the morning.

๒๔.๕ แบบฝึกหัดการสลับเสียงสูงต่ำ

ก.

มีทรายกี่เม็ด   ได้ลูกหินกี่ลูก
    มีทรายสามเม็ด   ได้ลูกหินสามลูก

ใช้กระดาษกี่แผ่น   สั่งแก้วกี่ใบ
    ใช้กระดาษสามแผ่น   สั่งแก้วสามใบ

เห็นผมกี่เส้น
    เห็นผมสามเส้น

ก.

ได้ทรายสี่เม็ด (กระดาษ)   เห็นผมสี่เส้น (กระดาษ)
ได้กระดาษสี่แผ่น (แก้ว)   เห็นกระดาษสี่แผ่น (ทราย)
ได้แก้วสี่ใบ (ลูกหิน)   เห็นทรายสี่เม็ด (แก้ว)
ได้ลูกหินสี่ลูก (เห็น)   เห็นแก้วสี่ใบ
เห็นลูกหินสี่ลูก (ผม)

๒๔.๖ แบบฝึกหัดการออกเสียงสระและพยัญชนะ

ก.   ใน   นาย   เรา   ราว   ไข่   ข่าย   เข่า   ข่าว

ข.   ยุบ   ยุด   ยุก   ยุ   กับ   กัด   กัก   กะ

๒๔.๗ แบบฝึกหัดไวยากรณ์

ก.

เนื้อทอด (ไก่)   หมูทอด (อบ)
ไก่ทอด (กุ้ง)   หมูอบ (เนื้อ)
กุ้งทอด (ปลา)   เนื้ออบ (ไก่)
ปลาทอด (หมู)   ไก่อบ

24.5 Tone manipulation.

a. Response drill.

mii saay kìi mét. How many grains of sand do you have?

  mii saay sǎam mét. I have three grains of sand.

cháy kradàat kìi phèn. How many sheets of paper did you use?

  cháy kradàat sǎam phèn. I used three sheets of paper.

hěn phǒm kìi sên. How many hairs did you see?

  hěn phǒm sǎam sên. I saw three hairs.

dây lûuk hǐn kìi lûuk. How many marbles did you get?

  dây lûuk hǐn sǎam lûuk. I got three marbles.

sàŋ kɛ̂ɛw kìi bay. How many glasses did you order?

  sàŋ kɛ̂ɛw sǎam bay. I ordered three glasses.

b. Response drill. Same as above but answer with 'five'.

c. Substitution drill.

dây saay sìi mét. (kradàat) I got four grains of sand. (paper)

dây kradàat sìi phèn. (kɛ̂ɛw) I got four sheets of paper. (glass)

dây kɛ̂ɛw sìi bay. (lûuk hǐn) I got four glasses. (marbles)

dây lûuk hǐn sìi lûuk. (hěn) I got four marbles. (see)

hěn lûuk hǐn sìi lûuk. (phǒm) I saw four marbles. (hair)

hěn phǒm sìi sên. (kradàat) I saw four hairs. (paper)

hěn kradàat sìi phèn. (saay) I saw four sheets of paper. (sand)

hěn saay sìi mét. (kɛ̂ɛw) I saw four grains of sand. (glass)

hěn kɛ̂ɛw sìi bay. I saw four glasses.

24.6 Vowel and consonant drills.

a. ay-aay and aw-aaw contrast drills.

nay	raw	khày	khàw
naay	raaw	khàay	khàaw

b. Final p-t-k-ʔ contrast drills.

yúp   yút   yúk   yúʔ   kàp   kàt   kàk   kàʔ

24.7 Grammar drills.

a. Substitution drill.

núa thɔ̂ɔt. (kày) Fried beef, steak. (chicken)

kày thɔ̂ɔt. (kûŋ) Fried chicken. (shrimps)

kûŋ thɔ̂ɔt. (plaa) Fried shrimps. (fish)

plaa thɔ̂ɔt. (mǔu) Fried fish. (pork)

mǔu thɔ̂ɔt. (ʔòp) Fried pork. (roast)

mǔu ʔòp. (núa) Roast pork. (beef)

núa ʔòp. (kày) Roast beef. (chicken)

kày ʔòp. Roast chicken.

53

ข.

แกงไก่ (เนื้อ)   ผัดกุ้ง (เผ็ด)

แกงเนื้อ (ผัด)   ผัดเผ็ด (แกง)

ผัดเนื้อ (หมู)   แกงเผ็ด (จืด)

ผัดหมู (กุ้ง)   แกงจืด

ค.

วันนี้ไม่ต้องทำอาหารเย็น (ไปตลาด)

วันนี้ไม่ต้องไปตลาด (ทำงาน)

วันนี้ไม่ต้องทำงาน (เรียนภาษาไทย)

วันนี้ไม่ต้องเรียนภาษาไทย (ไปซื้อของ)

วันนี้ไม่ต้องไปซื้อของ

ง.

เราจะไปกินข้างนอก (ที่บ้านคุณยัง)

เราจะไปกินที่บ้านคุณยัง (ที่ร้านอาหารนิด)

เราจะไปกินที่ร้านอาหารนิด (ข้างนอก)

เราจะไปกินข้างนอก (ที่ที่ทำงาน)

เราจะไปกินที่ที่ทำงาน

จ.

ถ้ามาไม่ได้จะโทรมาบอก (ไปเที่ยว)

ถ้าไปเที่ยวไม่ได้จะโทรมาบอก (ทำงาน)

ถ้าทำงานไม่ได้จะโทรมาบอก (เรียนภาษาไทย)

ถ้าเรียนภาษาไทยไม่ได้จะโทรมาบอก (ซื้อวิทยุ)

ถ้าซื้อวิทยุไม่ได้จะโทรมาบอก

b. Substitution drill.

keeŋ kày. (núa)	Chicken curry. (beef)
keeŋ núa. (phàt)	Beef curry. (a fried mixture)
phàt núa. (mǔu)	Fried beef and vegetables. (pork)
phàt mǔu. (kûŋ)	Fried pork and vegetables. (shrimps)
phàt kûŋ. (phèt)	Fried shrimps and vegetables. (hot)
phàt phèt. (keeŋ)	A hot fried mixture. (curry)
keeŋ phèt. (cùut)	Hot curry. (tasteless)
keeŋ cùut.	Thai soup.

c. Substitution drill.

wanníi mây tôŋ tham ʔaahǎan yen. (pay talàat)	You don't have to cook dinner today. (go to the market)
wan níi mây tôŋ pay talàat. (tham ŋaan)	You don't have to go to the market today. (work)
wan níi mây tôŋ tham ŋaan. (rian phasǎa thay)	You don't have to work today. (study Thai)
wan níi mây tôŋ rian phasǎa thay. (pay súu khɔ̌ɔŋ)	You don't have to study Thai today. (go shopping)
wan níi mây tôŋ pay súu khɔ̌ɔŋ.	You don't have to go shopping today.

d. Substitution drill.

raw ca pay kin khâŋ nɔ̂ɔk. (thîi bâan khun yaŋ)	We're going to eat out. (at Mr. Young's house)
raw ca pay kin thîi bâan khun yaŋ. (thîi ráan ʔaahǎan ník)	We're going to eat at Mr. Young's house. (at Nick's Restaurant)
raw ca pay kin thîi ráan ʔaahǎan ník. (khâŋ nɔ̂ɔk)	We're going to eat at Nick's Restaurant. (out)
raw ca pay kin khâŋ nɔ̂ɔk. (thîi thîi tham ŋaan)	We're going to eat out. (at the office)
raw ca pay kin thîi thîi tham ŋaan.	We're going to eat at the office.

e. Substitution drill.

thâa maa mây dây ca thoo maa bɔ̀ɔk. (pay thîaw)	If I can't come, I'll phone and tell you. (go out)
thâa pay thîaw mây dây ca thoo maa bɔ̀ɔk. (tham ŋaan)	If I can't go out, I'll phone and tell you. (work)
thâa tham ŋaan mây dây ca thoo maa bɔ̀ɔk. (rian phasǎa thay)	If I can't work, I'll phone and tell you. (study Thai)
thâa rian phasǎa thay mây dây ca thoo maa bɔ̀ɔk. (súu wítthayú?)	If I can't study Thai. I'll phone and tell you. (buy a radio)
thâa súu wítthayú? mây dây ca thoo maa bɔ̀ɔk.	If I can't buy a radio, I'll phone and tell you.

ฉ.

แปลว่าจะกลับมากิน (ไปกินข้างนอก)
แปลว่าจะไปกินข้างนอก (ทำงานที่บ้าน)
แปลว่าจะทำงานที่บ้าน (ไปหาคุณประสงค์)
แปลว่าจะไปหาคุณประสงค์ (ไม่อยู่ที่ที่ทำงาน)
แปลว่าจะไม่อยู่ที่ที่ทำงาน

๒๔.๘ เวลา

อีกสิบห้านาทีตีหนึ่ง	ตีสาม
ตีหนึ่ง	อีกยี่สิบห้านาทีตีสี่
ตีหนึ่งสิบนาที	ตีสี่ห้านาที
ตีสอง	อีกห้านาทีตีห้า
ตีสองครึ่ง	อีกสิบนาทีหกโมง (เช้า)

๒๔.๙ การสนทนาโต้ตอบ

ถ้า .... อยากได้ ...., เขาต้องทำยังไง

ถ้า .... อยากจะให้ ...., เขาต้องทำยังไง

f. Substitution drill.

plɛɛ wâa ca klàp maa kin.	It means I'll come home to eat.
(pay kin khâŋ nɔ̂ɔk)	(go eat out)
plɛɛ wâa ca pay kin khâŋ nɔ̂ɔk.	It means I'll go out to eat.
(tham ŋaan thîi bâan)	(work at home)
plɛɛ wâa ca tham ŋaan thîi bâan.	It means I'll work at home.
(pay hăa khun prasŏŋ)	(go see Khun Prasong)
plɛɛ wâa ca pay hăa khun prasŏŋ.	It means I'm going to go see Khun Prasong.
(mây yùu thîi thîi tham ŋaan)	(not be at the office)
plɛɛ wâa ca mây yùu thîi thîi tham ŋaan.	It means I won't be at the office.

24.8 Time of day.

12:45 a.m.	ʔìik sìp hâa naathii tii nɨ̀ŋ
1:00 a.m.	tii nɨ̀ŋ
1:10 a.m.	tii nɨ̀ŋ sìp naathii
2:00 a.m.	tii sɔ̆ɔŋ
2:30 a.m.	tii sɔ̆ɔŋ khrɨ̂ŋ
3:00 a.m.	tii săam
3:35 a.m.	ʔìik yîi sìp hâa naathii tii sìi
4:05 a.m.	tii sìi hâa naathii
4:55 a.m.	ʔìik hâa naathii tii hâa
5:50 a.m.	ʔìik sìp naathii hòk mooŋ (cháaw)

Practice reading the following times. Try to get the time under 45 seconds.

3:00 a.m.	4:40 a.m.	5:00 a.m.	1:55 a.m.	12:50 a.m.
12:35 a.m.	2:15 a.m.	3:45 a.m.	3:30 a.m.	2:00 a.m.
2:45 a.m.	5:30 a.m.	1:30 a.m.	4:05 a.m.	3:25 a.m.
1:00 a.m.	1:20 a.m.	4:00 a.m.	2:30 a.m.	5:50 a.m.

24.9 Conversation.

The teacher should read the narrative of lesson 20 (Book 1) to the students. Each student should then ask the teacher questions as suggested below.

thâa .... yàak dây ...., kháw tôŋ tham yaŋŋay.

thâa .... yàak ca hây ...., kháw tôŋ tham yaŋŋay.

๒๔.๑๐ การเขียน

เหลื๊อง	เกลื๊อ	เหมื๊อนกัน
เหลื๊อง	เชิ๊ง	คื๊น
เหลื๊อก	เชิด	คื๊อ
เหลื๊อ	เฉิด	คื๊บ
เกลื๊อ	เฉี๊ยด	เคลื๊อบ
กลั๊ว	เฉี๊ยง	เหลื๊อบ
หลั๊ว	เขี๊ยง	เหลอ
หลวง	เขี๊ยน	เกลอ
เหลิ๊ง	ขื๊น	เกลิก

24.10 Writing.

เหลือง	เกลือ	เหมือนกัน
lǔaŋ Yellow.	klʉa Salt.	mǔankan Likewise.

เหลือง	*lǔaŋ	เชิง	chəəŋ	คืน	khʉʉn
เหลือก	lʉ̀ak	เชิด	chə̂ət	คือ	khʉʉ
เหลือ	lʉ̌a	เฉิด	chə̀ət	คืบ	khʉ̂ʉp
เกลือ	*klʉa	เฉียด	chìat	เคลือบ	khlʉ̂ap
กลัว	klua	เฉียง	chǐaŋ	เหลือบ	lʉ̀ap
หลัว	lǔa	เขียง	khǐaŋ	เหลอ	*lə̌ə
หลวง	lǔaŋ	เขียน	*khǐan	เกลอ	kləə
เหลิง	lə̌əŋ	ขืน	khʉ̌ʉn	เกลิก	klə̀ək

59

บทที่ ๒๕

๒๕.บ

คุณสวัสดิ์เป็นคนไทย เขาชอบทานอาหารไทย เขาบอกว่าอาหารไทยอร่อย เขาไม่ชอบทานอาหารฝรั่ง เขาบอกว่าอาหารฝรั่งจืด

คุณยังเป็นฝรั่ง เขาชอบทานอาหารฝรั่ง เขาบอกว่าอาหารฝรั่งอร่อย เขาไม่ชอบทานอาหารไทย เขาบอกว่าอาหารไทยเผ็ด

ตอนเช้าคุณสวัสดิ์ทานข้าวต้ม คุณยังทานไข่กับหมูแฮมหรือหมูเบคอน

ตอนกลางวันคุณสวัสดิ์ทานก๋วยเตี๋ยวหรือข้าวผัด คุณยังทานซุบ, แซนวิช, กับมันทอด

ตอนเย็นคุณสวัสดิ์ทานข้าวกับแกง, น้ำพริกปลาทู และผัดอะไรอย่างหนึ่ง คุณยังทานเนื้อ, หมู หรือไก่ทอด หรืออบกับมันฝรั่ง, ผักและขนมปัง

คุณสวัสดิ์กับคุณยังชอบทานเบียร์ทั้งสองคน เขาไปทานเบียร์ด้วยกันบ่อยบ่อย

คุณสวัสดิ์เป็นคนไทยใช่ไหม
เขาชอบทานอาหารฝรั่งใช่ไหม
เขาบอกว่าอาหารไทยจืดใช่ไหม
เขาชอบทานอาหารฝรั่งใช่ไหม
เขาบอกว่าอาหารฝรั่งเผ็ดใช่ไหม
คุณยังเป็นคนไทยใช่ไหม
เขาชอบทานอาหารฝรั่งใช่ไหม
เขาบอกว่าอาหารฝรั่งไม่อร่อยใช่ไหม
เขาชอบทานอาหารไทยใช่ไหม
เขาบอกว่าอาหารไทยเผ็ดใช่ไหม
ตอนเช้าคุณสวัสดิ์ทานไข่ใช่ไหม

และคุณยังทานก๋วยเตี๋ยวใช่ไหม
ตอนกลางวันคุณสวัสดิ์ทานก๋วยเตี๋ยวหรือ
　ข้าวผัดใช่ไหม
และคุณยังทานแซนวิชกับมันทอดใช่ไหม
ตอนเย็นคุณสวัสดิ์ทานหมูอบกับมันฝรั่ง
　ใช่ไหม
และคุณยังทานน้ำพริกปลาทูใช่ไหม
คุณสวัสดิ์ชอบทานเบียร์ใช่ไหม
คุณยังไม่ชอบทานเบียร์ใช่ไหม
คุณยังกับคุณสวัสดิ์ไปเที่ยวด้วยกัน
　บ่อยบ่อยใช่ไหม

60

LESSON 25
(Review)

25.a Review sections 3, 5, 7, and 9 of lessons 21 - 24.

25.b Narrative.

khun sawàt pen khon thay. kháw chɔ̂ɔp thaan ʔaahǎan thay. kháw bɔ̀ɔk wâa ʔaahǎan thay ʔarɔ̀y. kháw mây chɔ̂ɔp thaan ʔaahǎan faràŋ. kháw bɔ̀ɔk wâa ʔaahǎan faràŋ cɯ̀ɯt.

khun yaŋ pen faràŋ. kháw chɔ̂ɔp thaan ʔaahǎan faràŋ. kháw bɔ̀ɔk wâa ʔaahǎan faràŋ ʔarɔ̀y. kháw mây chɔ̂ɔp thaan ʔaahǎan thay. kháw bɔ̀ɔk wâa ʔaahǎan thay phèt.

tɔɔn cháaw khun sawàt thaan khâaw tôm. khun yaŋ thaan khày kàp mǔu hɛm rɯ́ mǔu beekhɔ̂n.

tɔɔn klaaŋ wan khun sawàt thaan kúaytǐaw rɯ́ khâaw phàt. khun yaŋ thaan súp, sɛɛnwít, kàp man thɔ̂ɔt.

tɔɔn yen khun sawàt thaan khâaw kàp kɛɛŋ, nám phrík plaa thuu (*thuu* fish with shrimp-paste chili sauce), lɛ́ʔ phàt ʔaray yàaŋ nɯŋ (some kind of *phàt*). khun yaŋ thaan nɯ́a, mǔu, rɯ́ kày thɔ̂ɔt rɯ́ ʔɔ̀p, kàp man faràŋ, phàk lɛ́ʔ khanǒmpaŋ.

khun sawàt kàp khun yaŋ chɔ̂ɔp thaan bia tháŋ sɔ̌ɔŋ (all two, both) khon. kháw pay thaan bia dûaykan bɔ̀ybɔ̀y (often).

Answer the following questions with *chây* or *mây chây*.

khun sawàt pen khon thay chây máy.
kháw chɔ̂ɔp thaan ʔaahǎan faràŋ chây máy.
kháw bɔ̀ɔk wâa ʔaahǎan thay cɯ̀ɯt chây máy.
kháw chɔ̂ɔp thaan ʔaahǎan faràŋ chây máy.
kháw bɔ̀ɔk wâa ʔaahǎan faràŋ phèt chây máy.
khun yaŋ pen khon thay chây máy.
kháw chɔ̂ɔp thaan ʔaahǎan faràŋ chây máy.
kháw bɔ̀ɔk wâa ʔaahǎan faràŋ mây ʔarɔ̀y chây máy.
kháw chɔ̂ɔp thaan ʔaahǎan thay chây máy.
kháw bɔ̀ɔk wâa ʔaahǎan thay phèt chây máy.
tɔɔn cháaw khun sawàt thaan khày chây máy.
lɛ́ʔ khun yaŋ thaan kúaytǐaw chây máy.
tɔɔn klaaŋ wan khun sawàt thaan kúaytǐaw rɯ́ khâaw phàt chây máy.
lɛ́ʔ khun yaŋ thaan sɛɛnwít kàp man thɔ̂ɔt chây máy.
tɔɔn yen khun sawàt thaan mǔu ʔɔ̀p kàp man faràŋ chây máy.
lɛ́ʔ khun yaŋ thaan nám phrík plaa thuu chây máy.
khun sawàt chɔ̂ɔp thaan bia chây máy.
khun yaŋ mây chɔ̂ɔp thaan bia chây máy.
khun yaŋ kàp khun sawàt pay thîaw dûaykan bɔ̀ybɔ̀y chây máy.

คุณยังเป็นคนไทยหรือฝรั่ง
เขาชอบทานอาหารไทยหรืออาหารฝรั่ง
เขาบอกว่าอาหารฝรั่งอร่อยหรือไม่อร่อย
เขาไม่ชอบทานอาหารไทยหรืออาหารฝรั่ง
เขาบอกว่าอาหารไทยเผ็ดหรือจืด
ตอนเช้าเขาทานข้าวต้มหรือไข่กับหมูแฮม
ตอนกลางวันเขาทานแซนวิชหรือก๋วยเตี๋ยว
ตอนเย็นเขาทานข้าวหรือมันฝรั่ง
คุณสวัสดิ์เป็นคนไทยหรือฝรั่ง
เขาชอบทานอาหารไทยหรืออาหารฝรั่ง
เขาบอกว่าอาหารไทยอร่อยหรือไม่อร่อย
เขาบอกว่าอาหารฝรั่งเผ็ดหรือจืด
ตอนเช้าเขาทานไข่กับหมูเบคอนหรือ
    ข้าวต้ม
ตอนกลางวันเขาทานซุบหรือข้าวผัด
ตอนเย็นเขาทานเนื้อทอดหรือน้ำพริก
    ปลาทู
คุณสวัสดิ์กับคุณยังชอบกินเบียร์ทั้งสอง
    คนหรือคนเดียว
เขาไปเที่ยวกันบ่อยหรือไม่บ่อย

คุณสวัสดิ์เป็นคนชาติอะไร
เขาชอบทานอาหารอะไร
เขาบอกว่าอาหารไทยเป็นยังไง
คุณยังเป็นคนชาติอะไร
เขาชอบทานอาหารอะไร
เขาบอกว่าอาหารฝรั่งเป็นยังไง
เขาบอกว่าอาหารไทยเป็นยังไง
ตอนเช้าคุณสวัสดิ์ทานอะไร
แล้วคุณยังล่ะทานอะไร
ตอนกลางวันคุณยังทานอะไร
แล้วคุณสวัสดิ์ล่ะ, ทานอะไร
ตอนเย็นคุณสวัสดิ์ทานอะไร
แล้วตอนเช้าล่ะ, ทานอะไร
ตอนกลางวันคุณยังทานอะไร
แล้วตอนเย็นล่ะ, ทานอะไร
มีอะไรที่คุณสวัสดิ์และคุณยัง
    ชอบทานทั้งสองคน

Answer the following questions with the correct alternative.

khun yaŋ pen khon thay rú faràŋ.

kháw chɔ̂ɔp thaan ʔaahǎan thay rú ʔaahǎan faràŋ.

kháw bɔ̀ɔk wâa ʔaahǎan faràŋ ʔarɔ̀y rú mây ʔarɔ̀y.

kháw mây chɔ̂ɔp thaan ʔaahǎan thay rú ʔaahǎan faràŋ.

kháw bɔ̀ɔk wâa ʔaahǎan thay phèt rú cùut.

tɔɔn cháaw kháw thaan khâaw tôm rú khày ka mǔu hɛm.

tɔɔn klaaŋ wan kháw thaan sɛɛnwít rú kúaytǐaw.

tɔɔn yen kháw thaan khâaw rú man faràŋ.

khun sawàt pen khon thay rú faràŋ.

kháw chɔ̂ɔp thaan ʔaahǎan thay rú ʔaahǎan faràŋ.

kháw bɔ̀ɔk wâa ʔaahǎan thay ʔarɔ̀y rú mây ʔarɔ̀y.

kháw bɔ̀ɔk wâa ʔaahǎan faràŋ phèt rú cùut.

tɔɔn cháaw kháw thaan khày ka mǔu beekhɔ̂n rú khâaw tôm.

tɔɔn klaaŋ wan kháw thaan súp rú khâaw phàt.

tɔɔn yen kháw thaan núa thɔ̂ɔt rú nám phrík plaa thuu.

khun sawàt ka khun yaŋ chɔ̂ɔp kin bia thâŋ sɔ̌ɔŋ khon rú khon diaw.

kháw pay thîaw kan bɔ̀y rú mây bɔ̀y.

Answer the following questions with the shortest possible answers.

khun sawàt pen khon châat ʔaray. (*châat* means nationality.)

kháw chɔ̂ɔp thaan ʔaahǎan ʔaray.

kháw bɔ̀ɔk wâa ʔaahǎan thay pen yaŋŋay.

khun yaŋ pen khon châat ʔaray.

kháw chɔ̂ɔp thaan ʔaahǎan ʔaray.

kháw bɔ̀ɔk wâa ʔaahǎan faràŋ pen yaŋŋay.

kháw bɔ̀ɔk wâa ʔaahǎan thay pen yaŋŋay.

tɔɔn cháaw khun sawàt thaan ʔaray.

léɛw khun yaŋ lâ. thaan ʔaray.

tɔɔn klaaŋ wan khun yaŋ thaan ʔaray.

léɛw khun sawàt lâ. thaan ʔaray.

tɔɔn yen khun sawàt thaan ʔaray.

léɛw tɔɔn cháaw lâ. thaan ʔaray.

tɔɔn klaaŋ wan khun yaŋ thaan ʔaray.

léɛw tɔɔn yen lâ. thaan ʔaray.

mii ʔaray thîi khun sawàt lɛ́ʔ khun yaŋ chɔ̂ɔp thaan thâŋ sɔ̌ɔŋ khon.

คุณสวัสดิ์เป็นฝรั่งใช่ไหม
   ไม่ใช่, เขาเป็นคนไทย

เขาชอบทานอาหารฝรั่งใช่ไหม
   ไม่ใช่, เขาชอบทานอาหารไทย

เขาบอกว่าอาหารไทยไม่อร่อยใช่ไหม
   ไม่ใช่, เขาบอกว่าอาหารไทยอร่อย

เขาไม่ชอบทานอาหารฝรั่งใช่ไหม
   ใช่, เขาบอกว่าอาหารฝรั่งจืด

เขาบอกว่าอาหารฝรั่งเผ็ดใช่ไหม
   ไม่ใช่, เขาบอกว่าอาหารฝรั่งจืด

คุณยังเป็นคนไทยใช่ไหม
   ไม่ใช่, เขาเป็นฝรั่ง

เขาชอบทานอาหารฝรั่งใช่ไหม
   ใช่, เขาบอกว่าอาหารฝรั่งอร่อย

เขาบอกว่าอาหารฝรั่งไม่อร่อยใช่ไหม
   ไม่ใช่, เขาบอกว่าอาหารฝรั่งอร่อย

เขาชอบทานอาหารไทยใช่ไหม
   ไม่ใช่,   เขาไม่ชอบทานอาหารไทย
เขาบอกว่าเผ็ด

เขาบอกว่าอาหารไทยจืดใช่ไหม
   ไม่ใช่, เขาบอกว่าอาหารไทยเผ็ด

ตอนเช้าคุณยังทานข้าวต้มใช่ไหม
   ไม่ใช่, ตอนเช้าเขาทานไข่กับหมู

ตอนกลางวันเขาทานก๊วยเตี๋ยวใช่ไหม
   ไม่ใช่, ตอนกลางวันเขาทานแซนวิช
กับมันทอด

ตอนเย็นเขาทานเนื้อกับมันฝรั่งใช่ไหม
   ใช่, แล้วก็ผักกับขนมปังด้วย

ตอนเช้าคุณสวัสดิ์ทานไข่ใช่ไหม
   ไม่ใช่, ตอนเช้าเขาทานข้าวต้ม

ตอนเย็นเขาทานก๊วยเตี๋ยวหรือข้าวผัดใช่
ไหม
   ไม่ใช่,   ตอนเย็นเขาทานข้าวกับแกง,
ผัดและน้ำพริกปลาทู

ตอนกลางวันเขาทานแซนวิชใช่ไหม
   ไม่ใช่, ตอนกลางวันเขาทานก๊วยเตี๋ยว
หรือข้าวผัด

คุณสวัสดิ์ไม่รู้จักคุณยังใช่ไหม
   ไม่ใช่, เขารู้จัก

คุณสวัสดิ์กับคุณยังไม่ชอบ ทานเบียร์ทั้ง
สองคนใช่ไหม
   ไม่ใช่, เขาชอบทานทั้งสองคน

คุณยังกับคุณ สวัสดิ์ไม่ ชอบไปเที่ยวด้วย
กันใช่ไหม
   ไม่ใช่, เขาชอบ เขาไปเที่ยวด้วยกัน
บ่อยบ่อย

First read and then listen to the following questions and answers for comprehension only.

khun sawàt pen faràŋ chây máy.
    mây chây. kháw pen khon thay.

kháw chɔ̂ɔp thaan ʔaahǎan faràŋ chây máy.
    mây chây. kháw chɔ̂ɔp thaan ʔaahǎan thay.

kháw bɔ̀ɔk wâa ʔaahǎan thay mây ʔarɔ̀y chây máy.
    mây chây. kháw bɔ̀ɔk wâ̂a ʔaahǎan thay ʔarɔ̀y.

kháw mây chɔ̂ɔp thaan ʔaahǎan faràŋ chây máy.
    chây. kháw bɔ̀ɔk wâa ʔaahǎan faràŋ cùut.

kháw bɔ̀ɔk wâa ʔaahǎan faràŋ phèt chây máy.
    mây chây. kháw bɔ̀ɔk wâa ʔaahǎan faràŋ cùut.

khun yaŋ pen khon thay chây máy.
    mây chây. kháw pen faràŋ.

kháw chɔ̂ɔp thaan ʔaahǎan faràŋ chây máy.
    chây. kháw bɔ̀ɔk wâa ʔaahǎan faràŋ ʔarɔ̀y.

kháw bɔ̀ɔk wâa ʔaahǎan faràŋ mây ʔarɔ̀y chây máy.
    mây chây. kháw bɔ̀ɔk wâa ʔaahǎan faràŋ ʔarɔ̀y.

kháw chɔ̂ɔp thaan ʔaahǎan thay chây máy.
    mây chây. kháw mây chɔ̂ɔp thaan ʔaahǎan thay. kháw bɔ̀ɔk wâa phèt.

kháw bɔ̀ɔk wâa ʔaahǎan thay cùut chây máy.
    mây chây. kháw bɔ̀ɔk wâa ʔaahǎan thay phèt.

tɔɔn cháaw khun yaŋ thaan khâaw tôm chây máy.
    mây chây. tɔɔn cháaw kháw thaan khày ka mǔu.

tɔɔn klaaŋ wan kháw thaan kúaytǐaw chây máy.
    mây chây. tɔɔn klaaŋ wan kháw thaan sɛɛnwít ka man thɔ̂ɔt.

tɔɔn yen kháw thaan núa ka man faràŋ chây máy.
    chây. lɛ́ɛw kô phàk ka khanǒmpaŋ dûay.

tɔɔn cháaw khun sawàt thaan khày chây máy.
    mây chây. tɔɔn cháaw kháw thaan khâaw tôm.

tɔɔn yen kháw thaan kúaytǐaw rú khâaw phàt chây máy.
    mây chây. tɔɔn yen kháw thaan khâaw kàp kɛɛŋ, phàt, lɛ́ʔ nám phrík plaa thuu.

tɔɔn klaaŋ wan kháw thaan sɛɛnwít chây máy.
    mây chây. tɔɔn klaaŋ wan kháw thaan kúaytǐaw rú khâaw phàt.

khun sawàt mây rúucàk khun yaŋ chây máy.
    mây chây. kháw rúucàk.

khun sawàt ka khun yaŋ mây chɔ̂ɔp thaan bia tháŋ sɔ̌ɔŋ khon chây máy.
    mây chây. kháw chɔ̂ɔp thaan tháŋ sɔ̌ɔŋ khon.

khun yaŋ ka khun sawàt mây chɔ̂ɔp pay thîaw dûaykan chây máy.
    mây chây. kháw chɔ̂ɔp. kháw pay thîaw dûaykan bɔ̀ybɔ̀y.

๒๕.ก

ก. ทานอะไรบ้างครับ

ข. เอาแซนวิชไข่สองชิ้น, ข้าวผัดจานหนึ่ง แล้วก็ขอเบียร์เย็นเย็นขวดหนึ่งด้วย

ก. เบียร์ไม่มีครับ, มีน้ำชา, กาแฟ, น้ำมะนาว, น้ำผลไม้ครับ

ข. เอาชาเย็นแก้วหนึ่ง

ก. ทานอะไรอีกไหมครับ

ข. เท่านั้นพอแล้ว อ้อ, มีบุหรี่ไหม

ก. บุหรี่อะไรครับ, ไทยหรืออเมริกัน

ข. บุหรี่อเมริกัน

ก. มีครับ เอาไม้ขีดด้วยไหมครับ

ข. เอาด้วย ขอที่เขี่ยบุหรี่หน่อยได้ไหม

ก. นี่ครับ

ข. ขอบใจ, ทั้งหมดเท่าไร

ก. สามสิบแปดบาทครับ

25.c Dialog. (Ordering a meal.)

A. thaan ʔaray bâaŋ khráp.

   B. ʔaw sɛɛnwít khày sɔ̌ɔŋ chín, khâaw phàt caan nɯŋ,
      lɛ́ɛw kɔ̂ khɔ̌ɔ bia yenyen khùat nɯŋ dûay.

A. bia mây mii khráp.
   mii nám chaa, kaafɛɛ, nám manaaw, nám phɔ̌nlamáay khráp.

   B. ʔaw chaa yen kɛ̂ɛw nɯŋ.

A. thaan ʔaray ʔìik máy khráp.

   B. thâwnán phɔɔ lɛ́ɛw. ʔɔ̂ɔ, mii burìi máy.

A. burìi ʔaray khráp. thay rɯ́ ʔameerikan.

   B. burìi ʔameerikan.

A. mii khráp. ʔaw máykhìit dûay máy khráp.

   B. ʔaw dûay. khɔ̌ɔ thîi khìa burìi nɔ̀y dây máy.

A. nîi khráp.

   B. khɔ̀ɔpcay ('thanks' to a social inferior). tháŋmòt (altogether) thâwrày.

A. sǎam sìp pɛ̀ɛt bàat khráp.

บทที่ ๒๖

๒๖.๑ คำศัพท์

ยืน

คอย

คอยที่นี่

ยืนคอยที่นี่

รถ

รถยนต์

ถอยรถ

รับ

ถอยรถมารับ

จอด

จอดรถ

จอดที่โน่น

รถจอดอยู่ที่โน่น

เสีย

หลาย

หลายวันแล้ว

เสียมาหลายวันแล้ว

แก้

เอาไปแก้

เอาไปแก้ยังไม่เสร็จ

ขับ

ขับรถ

เอง

ขับเอง

ขับรถเอง

เป็น

ไหว

ได้

นาน

LESSON 26

26.1 Vocabulary and expansions.

yɯɯn	To stand.
khɔɔy	To wait for.
khɔɔy thîi nîi	To wait here.
yɯɯn khɔɔy thîi nîi	Stand and wait here.
rót	Any wheeled vehicle.
rót yon	Automobile.
thɔ̌y rót	To back up a car.
ráp	To receive, pick up someone.
thɔ̌y rót maa ráp	'Back up car come get.' Long strings of verbs can be used in Thai. In English at least one of the verbs in this example must be omitted: I'll come pick you up (backing). I'll back up and get you (coming).
cɔ̀ɔt	To park, bring to a stop.
cɔ̀ɔt rót	To park the car.
cɔ̀ɔt thîi nôon	Park over there.
rót cɔ̀ɔt yùu thîi nôon	The car is parked over there. *yùu* adds a tense-like modification to the verb. It focuses on the current duration of the verb's meaning and thus points up its relevance to the present situation (see below).
sǐa	To be spoiled, out of order.
lǎay	Several.
lǎay wan lɛ́ɛw	Several days now.
sǐa maa lǎay wan lɛ́ɛw	It has been out of order for several days now. *maa*, like *yùu*, adds a tense-like meaning to the main verb. It suggests a passage of the verb's meaning coming through a time period up until now. 'It *has been* out of order *coming through* several days up to now.' Compare this with *rót sǐa yùu*. Here the focus is not on the period of time that the car has been out of order, but rather on the fact that the car is out of order *now* and our present actions are affected (we'll have to take a bus).
kɛ̂ɛ	To repair, make right, to correct.
ʔaw pay kɛ̂ɛ	To take for repairs.
ʔaw pay kɛ̂ɛ yaŋ mây sèt	I took it to be fixed, but it isn't ready yet. 'Take, go, fix, still not finished.'
khàp	To drive.
khàp rót	To drive a car.
ʔeeŋ	Self.
khàp ʔeeŋ	To do one's own driving.
khàp rót ʔeeŋ	I drive the car myself.
pen	To be mentally able, to know how.
wǎy	To be physically able, to be up to.
dây	To be able, to have permission.
naan	To be long in time.
(More.)	

อา
น้ำ
ป้อน
แพ้

อาทิตย์
เดือน

ราย
การ
รายการ
รายการอาหาร

ตัง
สตางค์
คิด
คิดตังค์

๒๖.๒ โครงสร้างของประโยค

ถอยรถไม่เป็น
จอดรถไม่เป็น
ขับรถไม่เป็น
ขับรถไม่ได้
ขับรถไม่ไหว

เขาจะขับรถมารับคุณ
ฉันจะขับรถไปรับเขา

โทรศัพท์เสีย
วิทยุเสีย
นมเสีย
อาหารเสีย

ฉันคอยมาหลายวันแล้ว
ฉันไม่ได้พบเขามานานแล้ว
รถเสียมานานแล้ว

ฉันเอง
คุณเอง
เขาเอง

ฉันทำเอง
คุณทำเอง
เขาทำเอง

ʔaa	Father's younger sibling, aunt, uncle. (Because of translation difficulties, this will usually be referred to as *Ah* in English translations of drills.)
náa	Mother's younger sibling, aunt, uncle. *Nah* (see above). Note that one's parents' older siblings are differentiated by the sex of the person (luŋ, pâa) while the younger siblings are differentiated by the sex of the parent.
pɔ̂ɔn	To feed someone.
phɛ́ɛ	To lose to someone (as in a game).
ʔathít	Week.
dʉan	Month.
raay kaan	
raaykaan	A list of items.
raaykaan ʔaahǎan	Menu.
taŋ	The usual pronunciation of *sataaŋ*.
sataaŋ	One-hundredth part of a baht. Money.
khít	To figure, think.
khít taŋ	Figure up the bill.

26.2 Patterns.

thɔ̌y rót mây pen.	I don't know how to back up a car.
cɔ̀ɔt rót mây pen.	I don't know how to park a car.
khàp rót mây pen.	I don't know how to drive a car.
khàp rót mây dây.	I can't drive (I don't have a license).
khàp rót mây wǎy.	I can't drive (I'm feeling too weak).
kháw ca khàp rót maa ráp khun.	He'll drive here and pick you up.
chán ca khàp rót pay ráp kháw.	I'll drive there and pick him up.
thoorasàp sǐa.	The phone is out of order.
wítthayúʔ sǐa.	The radio doesn't work.
nom sǐa.	The milk is sour.
ʔaahǎan sǐa.	The food is spoiled.
chán khɔɔy maa lǎay wan lɛ́ɛw.	I've been waiting for several days now.
chán mây dây phóp kháw maa naan lɛ́ɛw.	I haven't seen him for a long time.
rót sǐa maa naan lɛ́ɛw.	The car has been out of order for a long time now.
chán ʔeeŋ.	I myself.
khun ʔeeŋ.	You yourself.
kháw ʔeeŋ.	He himself.
chán tham ʔeeŋ.	I did it myself.
khun tham ʔeeŋ.	You did it yourself.
kháw tham ʔeeŋ.	He did it himself.

71

๒๖.๓ บทสนทนา

ก. คุณยืนคอยที่นี่ก่อน เดี๋ยวผมจะถอยรถมารับ

    ข. รถจอดอยู่ที่ไหน

ก. จอดอยู่ที่โน่น ที่นี่จอดรถไม่ได้

    ข. ไม่เป็นไร ผมจะเดินไปกับคุณ

       รถผมเสียมาหลายวันแล้ว เอาไปแก้ยังไม่เสร็จ

ก. คุณขับรถเองหรือ

    ข. เปล่า, ผมขับไม่เป็น

๒๖.๔ แบบฝึกหัดการฟังและการออกเสียงสูงต่ำ

ก.

ค้นคว้า   เชียงใหม่   ส้มโอ   หมู่บ้าน   หัวหิน

ข.

ประชุมเตือนอาใช่ไหม   ประสงค์ถามป้าใช่ไหม

    ไม่ใช่, อาเตือนประชุม   ไม่ใช่, ป้าถามประสงค์

ประเสริฐบอกปู่ใช่ไหม   ประพัทธ์ทักน้าใช่ไหม

    ไม่ใช่, ปู่บอกประเสริฐ   ไม่ใช่, น้าทักประพัทธ์

ประภาสพูดกับป้าใช่ไหม

    ไม่ใช่, ป้าพูดกับประภาส

26.3 Dialog.

A. khun yʉʉn khɔɔy thîi nîi kɔɔn.　　　You stand here and wait. (*kɔɔn* implies 'while I go'.)
　　dǐaw phǒm ca thɔ̌y rót maa ráp.　　　I'll come pick you up in a minute.

　B. rót còɔt yùu thîi nǎy.　　　　　Where's your car parked?

A. còɔt yùu thîi nôon.　　　　　It's parked over there.
　　thîi nîi còɔt rót mây dây.　　　Parking isn't allowed here.

　B. mây pen ray.　　　　　　Never mind.
　　phǒm ca dəən pay kàp khun.　　　I'll walk along with you.
　　rót phǒm sǐa maa lǎay wan lɛ́ɛw.　　My car has been out of order for several days
　　ʔaw pay kɛ̂ɛ yaŋ mây sèt.　　　now.　I took it to be fixed, but it isn't ready yet.

A. khun khàp rót ʔeeŋ lɔ̌ə.　　　　Do you do your own driving?

　B. plàaw. phǒm khàp mây pen.　　　No. I can't drive.

26.4　Tone identification and production.

a.　Identify the tones and record the number of repetitions required.

To research.	khon khwaa	....	....
Chiang Mai.	chiaŋ may	....	....
Pomelo.	som ʔoo	....	....
Village.	muu baan	....	....
Hua Hin.	hua hin	....	....

b. Response drill.

prachum tʉan ʔaa chây máy.　　　Prachum warned Ah, didn't he?
　mây chây. ʔaa tʉan prachum.　　　No.　Ah warned Prachum.

prasəət bɔ̀ɔk pùu chây máy.　　　Prasert told Grandpa, didn't he?
　mây chây.　pùu bɔ̀ɔk prasəət.　　　No. Grandpa told Prasert.

praphâat phûut kàp pâa chây máy.　　Prapart talked to Auntie, didn't he?
　mây chây.　pâa phûut kàp praphâat.　No. Auntie talked to Prapart.

prasǒŋ thǎam pǎa chây máy.　　　Prasong asked Papa, didn't he?
　mây chây.　pǎa thǎam prasǒŋ.　　　No.　Papa asked Prasong.

praphát thák náa chây máy.　　　Prapat greeted Nah, didn't he?
　mây chây.　náa thák praphát.　　　No.　Nah greeted Prapat.

๒๖.๕ แบบฝึกหัดการสลับเสียงสูงต่ำ

ก.

มีไหม, เนื้อ มีเนื้อไหม (ไก่)
มีไหม, ไก่ มีไก่ไหม (กุ้ง)
มีไหม, กุ้ง มีกุ้งไหม (เห็น)
เห็นไหม, กุ้ง เห็นกุ้งไหม (เนื้อ)
เห็นไหม, เนื้อ เห็นเนื้อไหม (ใส่)
ใส่ไหม, เนื้อ ใส่เนื้อไหม (หมู)
ใส่ไหม, หมู ใส่หมูไหม (ชอบ)
ชอบไหม, หมู ชอบหมูไหม (ซื้อ)
ซื้อไหม, หมู ซื้อหมูไหม (ปลา)
ซื้อไหม, ปลา ซื้อปลาไหม (มี)
มีไหม, ปลา มีปลาไหม (หมู)
มีไหม, หมู มีหมูไหม (เห็น)
เห็นไหม, หมู เห็นหมูไหม (ปลา)

เห็นไหม, ปลา เห็นปลาไหม (ใส่)
ใส่ไหม, ปลา ใส่ปลาไหม (ชอบ)
ชอบไหม, ปลา ชอบปลาไหม (ไก่)
ชอบไหม, ไก่ ชอบไก่ไหม (ซื้อ)
ซื้อไหม, ไก่ ซื้อไก่ไหม (กุ้ง)
ซื้อไหม, กุ้ง ซื้อกุ้งไหม (เนื้อ)
ซื้อไหม, เนื้อ ซื้อเนื้อไหม (ชอบ)
ชอบไหม, เนื้อ ชอบเนื้อไหม (กุ้ง)
ชอบไหม, กุ้ง ชอบกุ้งไหม (ใส่)
ใส่ไหม, กุ้ง ใส่กุ้งไหม (ไก่)
ใส่ไหม, ไก่ ใส่ไก่ไหม (เห็น)
เห็นไหม, ไก่ เห็นไก่ไหม

๒๖.๖ แบบฝึกหัดการออกเสียงสระและพยัญชนะ

ก.   เห็ด   เหตุ   สด   โสด

26.5 Tone manipulation.

a. Substitution drill.

mii máy. núa. mii núa máy. (kày)

mii máy. kày. mii kày máy. (kûŋ)

mii máy. kûŋ. mii kûŋ máy. (hěn)

hěn máy. kûŋ. hěn kûŋ máy. (núa)

hěn máy. núa. hěn núa máy. (sày)

sày máy. núa. sày núa máy. (mǔu)

sày máy. mǔu. sày mǔu máy. (chɔ̂ɔp)
chɔ̂ɔp máy. mǔu. chɔ̂ɔp mǔu máy. (súu)
súu máy. mǔu. súu mǔu máy. (plaa)
súu máy. plaa. súu plaa máy. (mii)
mii máy. plaa. mii plaa máy. (mǔu)
mii máy. mǔu. mii mǔu máy. (hěn)
hěn máy. mǔu. hěn mǔu máy. (plaa)
hěn máy. plaa. hěn plaa máy. (sày)
sày máy. plaa. sày plaa máy. (chɔ̂ɔp)
chɔ̂ɔp máy. plaa. chɔ̂ɔp plaa máy. (kày)
chɔ̂ɔp máy. kày. chɔ̂ɔp kày máy. (súu)
súu máy. kày. súu kày máy. (kûŋ)
súu máy. kûŋ. súu kûŋ máy. (núa)
súu máy. núa. súu núa máy. (chɔ̂ɔp)
chɔ̂ɔp máy. núa. chɔ̂ɔp núa máy. (kûŋ)
chɔ̂ɔp máy. kûŋ. chɔ̂ɔp kûŋ máy. (sày)
sày máy. kûŋ. sày kûŋ máy. (kày)
sày máy. kày. sày kày máy. (hěn)
hěn máy. kày. hěn kày máy.

Do you have any? Beef, that is.
Do you have any beef? (chicken)
Do you have any? Chicken, that is.
Do you have any chicken? (shrimps)
Do you have any? Shrimps, that is.
Do you have any shrimps? (see)
Do you see any? Shrimps, that is.
Do you see any shrimps? (beef)
Do you see any? Beef, that is.
Do you see any beef? (put in)
Shall I put in some? Beef, that is.
Shall I put in some beef? (pork)
Shall I put in some pork? (like)
Do you like pork? (buy)
Do you want to buy pork? (fish)
Do you want to buy fish? (have)
Do you have any fish? (pork)
Do you have any pork? (see)
Do you see any pork? (fish)
Do you see any fish? (put in)
Shall I put in some fish? (like)
Do you like fish? (chicken)
Do you like chicken? (buy)
Do you want to buy chicken? (shrimps)
Do you want to buy shrimps? (beef)
Do you want to buy beef? (like)
Do you like beef? (shrimps)
Do you like shrimps? (put in)
Shall I put in some shrimps? (chicken)
Shall I put in some chicken? (see)
Do you see any chicken?

26.6 Vowel and consonant drills.

a. e-ee and o-oo contrast drills.

hèt	sòt
hèet	sòot

75

ข.

บิ๋มบอกบ้า

      บ้าบอกบิ๋ม

พ่อแพ้บ้า

      บ้าแพ้พ่อ

บ้าป้อนบิ๋ม

      บิ๋มป้อนบ้า

บ้าป้อนพ่อ

      พ่อป้อนบ้า

เบิ๊มป้อนปู่

      ปู่ป้อนเบิ๊ม

พี่ป้อนปู่

      ปู่ป้อนพี่

ปู่บอกเบิ๊ม

      เบิ๊มบอกปู่

ปู่แพ้พี่

      พี่แพ้ปู่

๒๖.๗ แบบฝึกหัดไวยากรณ์

ก.

รถเสียมาหลายวันแล้ว (อาหาร)   วิทยุเสียมาอาทิตย์หนึ่งแล้ว (สองเดือน)

อาหารเสียมาหลายวันแล้ว (นาน)   วิทยุเสียมาสองเดือนแล้ว (โทรศัพท์)

อาหารเสียมานานแล้ว (ประตู)   โทรศัพท์เสียมาสองเดือนแล้ว (รถ)

ประตูเสียมานานแล้ว (อาทิตย์หนึ่ง)   รถเสียมาสองเดือนแล้ว

ประตูเสียมาอาทิตย์หนึ่งแล้ว (วิทยุ)

b. Transformation drill. (p, b, and ph).

bǐm bɔ̀ɔk pâa.	Bim told Auntie.
pâa bɔ̀ɔk bǐm.	Auntie told Bim.
pâa pɔ̂ɔn bǐm.	Auntie fed Bim.
bǐm pɔ̂ɔn pâa.	Bim fed Auntie.
bâm pɔ̂ɔn pùu.	Berm fed Grandpa.
pùu pɔ̂ɔn bâm.	Grandpa fed Berm.
pùu bɔ̀ɔk bâm.	Grandpa told Berm,
bâm bɔ̀ɔk pùu.	Berm told Grandpa.
phɔ̂ɔ phɛ́ɛ pâa.	Father lost to Auntie.
pâa phɛ́ɛ phɔ̂ɔ.	Auntie lost to Father.
pâa pɔ̂ɔn phɔ̂ɔ.	Auntie fed Father.
phɔ̂ɔ pɔ̂ɔn pâa.	Father fed Auntie.
phǐi pɔ̂ɔn pùu.	Older One fed Grandpa.
pùu pɔ̂ɔn phǐi.	Grandpa fed Older One.
pùu phɛ́ɛ phǐi.	Grandpa lost to Older One.
phǐi phɛ́ɛ pùu.	Older One lost to Grandpa.

26.7 Grammar drills.

a. Substitution drill.

rót sǐa maa lǎay wan lɛ́ɛw. (ʔaahǎan)	The car has been out of order for several days now. (food)
ʔaahǎan sǐa maa lǎay wan lɛ́ɛw. (naan)	The food has been spoiled for several days now. (long time)
ʔaahǎan sǐa maa naan lɛ́ɛw. (pratuu)	The food has been spoiled for a long time now. (door)
pratuu sǐa maa naan lɛ́ɛw. (ʔathít nɯŋ)	The door has been broken for a long time now. (a week)
pratuu sǐa maa ʔathít nɯŋ lɛ́ɛw. (wítthayú?)	The door has been broken for a week now. (radio)
wítthayú? sǐa maa ʔathít nɯŋ lɛ́ɛw. (sɔ̌ɔŋ dɯan)	The radio has been out of order for a week now. (two months)
wítthayú? sǐa maa sɔ̌ɔŋ dɯan lɛ́ɛw. (thɔɔrasàp)	The radio has been out of order for two months now. (telephone)
thɔɔrasàp sǐa maa sɔ̌ɔŋ dɯan lɛ́ɛw. (rót)	The telephone has been out of order for two months now. (car)
rót sǐa maa sɔ̌ɔŋ dɯan lɛ́ɛw.	The car has been out of order for two months now.

77

ข.

จอดที่นี่
  ที่นี่จอดรถไม่ได้

จอดที่สี่แยก
  ที่สี่แยกจอดรถไม่ได้

จอดที่โน่น
  ที่โน่นจอดรถไม่ได้

จอดข้างหน้าร้าน
  ข้างหน้าร้านจอดรถไม่ได้

จอดข้างหลังบ้าน
  ข้างหลังบ้านจอดรถไม่ได้

จอดที่ตลาด
  ที่ตลาดจอดรถไม่ได้

ค.

ใครขับรถให้
  ฉันขับเอง

ใครสั่งอาหารให้
  ฉันสั่งเอง

ใครเปิดประตูให้
  ฉันเปิดเอง

ใครซื้อบุหรี่ให้เขา
  เขาซื้อเอง

ใครทำอาหารให้คุณยัง
  เขาทำเอง

ใครแก้รถให้คุณประภาส
  เขาแก้เอง

ง.

คุณขับรถเองหรือ
  เปล่า, ขับไม่เป็น

คุณทำอาหารเองหรือ
  เปล่า, ทำไม่เป็น

คุณแก้รถเองหรือ
  เปล่า, แก้ไม่เป็น

คุณเปิดวิทยุเองหรือ
  เปล่า, เปิดไม่เป็น

คุณประเสริฐทำแซนวิชเองหรือ
  เปล่า, เขาทำไม่เป็น

b. Response drill.

còɔt thîi níi.
  thîi níi còɔt rót mây dây.
           Park here.
             Parking isn't allowed here.

còɔt thîi sìiyêɛk.
  thîi sìiyêɛk còɔt rót mây dây.
           Park at the intersection.
             Parking isn't allowed at the intersection.

còɔt thîi nôon.
  thîi nôon còɔt rót mây dây.
           Park over there.
             You can't park over there.

còɔt khâŋ nâa ráan.
  khâŋ nâa ráan còɔt rót mây dây.
           Park in front of the shop.
             You can't park in front of the shop.

còɔt khâŋ lǎŋ bâan.
  khâŋ lǎŋ bâan còɔt rót mây dây.
           Park behind the house.
             You can't park behind the house.

còɔt thîi talàat.
  thîi talàat còɔt rót mây dây.
           Park at the market.
             Parking isn't allowed at the market.

c. Response drill

khray khàp rót hây.
  chán khàp ʔeeŋ.
           Who drives for you?
             I drive myself.

khray sàŋ ʔaahǎan hây.
  chán sàŋ ʔeeŋ.
           Who ordered the food for you?
             I ordered it myself.

khray pɔ̀ɔt pratuu hây.
  chán pɔ̀ɔt ʔeeŋ.
           Who opened the gate for you?
             I opened it myself.

khray súu burìi hây kháw.
  kháw súu ʔeeŋ.
           Who bought the cigarets for him?
             He bought them himself.

khray tham ʔaahǎan hây khun yaŋ.
  kháw tham ʔeeŋ.
           Who prepared the food for Mr. Young?
             He prepared it himself.

khray kɛ̂ɛ rót hây khun praphâat.
  kháw kɛ̂ɛ ʔeeŋ.
           Who fixed the car for Khun Prapart?
             He fixed it himself.

d. Response drill.

khun khàp rót ʔeeŋ lɔ̌ɔ.
  plàaw. khàp mây pen.
           Do you drive yourself?
             No. I don't know how to drive.

khun tham ʔaahǎan ʔeeŋ lɔ̌ɔ.
  plàaw. tham mây pen.
           Did you cook yourself?
             No. I don't know how.

khun kɛ̂ɛ rót ʔeeŋ lɔ̌ɔ.
  plàaw. kɛ̂ɛ mây pen.
           Did you fix the car yourself?
             No. I don't know how to fix it.

khun pɔ̀ɔt wítthayúʔ ʔeeŋ lɔ̌ɔ.
  plàaw. pɔ̀ɔt mây pen.
           Did you turn the radio on yourself?
             No. I don't know how to turn it on.

khun prasɔ̀ɔt tham sɛɛnwít ʔeeŋ lɔ̌ɔ.
  plàaw. kháw tham mây pen.
           Did Khun Prasert make the sandwiches himself?
             No. He doesn't know how to make them.

จ.

ขับไม่เป็น (ได้)   ทำไม่ได้ (กิน)
ขับไม่ได้ (ไหว)   กินไม่ได้ (ไหว)
ขับไม่ไหว (ทำ)   กินไม่ไหว (เป็น)
ทำไม่ไหว (เป็น)   กินไม่เป็น
ทำไม่เป็น (ได้)

๒๖.๘ เวลา

๒๑๔๕ ยี่สิบเอ็ดนาฬิกาสี่สิบห้านาที   อีกสิบห้านาทีสี่ทุ่ม

๒๖.๕ การสนทนาโต้ตอบ

นี่, ขอดูรายการอาหาร
        ครับ
เอา ...., ..., แล้วก็ ....,
        ครับ
นี่, เอา ...., มาอีก .... หนึ่ง
        ครับ
คิดตังค์ซิ
        ครับ, ... บาท .... ตังค์

e. Substitution drill.

khàp mây pen. (dây)	I don't know how to drive.
khàp mây dây. (wǎy)	I'm not allowed to drive.
khàp mây wǎy. (tham)	I don't feel up to driving.
tham mây wǎy. (pen)	I'm too weak to do it.
tham mây pen. (dây)	I don't know how to do it.
tham mây dây. (kin)	I can't do it.
kin mây dây. (wǎy)	I can't eat it.
kin mây wǎy. (pen)	I'm too full to eat it.
kin mây pen.	I don't eat it. (It's something that I'm not accustomed to eating.)

26.8 Time of day.

2145   yîi sìp ʔèt naalikaa sìi sìp hâa naathii
       ʔìik sìp hâa naathii sìi thûm

Practice reading the following times by both the 24 hour system (under 1 minute) and the 6 hour system (under 2 minutes 30 seconds).

2035	1205	0130	0945	1300	2320
0715	1625	2400	1440	0410	1755
1050	0235	0550	2105	1840	0830
2210	1915	1125	0355	0620	1545

26.9 Conversation.

Use the following framework to practice ordering meals.

nîi. khɔ̌ɔ duu raaykaan ʔaahǎan.	Waiter! Let me see a menu.
khráp.	Yes sir.
ʔaw ...., ..., lɛ́ɛw kɔ̂	I'll have ...., ..., and ....
khráp.	Yes sir.
nîi. ʔaw .... maa ʔìik .... nɯ̀ŋ.	Waiter! Bring me another ....
khráp.	Yes sir.
khít taŋ sí.	Figure up the money.
khráp. .... bàat .... taŋ.	Yes sir. .... baht .... satang.

๒๖.๑๐ การเขียน

ที่เขี่ยบุหรี่		ไข่ไก่
ขวด	ก่อน	บ่าย
ข่วน	กอด	ช่วย
เที่ยง	ว่าง	หนึ่ง
เทียบ	วาด	ไม่
กว่า	เขี่ย	กี่
กวาด	เขียด	นั่ง
มาก	ง่วง	หมื่น
ม่าน	งวด	เที่ยว
ส่ง	ปี่	ไข่
สด	ปีก	โน่น

26.10 Writing.

ที่เขี่ยบุหรี่

thîi khìa burìi
Ash tray.

ไข่ไก่

khày kày
Chicken eggs.

The first tone marker (máy ?èek) has the same affect on a syllable's tone as an abruptly stopped ending (p, t, k, ?).

ขวด	*khùat	ก่อน	*kɔ̀ɔn	บ่าย	*bàay
ข่วน	*khùan	กอด	kɔ̀ɔt	ช่วย	*chûay
เที่ยง	*thîaŋ	ว่าง	*wâaŋ	หนึ่ง	*nɯ̀ŋ
เทียบ	thîap	วาด	wâat	ไม่	*mây
กว่า	*kwàa	เขี่ย	*khìa	กี่	*kìi
กวาด	kwàat	เขียด	khìat	นั่ง	*nâŋ
มาก	*mâak	ง่วง	*ŋûaŋ	หมื่น	*mɯ̀ɯn
ม่าน	mâan	งวด	ŋûat	เที่ยว	*thîaw
ส่ง	*sòŋ	บี่	*pìi	ไข่	*khày
สด	sòt	บีก	pìik	โน่น	*nôon

83

บทที่ ๒๗

๒๗.๑ คำศัพท์

ลง	ชั่ว
	ชั่วโมง
เลย	ครึ่งชั่วโมง
เลยไป	อีกครึ่งชั่วโมง
กลับรถ	เพราะ
ตำ	เมล์
หรวด	รถเมล์
ตำรวจ	แท๊กซี่
ตู้	
ยาม	หมา
ตู้ยาม	ยา
ตู้ยามตำรวจ	
	กางเกง
สถา	
สถานี	ตัว
รถไฟ	
สถานีรถไฟ	เล่ม
	หลัง
	ด่า
	แทง

LESSON 27

27.1 Vocabulary and expansions.

loŋ	To descend, go down, get off.
lɔɔy	To be beyond.
lɔɔy pay	To go beyond, to go past.
klàp rót	To turn the car around.
tam	
rùat	
tamrùat	Police.
tûu	A cabinet, closet.
yaam	A guard, watchman.
tûu yaam	
tûu yaam tamrùat	A police box.
sathǎa	
sathǎanii	Station.
rót fay	Train.
sathǎanii rót fay	Railway station.
chûa	
chûamooŋ	An hour.
khrɯ̂ŋ chûamooŋ	A half hour.
ʔìik khrɯ̂ŋ chûamooŋ	In half an hour.
phrɔ́ʔ	Because.
mee	(From the English word 'mail'.)
rót mee	Bus.
théksîi	Taxi.
mǎa	Dog.
yaa	Medicine.
kaŋkeeŋ	Trousers.
tua	Body. Classifier for animals, chairs, tables, and articles of clothing.
lêm	Classifier for books.
lǎŋ	Classifier for houses.
dàa	To curse, scold.
theeŋ	To stab.

85

๒๗.๒ โครงสร้างของประโยค

ต้องกลับรถก่อน

ต้องกินข้าวก่อน

ต้องบอกเขาก่อน

ตรงหน้าบ้าน

ตรงหลังบ้าน

ตรงข้างบ้าน

ตรงหน้าประตู

ตรงหน้าตู้ยามตำรวจ

ครึ่งชั่วโมง

ครึ่งวัน

ครึ่งขวด

ครึ่งแก้ว

อีกครึ่งชั่วโมง

อีกชั่วโมงหนึ่ง

อีกสองชั่วโมง

อีกสามวัน

อีกอาทิตย์หนึ่ง

ไปแท๊กซี่ดีกว่า

นั่งที่โน่นดีกว่า

ขับเองดีกว่า

รถยนต์

รถไฟ

รถเมล์

รถแท๊กซี่

๒๗.๓ บทสนทนา

ก. จะลงที่ไหน

ข. เลยไปอีกหน่อย, แล้วจอดทางขวา

ก. ถ้ายังงั้นต้องกลับรถก่อน   จอดตรงหน้าตู้ยามตำรวจใช่ไหม

ข. ใช่, ขอบคุณมาก

ก. ผมจะคอยที่โน่นนะ

ข. ไปได้แล้ว, ไม่ต้องคอย

ก. ถ้ายังงั้นจะไปสถานีรถไฟก่อน,   อีกครึ่งชั่วโมงจะกลับมารับ

ข. ไม่ต้อง, เพราะไม่แน่ว่าจะกลับเมื่อไหร่ ไปแท๊กซี่ดีกว่า

27.2 Patterns.

tôŋ klàp rót kòɔn.	I have to turn the car around first.
tôŋ kin khâaw kòɔn.	I have to eat first.
tôŋ bɔ̀ɔk kháw kòɔn.	I have to tell him first.

troŋ nâa bâan.	Right in front of the house.
troŋ lǎŋ bâan.	Right in back of the house.
troŋ khâaŋ bâan.	Right beside the house.
troŋ nâa pratuu.	Right in front of the gate.
troŋ nâa tûu yaam tamrùat.	Right in front of the police box.

khrɤ̂ŋ chûamooŋ.	Half an hour.
khrɤ̂ŋ wan.	Half a day.
khrɤ̂ŋ khùat.	Half a bottle.
khrɤ̂ŋ kɛ̂ɛw.	Half a glass.

ʔìik khrɤ̂ŋ chûamooŋ.	In half an hour.
ʔìik chûamooŋ nɤŋ.	In an hour.
ʔìik sɔ̌ɔŋ chûamooŋ.	In two hours.
ʔìik sǎam wan.	In three more days.
ʔìik ʔathít nɤŋ.	In another week.

pay théksîi dii kwàa.	I'd better take a taxi.
nâŋ thîi nôon dii kwàa.	It's better to sit over there.
khàp ʔeeŋ dii kwàa.	I'd rather drive myself.

rót yon.	Automobile.
rót fay.	Train.
rót mee.	Bus.
rót théksîi.	Taxi.

27.3 Dialog.

A. ca loŋ thîi nǎy.

Where do you want to get off?

B. lɔɔy pay ʔìik nɔ̀y
lɛ́ɛw còɔt thaaŋ khwǎa.

Go a little further,
then stop on the right.

A. thâa yaŋŋán tôŋ klàp rót kòɔn.
còɔt troŋ nâa tûu yaam tamrùat,
chây máy.

I'll have to turn around first, then.
Stop right in front of the police box,
right?

B. chây. khɔ̀ɔpkhun mâak.

Yes. Thanks a lot.

A. phǒm ca khɔɔy thîi nôon ná.

I'll wait for you over there. Okay?

B. pay dây lɛ́ɛw. mây tôŋ khɔɔy.

You can go on. You don't have to wait.

A. thâa yaŋŋán
ca pay sathǎanii rót fay kòɔn.
ʔìik khrɤ̂ŋ chûamooŋ
ca klàp maa ráp.

In that case
I'll go on to the railway station.
I'll come back and pick you up
in half an hour.

B. mây tôŋ,
phrɔ́ʔ mây nɛ̂ɛ wâa
ca klàp mɤ̂arày.
pay théksîi dii kwàa.

That won't be necessary.
Because I'm not sure when I'll be
going back.
It's better that I take a taxi.

๒๗.๔ แบบฝึกหัดการฟังและการออกเสียงสูงต่ำ

ก.　　โคราช　　　　ลิ้นจี่　　　　ปากกา　　　　เสื้อเชิ้ต　　　　ผิวหนัง

ข.

ให้อาเตือนประชุม
　อาเตือนประชุมหน่อยได้ไหม, อา

ให้ปู่บอกประเสริฐ
　ปู่บอกประเสริฐหน่อยได้ไหม, ปู่

ให้ป้าพูดกับประภาส
　ป้าพูดกับประภาสหน่อยได้ไหม, ป้า

ให้ป้าถามประสงค์
　ป้าถามประสงค์หน่อยได้ไหม, ป้า

ให้น้าทักประพัทธ์
　น้าทักประพัทธ์หน่อยได้ไหม, น้า

๒๗.๕ แบบฝึกหัดการสลับเสียงสูงต่ำ

ก.

เห็นหมากี่ตัว　　　　　　　　มีบ้านกี่หลัง
　เห็นหมาสามตัว　　　　　　　มีบ้านสามหลัง

ซื้อเบียร์กี่ขวด　　　　　　　ซื้อแก้วกี่ใบ
　ซื้อเบียร์สามขวด　　　　　　ซื้อแก้วสามใบ

อ่านหนังสือกี่เล่ม　　　　　　ได้กระดาษกี่แผ่น
　อ่านหนังสือสามเล่ม　　　　　ได้กระดาษสามแผ่น

สั่งยากี่เม็ด　　　　　　　　ขายกางเกงกี่ตัว
　สั่งยาสามเม็ด　　　　　　　ขายกางเกงสามตัว

27.4 Tone identification and production.

a. Identify the tones and record the number of repetitions required.

Korat.	khooraat	....
Litchi, lichee nuts.	lincii	....
Pen.	pakkaa	....
Dress shirt.	sɯa chɔɔt	....
Skin.	phiw naŋ	....

b. Response drill.

hây ʔaa tɯan prachum.	Have Ah remind Prachum.
ʔaa tɯan prachum nɔ̀y dây máy, ʔaa.	Can you remind Prachum, Ah?
hây pùu bɔ̀ɔk prasɔ̀ɔt.	Have Grandpa tell Prasert.
pùu bɔ̀ɔk prasɔ̀ɔt nɔ̀y dây máy, pùu.	Can you tell Prasert, Grandpa?
hây pâa phûut kàp praphâat.	Have Auntie speak to Prapart.
pâa phûut ka praphâat nɔ̀y dây máy, pâa.	Can you speak to Prapart, Auntie?
hây pǎa thǎam prasǒŋ.	Have Papa ask Prasong.
pǎa thǎam prasǒŋ nɔ̀y dây máy, pǎa.	Can you ask Prasong, Papa?
hây náa thák praphát.	Have Nah greet Prapat.
náa thák praphát nɔ̀y dây máy, náa.	Can you greet Prapat, Nah?

27.5 Tone manipulation.

a. Response drill.

hěn mǎa kìi tua.	How many dogs do you see?
hěn mǎa sǎam tua.	I see three dogs.
sɯ́ɯ bia kìi khùat.	How many bottles of beer did you buy?
sɯ́ɯ bia sǎam khùat.	I bought three bottles of beer.
ʔàan naŋsɯ́ɯ kìi lêm.	How many books did you read?
ʔàan naŋsɯ́ɯ sǎam lêm.	I read three books.
sàŋ yaa kìi mét.	How many pills did you order?
sàŋ yaa sǎam mét.	I ordered three pills.
mii bâan kìi lǎŋ.	How many houses do you have?
mii bâan sǎam lǎŋ.	I have three houses.
sɯ́ɯ kɛ̂ɛw kìi bay.	How many glasses did you buy?
sɯ́ɯ kɛ̂ɛw sǎam bay.	I bought three glasses.
dây kradàat kìi phɛ̀n.	How many sheets of paper did you get?
dây kradàat sǎam phɛ̀n.	I got three sheets of paper.
khǎay kaŋkeeŋ kìi tua.	How many pairs of trousers did you sell?
khǎay kaŋkeeŋ sǎam tua.	I sold three pairs of trousers.

๒๗.๖ แบบฝึกหัดการออกเสียงสระและพยัญชนะ

ก.

เข็น	ขน	เอ็น	จน
เขน	โขน	เอน	โจน

ข.

แดงด่าต้อย
  ต้อยด่าแดง

ต้อยตี๋แดง
  แดงตี๋ต้อย

ดำตี๋ติ่ม
  ติ่มตี๋ดำ

ติ่มด่าดำ
  ดำด่าติ่ม

แถมแทงต้อย
  ต้อยแทงแถม

ต้อยตี๋แถม
  แถมตี๋ต้อย

ทอมตี๋ติ่ม
  ติ่มตี๋ทอม

ติ่มแทงทอม
  ทอมแทงติ่ม

๒๗.๗ แบบฝึกหัดไวยากรณ์

ก.

คุณจะลงที่ไหน (ซ้าย)
  เลยไปอีกหน่อยแล้วจอดทางซ้าย

คุณจะลงที่ไหน (ขวา)
  เลยไปอีกหน่อยแล้วจอดทางขวา

คุณจะลงที่ไหน (ตรงหน้าตู้ยามตำรวจ)
  เลยไปอีกหน่อยแล้วจอดตรงหน้าตู้ยามตำรวจ

b. Response drill. Same as above but answer with 'four'.

c. Response drill. Same as above but answer with 'five'.

27.6 Vowel and consonant drills.

a. e-ee and o-oo contrast drills.

khěn	khǒn	ʔen	con
khěen	khǒon	ʔeen	coon

b. Transformation drill. (t, d, and th).

deɛŋ dàa tôy.   Daeng cursed Toy.
  tôy dàa deɛŋ.   Toy cursed Daeng.

tôy tii deɛŋ.   Toy beat Daeng.
  deɛŋ tii tôy.   Daeng beat Toy.

dam tii tǐm.   Dum beat Tim.
  tǐm tii dam.   Tim beat Dum.

tǐm dàa dam.   Tim cursed Dum.
  dam dàa tǐm.   Dum cursed Tim.

thěɛm theɛŋ tôy.   Tam stabbed Toy.
  tôy theɛŋ thěɛm.   Toy stabbed Tam.

tôy tii thěɛm.   Toy beat Tam.
  thěɛm tii tôy.   Tam beat Toy.

thɔɔm tii tǐm.   Tom beat Tim.
  tǐm tii thɔɔm.   Tim beat Tom.

tǐm theɛŋ thɔɔm.   Tim stabbed Tom.
  thɔɔm theɛŋ tǐm.   Tom stabbed Tim.

27.7 Grammar drills.

a. Response drill.

khun ca loŋ thîi nǎy.   Where do you want to get off?
(sáay)   (left)
  lɔɔy pay ʔìik nɔ̀y   Go a little further on,
  lɛ́ɛw cɔ̀ɔt thaaŋ sáay.   then park on the left.

khun ca loŋ thîi nǎy.   Where do you want to get off?
(khwǎa)   (right)
  lɔɔy pay ʔìik nɔ̀y   Go a little further on,
  lɛ́ɛw cɔ̀ɔt thaaŋ khwǎa.   then park on the right.

khun ca loŋ thîi nǎy.   Where do you want to get off?
(troŋ nâa tûu yaam tamrùat)   (right in front of the police box)
  lɔɔy pay ʔìik nɔ̀y   Go a little further on,
  lɛ́ɛw cɔ̀ɔt troŋ nâa   then park right in front of the
  tûu yaam tamrùat.   police box.

91

ข.

ถ้ายังงั้นต้องกลับรถก่อน
(พูดโทรศัพท์)

ถ้ายังงั้นต้องไปตลาดก่อน
(กินข้าว)

ถ้ายังงั้นต้องพูดโทรศัพท์ก่อน
(บอกเขา)

ถ้ายังงั้นต้องกินข้าวก่อน
(เรียนภาษาไทย)

ถ้ายังงั้นต้องบอกเขาก่อน
(ไปตลาด)

ถ้ายังงั้นต้องเรียนภาษาไทยก่อน

ค.

อีกครึ่งชั่วโมงจะกลับมารับ
(สองชั่วโมง)

อีกยี่สิบนาทีจะกลับมารับ
(สี่ชั่วโมง)

อีกสองชั่วโมงจะกลับมารับ
(ชั่วโมงหนึ่ง)

อีกสี่ชั่วโมงจะกลับมารับ
(สี่สิบห้านาที)

อีกชั่วโมงหนึ่งจะกลับมารับ
(ยี่สิบนาที)

อีกสี่สิบห้านาทีจะกลับมารับ

ง.

ไม่แน่ว่าจะกลับเมื่อไหร่
(กินข้าว)

ไม่แน่ว่าจะเปิดเมื่อไหร่
(ช่วย)

ไม่แน่ว่าจะกินข้าวเมื่อไหร่
(ขาย)

ไม่แน่ว่าจะช่วยเมื่อไหร่
(ทำ)

ไม่แน่ว่าจะขายเมื่อไหร่
(ใช้)

ไม่แน่ว่าจะทำเมื่อไหร่

ไม่แน่ว่าจะใช้เมื่อไหร่
(เปิด)

b. Substitution drill.

thâa yaŋŋán tôŋ klàp rót kɔ̀ɔn.
(phûut thoorasàp)

Then I'll have to turn the car around first.
(make a phone call)

thâa yaŋŋán tôŋ phûut thoorasàp kɔ̀ɔn.
(bɔ̀ɔk kháw)

Then I'll have to make a phone call first.
(tell him)

thâa yaŋŋán tôŋ bɔ̀ɔk kháw kɔ̀ɔn.
(pay talàat)

Then I'll have to tell him first.
(go to the market)

thâa yaŋŋán tôŋ pay talàat kɔ̀ɔn.
(kin khâaw)

Then I'll have to go to the market first.
(eat)

thâa yaŋŋán tôŋ kin khâaw kɔ̀ɔn.
(rian phasǎa thay)

Then I'll have to eat first.
(study Thai)

thâa yaŋŋán tôŋ rian phasǎa thay kɔ̀ɔn.

Then I'll have to study Thai first.

c. Substitution drill.

ʔìik khrɐ̂ŋ chûamooŋ ca klàp maa ráp.
(sɔ̌ɔŋ chûamooŋ)

I'll come back and pick you up in half an hour.
(two hours)

ʔìik sɔ̌ɔŋ chûamooŋ ca klàp maa ráp.
(chûamooŋ nɐŋ)

I'll come back and get you in two hours.
(an hour)

ʔìik chûamooŋ nɐŋ ca klàp maa ráp.
(yîi sìp naathii)

I'll come back and get you in an hour.
(twenty minutes)

ʔìik yîi sìp naathii ca klàp maa ráp.
(sìi chûamooŋ)

I'll come back and get you in twenty minutes.
(four hours)

ʔìik sìi chûamooŋ ca klàp maa ráp.
(sìi sìp hâa naathii)

I'll come back and get you in four hours.
(45 minutes)

ʔìik sìi sìp hâa naathii ca klàp maa ráp.

I'll come back and get you in 45 minutes.

d. Substitution drill.

mây nɛ̂ɛ wâa ca klàp mɐ̂arày.
(kin khâaw)

I'm not sure when I'll be back.
(eat)

mây nɛ̂ɛ wâa ca kin khâaw mɐ̂arày.
(khǎay)

I'm not sure when I'll eat.
(sell it)

mây nɛ̂ɛ wâa ca khǎay mɐ̂arày.
(cháy)

I'm not sure when I'll sell it.
(use it)

mây nɛ̂ɛ wâa ca cháy mɐ̂arày.
(pɔ̀ɔt)

I'm not sure when I'll use it.
(open)

mây nɛ̂ɛ wâa ca pɔ̀ɔt mɐ̂arày.
(chûay)

I'm not sure when it'll open.
(help)

mây nɛ̂ɛ wâa ca chûay mɐ̂arày.
(tham)

I'm not sure when they'll help.
(do it)

mây nɛ̂ɛ wâa ca tham mɐ̂arày.

I'm not sure when I'll do it.

๒๓.๔ วัน

วันจันทร์	วันศุกร์
วันอังคาร	วันเสาร์
วันพุธ	วันอาทิตย์
วันพฤหัส	

๒๓.๕ การสนทนาโต้ตอบ

ปกติตอนเช้าคุณทานอะไรคะ อาหารไทยหรืออาหารฝรั่ง
ทานอะไรบ้างคะ   แล้ววันนี้ทานอะไรคะ

แล้วกลางวันล่ะคะ ทานอาหารไทยหรืออาหารฝรั่ง
ทานอะไรบ้างคะ   แล้ววันนี้ (จะ) ทานอะไรคะ

แล้วตอนเย็นล่ะคะ ทานอาหารไทยหรืออาหารฝรั่ง
ทานอะไรบ้างคะ   แล้ววันนี้ (จะ) ทานอะไรคะ

อาหารไทย

ข้าวต้ม   (ปลา, กุ้ง, ไก่, หมู)
ข้าวผัด   (กุ้ง, หมู, เนื้อ, ปู)
ก๋วยเตี๋ยว   (ไก่, เป็ด, เนื้อ, หมู, ปู)
แกง   (เผ็ด) (เนื้อ, ไก่)
ผัดเผ็ด   (เนื้อ, หมู, กุ้ง, ไก่, ปลา)
แกงจืด
ต้มยำ   (กุ้ง, ปลา, เนื้อ, ไก่)
น้ำพริกปลาทู
กุ้งทอด   (เนื้อ, หมู, ปลา)

อาหารฝรั่ง

ไข่   (ต้ม, ดาว, ลวก)
หมู   (แฮม, เบคอน)
ขนมปัง   (ปิ้ง) เนย
แซนวิช   (ไก่, เนื้อ, ไข่, เนยแข็ง)
ซุบ   (ไก่, เนื้อ)
สลัด   (ผัก, มันฝรั่ง, กุ้ง, ไก่, เนื้อ)
เนื้อทอด   (ไก่, หมู, ปลา)
เนื้ออบ   (ไก่, หมู)
มันฝรั่ง, ผัก

27.8 Days of the week.

wan can	Monday.	wan sùk	Friday.
wan ʔaŋkhaan	Tuesday.	wan ˌsǎw	Saturday.
wan phút	Wednesday.	wan ʔathít	Sunday.
wan phárɯhàt	Thursday.		

Practice translating the following days of the week into Thai. Try to get the time under 45 seconds.

Tuesday	Sunday	Thursday	Saturday	Friday	Monday	Wednesday
Friday	Saturday	Tuesday	Thursday	Sunday	Wednesday	Monday
Sunday	Thursday	Wednesday	Friday	Monday	Saturday	Tuesday
Monday	Wednesday	Friday	Tuesday	Saturday	Thursday	Sunday
Wednesday	Tuesday	Monday	Sunday	Thursday	Friday	Saturday

27.9 Conversation.

The teacher should use sentences like those below to ask each student about his eating habits. The student can refer to the lists of food for answers.

pòkkatìʔ tɔɔn cháaw khun thaan ʔaɾay khá, ʔaahǎan thay ɾɯ́ ʔaahǎan faràŋ.

thaan ʔaray bâaŋ khá.

lɛ́ɛw wan níi thaan ʔaray khá.

lɛ́ɛw klaaŋ wan la khá, thaan ʔaahǎan thay ɾɯ́ ʔaahǎan faɾàŋ.

thaan ʔaray bâaŋ khá.

lɛ́ɛw wan níi (ca) thaan ʔaray khá.

lɛ́ɛw tɔɔn yen la khá, thaan ʔaahǎan thay ɾɯ́ ʔaahǎan faràŋ.

thaan ʔaray bâaŋ khá.

lɛ́ɛw wan níi (ca) thaan ʔaray khá.

ʔaahǎan thay

khâaw tôm (plaa, kûŋ, kày, mǔu)
khâaw phàt (kûŋ, mǔu, nɯ́a, puu)
kúaytǐaw (kày, pèt, nɯ́a, mǔu, puu)
kɛɛŋ (phèt) (nɯ́a, kày)
phàt phèt (nɯ́a, mǔu, kûŋ, kày, plaa)
kɛɛŋ cɯ̀ɯt
tôm yam (kûŋ, plaa, nɯ́a, kày)
nám phrík plaa thuu
kûŋ thɔɔt (nɯ́a, mǔu, plaa)

ʔaahǎan faràŋ

khày (tôm, daaw, lûak)
mǔu (hɛm, beekhɔ̂n)
khanǒmpaŋ (pîŋ), nəəy
sɛɛnwít (kày, nɯ́a, khày, nəəykhɛ̌ŋ)
súp (kày, nɯ́a)
salàt (phàk, man faràŋ, kûŋ, kày, nɯ́a)
nɯ́a thɔ̀ɔt (kày, mǔu, plaa)
nɯ́a ʔòp (kày, mǔu)
man faràŋ, phàk

New words

pòkkatìʔ	Normally.	khày daaw	Fried eggs ('star' eggs).
puu	Crab.	lûak	To scald.
pèt	Duck.	khày lûak	Very soft boiled eggs. ,
tôm yam	A hot, sour soup.	pîŋ	To toast.
		salàt	Salad.

This is the first time the student has been asked to think, and at first his answers will be labored and his tones will tend to be destroyed. When this happens, the teacher should immediately give three fast repetitions of the correct answer and ask the question again, and again, until the answer is correct and without hesitation. The student shouldn't try to say things beyond his capability. If he doesn't know the Thai for something he wants to say, he can say *ríak mây thùuk* or *mây rúu phasǎa thay ríak wâa ʔaray*, or he can stay within his vocabulary by lying.

๒๗.๑๐ การเขียน

เท่าไหร่	ทำไม	ใหม่
ไก่	ดำ	เขียด
ไม่	ต่ำ	เขียน
ใส่	ทำ	เขี่ย
ไหน	ค่ำ	ยื่น
ใน	ขำ	ยืด
ไข่	เอา	ยืน
ไฟ	เป่า	กลับ
ใหม่	เท่า	กลั่น
ไป	เผา	กลัว

เท่าไหร่   ทำไม   ใหม่

thâwrày   thammay   mày
How much.   Why.   New.

Note that *aw*, *ay*, and *am* are not spelled, as might be expected, with the symbol for *a* plus the final consonant. They have, instead, their own special symbols. *ay*, in fact has two different symbols: *máy malay*, as in *thâwrày*, and *máy múan*, as in *mày*. Actually, a few words of foreign origin with the sounds *ay* and *am* are written with the symbol for *a* plus that for final *y* or *m*, but these should be considered exceptions. *aw*, of course, can never be written with *a* plus *w*, as this combination is used for *ua*.

ไก่	*kày	ดำ	*dam	เขียด	khìat
ไม่	*mây	ต่ำ	tàm	เขียน	*khĭan
ใส่	*sày	ทำ	*tham	เขี่ย	*khìa
ไหน	*nǎy	ค่ำ	khâm	ยืน	yə̂ɯn
ใน	*nay	ขำ	khăm	ยืด	yə̀ɯt
ไข่	*khày	เอา	*ʔaw	ยืน	*yəɯn
ไฟ	*fay	เบ่า	*pàw	กลับ	*klàp
ใหม่	*mày	เท่า	*thâw	กลั่น	klàn
ไป	*pay	เผา	phăw	กลัว	klua

บทที่ ๒๘

๒๘.๑ คำศัพท์

ล้อ	จับ
สามล้อ	
คัน	เกา
สามล้อคันหนึ่ง	
	ไกล
ธนา	
คาน	หนัก
ธนาคาร	
	เมตร
กรุงเทพ ฯ	กิโล (เมตร)
ธนาคารกรุงเทพ ฯ	
	กิโล (กรัม)
แบงค์	
แบงค์อเมริกา	ลิตร
	มัน
ไปร	น้ำมัน
สะนี	
ไปรษณีย์	เชือก
	วาน
ราว	เมื่อวานนี้
ราวราว	
	พรุ่ง
แพง	พรุ่งนี้
ถูก	

LESSON 28

28.1 Vocabulary and expansions.

lɔ́ɔ	Wheel.
săamlɔ́ɔ	Samlor, tricycle taxi.
khan	Classifier for *rót*.
săamlɔ́ɔ khan nɯ̀ŋ	A samlor.
thanaa	
khaan	
thanaakhaan	Bank.
kruŋthêep	Bangkok.
thanaakhaan kruŋthêep	Bangkok Bank.
bɛ́ŋ	Bank.
bɛ́ŋ ʔameerikaa	Bank of America.
pray	
sanii	
praysanii	Post office.
raaw	Approximately.
rawraaw	
phɛɛŋ	Expensive.
thùuk	Cheap.
càp	To catch, grab.
kaw	To scratch lightly.
klay	To be far.
nàk	To be heavy.
méet	Meter (39.37 inches).
kiloo (méet)	Kilometer (.621 mile).
kiloo (kram)	Kilogram (2.205 pounds).
lít	Liter (1.057 quarts).
man	The fat of an animal.
námman	Oil, gasoline.
chûak	Rope.
waan	
mûa waan níi	Yesterday.
phrûŋ	
phrûŋ níi	Tomorrow.

99

๒๘.๒ โครงสร้างของประโยค

รถยนต์สามคัน	ราวราวห้านาที
รถเมล์สองคัน	ราวราวยี่สิบวัน
รถแท๊กซี่ห้าคัน	ราวราวครึ่งแก้ว
รถสามล้อสี่คัน	ราวราวร้อยบาท

ไปร้านก่อน, แล้วไปสถานทูต	แพงไป
ไปธนาคารก่อน, แล้วไปบ้าน	มากไป
กินเบียร์ก่อน, แล้วกินข้าว	ใหญ่ไป
ใส่น้ำตาลก่อน, แล้วใส่นม	เล็กไป
เอาไปโน่นก่อน, แล้วเอามานี่	

คอยนานไหม
รู้จักกันนานไหม
พูดกับเขานานไหม

๒๘.๓ บทสนทนา

ก. ช่วยเรียกสามล้อให้หน่อย,
  บอกเขาว่าไปแบงค์อเมริกาก่อน, แล้วไปไปรษณีย์

  ข. ต้องคอยนานไหมครับ

ก. ไม่นาน ราวราวห้านาทีเท่านั้น

  ข. สามล้อมาแล้วครับ

ก. เขาจะเอากี่บาท

  ข. สิบบาทครับ

ก. แพงไป ถามเขาว่าแปดบาทได้ไหม

100

28.2 Patterns.

rót yon săam khan.	Three automobiles.
rót mee sɔ̌ɔŋ khan.	Two busses.
rót thɛ́ksîi hâa khan.	Five taxis.
rót săamlɔ́ɔ sìi khan.	Four samlors.

pay ráan kɔ̀ɔn, lɛ́ɛw pay sathǎanthûut.	First go to the shop, then to the Embassy.
pay thanaakhaan kɔ̀ɔn, lɛ́ɛw pay bâan.	First go to the bank, then go home.
kin bia kɔ̀ɔn, lɛ́ɛw kin khâaw.	First have some beer, then eat.
sày námtaan kɔ̀ɔn, lɛ́ɛw sày nom.	Put sugar in first, then add cream.
ʔaw pay nôon kɔ̀ɔn, lɛ́ɛw ʔaw maa nîi.	Take it there first, then bring it here.

khɔɔy naan máy.	Did you wait long?
rúucàk kan naan máy.	Have you known each other long?
phûut kàp kháw naan máy.	Did you talk with him long?

rawraaw hâa naathii.	About five minutes.
rawraaw yîi sìp wan.	About twenty days.
rawraaw khrɐ̂ŋ kɛ̂ɛw.	About half a glass.
rawraaw rɔ́ɔy bàat.	About a hundred baht.

phɛɛŋ pay.	Too expensive.
mâak pay.	Too much.
yày pay.	Too big.
lék pay.	Too little.

28.3 Dialog.

A. chûay rîak săamlɔ́ɔ hây nɔ̀y. bɔ̀ɔk kháw wâa pay bɛ́ŋ ʔameerikaa kɔ̀ɔn, lɛ́ɛw pay praysanii.	Please call me a samlor. Tell him to go to the Bank of America first, then to go to the post office.
B. tôŋ khɔɔy naan máy khráp.	Will he have to wait long?
A. mây naan. rawraaw hâa naathii thâwnán.	No, not long. Only about five minutes.
B. săamlɔ́ɔ maa lɛ́ɛw khráp.	Here's the samlor.
A. kháw ca ʔaw kìi bàat.	How much does he want?
B. sìp bàat khráp.	Ten baht.
A. phɛɛŋ pay. thǎam kháw wâa pɛ̀ɛt bàat dây máy.	That's too much. Ask him if he'll take eight.

101

๒๘.๔ แบบฝึกหัดการฟังและการออกเสียงสูงต่ำ

ก.

รองเท้า   สามี   เยี่ยมเพื่อน   คุกเข่า   เหมาะสม

ข.

ช่วยถามอาหน่อยนะว่า   ช่วยถามน้ำหน่อยนะว่า
ประชุมกินปลาทูแล้วหรือยัง   ประพัทธ์ซื้อเนื้อแพะแล้วหรือยัง
    ประชุมกินปลาทู   ประพัทธ์ซื้อเนื้อแพะ
    แล้วหรือยัง, อา   แล้วหรือยัง, น้ำ

ช่วยถามปู่หน่อยนะว่า   ช่วยถามป้าหน่อยนะว่า
ประเสริฐสั่งไก่อบแล้วหรือยัง   ประสงค์ขายหมูหวานแล้วหรือยัง
    ประเสริฐสั่งไก่อบ   ประสงค์ขายหมูหวาน
    แล้วหรือยัง, ปู่   แล้วหรือยัง, ป้า

ช่วยถามป้าหน่อยนะว่า
ประภาสทอดกุ้งแห้งแล้วหรือยัง
    ประภาสทอดกุ้งแห้ง
    แล้วหรือยัง, ป้า

๒๘.๕ แบบฝึกหัดการสลับเสียงสูงต่ำ

รถสองคันพอไหม   กระดาษหกแผ่นพอไหม
    ไม่พอ เอาสามคันดีกว่า   ไม่พอ เอาเจ็ดแผ่นดีกว่า

ยาแปดเม็ดพอไหม   หนังสือหนึ่งเล่มพอไหม
    ไม่พอ เอาเก้าเม็ดดีกว่า   ไม่พอ เอาสองเล่มดีกว่า

บ้านสามหลังพอไหม   ไข่เก้าสิบเก้าลูกพอไหม
    ไม่พอ เอาสี่หลังดีกว่า   ไม่พอ เอาร้อยลูกดีกว่า

102

28.4 Tone identification and production.

a. Identify the tones and record the number of repetitions required.

Shoes.	rɔŋ thaaw	....	....
Husband.	saamii	....	....
To visit friends.	yiam phʉan	....	....
To kneel.	khuk khaw	....	....
To be appropriate.	mɔʔ som	....	....

b. Response drill.

chûay thăam ʔaa nɔ̀y ná wâa
prachum kin plaa thuu lɛ́ɛw rʉ́ yaŋ.
  prachum kin plaa thuu
  lɛ́ɛw rʉ́ yaŋ, ʔaa.

Please ask Ah if Prachum has eaten the mackerel yet.
  Has Prachum eaten the mackerel yet, Ah?

chûay thăam pùu nɔ̀y ná wâa
prasɔ̀ət sàŋ kày ʔɔ̀p lɛ́ɛw rʉ́ yaŋ.
  prasèet sàŋ kày ʔɔ̀p
  lɛ́ɛw rʉ́ yaŋ, pùu.

Please ask Grandpa if Prasert has ordered the roast chicken yet.
  Has Prasert ordered the roast chicken yet, Grandpa?

chûay thăam pâa nɔ̀y ná wâa
praphâat thɔ̂ɔt kûŋ hɛ̂ɛŋ lɛ́ɛw rʉ́ yaŋ.
  praphâat thɔ̂ɔt kûŋ hɛ̂ɛŋ
  lɛ́ɛw rʉ́ yaŋ, pâa.

Please ask Auntie if Prapart has fried the dried shrimps yet.
  Has Prapart fried the dried shrimps yet, Auntie?

chûay thăam náa nɔ̀y ná wâa
praphát sʉ́ʉ nʉ́a phɛ́ʔ lɛ́ɛw rʉ́ yaŋ.
  praphát sʉ́ʉ nʉ́a phɛ́ʔ
  lɛ́ɛw rʉ́ yaŋ, náa.

Please ask Nah if Prapat has bought the goat meat yet.
  Has Prapat bought the goat meat yet, Nah?

chûay thăam păa nɔ̀y ná wâa
prasŏŋ khăay mŭu wăan lɛ́ɛw rʉ́ yaŋ.
  prasŏŋ khăay mŭu wăan
  lɛ́ɛw rʉ́ yaŋ, păa.

Please ask Papa if Prasong has sold the sweet pork yet.
  Has Prasong sold the sweet pork yet, Papa?

28.5 Tone manipulation.

a. Response drill.

rót sɔ̌ɔŋ khan phɔɔ máy.
  mây phɔɔ. ʔaw săam khan dii kwàa.

Will two cars be enough?
  No. Better make it three.

yaa pɛ̀ɛt mét phɔɔ máy.
  mây phɔɔ. ʔaw kâaw mét dii kwàa.

Will eight pills be enough?
  No. Better make it nine.

bâan săam lăŋ phɔɔ máy.
  mây phɔɔ. ʔaw sìi lăŋ dii kwàa.

Will three houses be enough?
  No. Better make it four.

kradàat hòk phɛ̀n phɔɔ máy.
  mây phɔɔ. ʔaw cèt phɛ̀n dii kwàa.

Will six sheets of paper be enough?
  No. Better make make it seven.

naŋsʉ̌ʉ nʉ̀ŋ lêm phɔɔ máy.
  mây phɔɔ. ʔaw sɔ̌ɔŋ lêm dii kwàa.

Will one book be enough?
  No. Better make it two.

khày kâaw sìp kâaw lûuk phɔɔ máy.
  mây phɔɔ. ʔaw rɔ́ɔy lûuk dii kwàa.

Will ninety nine eggs be enough?
  No. Better make it a hundred.

๒๘.๖ แบบฝึกหัดการออกเสียงสระและพยัญชนะ

ก.

จิบ	ขุด	สิน	ทุน
จีบ	ขูด	ศีล	ทูน

ข.

ชมช่วยแจ๋ว
  แจ๋วช่วยชม

แขกคอยเกียรติ
  เกียรติคอยแขก

จอนจับชด
  ชดจับจอน

โกเกาเข็ม
  เข็มเกาโก

ชดจับแจ๋ว
  แจ๋วจับชด

เข็มเกาเกียรติ
  เกียรติเกาเข็ม

จอนช่วยชม
  ชมช่วยจอน

โกคอยแขก
  แขกคอยโก

๒๘.๗ แบบฝึกหัดไวยากรณ์

ก.

ไปแบงค์อเมริกาก่อน
(สถานีรถไฟ)

ไปสถานีรถไฟก่อน
(ธนาคารกรุงเทพฯ)

ไปธนาคารกรุงเทพ ฯ ก่อน
(แบงค์อเมริกา)

ข.

แล้วไปไปรษณีย์
(สถานทูตอังกฤษ)

แล้วไปสถานทูตอังกฤษ
(โรงแรมเอราวัณ)

แล้วไปโรงแรมเอราวัณ
(ไปรษณีย์)

104

28.6 Vowel and consonant drills.

a. i-ii and u-uu contrast drills.

cìp	khùt	sĭn	thun
cìip	khùut	sĭin	thuun

b. Transformation drill. (c and ch, k and kh).

chom chûay cĕw.	Chom helped Jaeo.
cĕw chûay chom.	Jaeo helped Chom.
cɔɔn càp chót.	John grabbed Chote.
chót càp cɔɔn.	Chote grabbed John.
chót càp cĕw.	Chote grabbed Jaeo.
cĕw càp chót.	Jaeo grabbed Chote.
cɔɔn chûay chom.	John helped Chom.
chom chûay cɔɔn.	Chom helped John.
khὲɛk khɔɔy kìat.	Kaek waited for Kiat.
kìat khɔɔy khὲɛk.	Kiat waited for Kaek.
koo kaw khĕm.	Ko scratched Kem.
khĕm kaw koo.	Kem scratched Ko.
khĕm kaw kìat.	Kem scratched Kiat.
kìat kaw khĕm.	Kiat scratched Kem.
koo khɔɔy khὲɛk.	Ko waited for Kaek.
khὲɛk khɔɔy koo.	Kaek waited for Ko.

28.7 Grammar drills.

a. Substitution drill.

pay bέŋ ʔameerikaa kɔ̀ɔn.	Go to the Bank of America first.
(sathăanii rót fay)	(the railway station)
pay sathăanii rót fay kɔ̀ɔn.	Go to the railway station first.
(thanaakhaan kruŋthêep)	(Bangkok Bank)
pay thanaakhaan kruŋthêep kɔ̀ɔn.	Go to Bangkok Bank first.
(bέŋ ʔameerikaa)	(the Bank of America)

b. Substitution drill.

lέɛw pay praysanii.	Then go to the post office.
(sathăanthûut ʔaŋkrìt)	(the British Embassy)
lέɛw pay sathăanthûut ʔaŋkrìt.	Then go to the British Embassy.
(rooŋrɛɛm ʔeerawan)	(the Erawan Hotel)
lέɛw pay rooŋrɛɛm ʔeerawan.	Then go to the Erawan Hotel.
(praysanii)	(the post office)

105

ค.

ไปไปรษณีย์ก่อน
แล้วไปธนาคารกรุงเทพฯ
(สถานทูตอเมริกัน)
(สถานีรถไฟ)

ไปสถานทูตอเมริกันก่อน
แล้วไปสถานีรถไฟ
(ตู้ยามตำรวจ)
(สี่แยกราชประสงค์)

ไปตู้ยามตำรวจก่อน
แล้วไปสี่แยกราชประสงค์
(ตลาด)
(แบงค์อเมริกา)

ไปตลาดก่อนแล้ว
ไปแบงค์อเมริกา
(ร้านตัดผมสวัสดิ์)
(ร้านอาหารนิค)

ไปร้านตัดผมสวัสดิ์ก่อน
แล้วไปร้านอาหารนิค
(สถานทูตจีน)
(โรงแรมเอราวัณ)

ไปสถานทูตจีนก่อน
แล้วไปโรงแรมเอราวัณ

.

ง.

ต้องคอยนานไหม
 ไม่นาน ราวราวห้านาทีเท่านั้น

ที่ทำงานอยู่ไกลไหม
 ไม่ไกล ราวราวห้ากิโลเท่านั้น

เชือกยาวไหม
 ไม่ยาว ราวราวห้าเมตรเท่านั้น

ไปแท๊กซี่แพงไหม
 ไม่แพง ราวราวห้าบาทเท่านั้น

ต้องใช้น้ำมันมากไหม
 ไม่มาก ราวราวห้าลิตรเท่านั้น

โต๊ะหนักไหม
 ไม่หนัก ราวราวห้ากิโลเท่านั้น

c. Substitution drill.

pay praysanii kɔ̀ɔn,
lɛ́ɛw pay thanaakhaan kruŋthêep.
(sathǎanthûut ʔameerikan)
(sathǎanii rót fay)

Go to the post office first,
then go to Bangkok Bank.
(the American Embassy)
(the railway station)

pay sathǎanthûut ʔameerikan kɔ̀ɔn,
lɛ́ɛw pay sathǎanii rót fay.
(tûu yaam tamrùat)
(sìiyɛ̂ɛk râatprasɔ̌ŋ)

Go to the American Embassy first,
then go to the railway station.
(the police box)
(Rajprasong Intersection)

pay tûu yaam tamrùat kɔ̀ɔn,
lɛ́ɛw pay sìiyɛ̂ɛk râatprasɔ̌ŋ.
(talàat)
(bɛ́ŋ ʔameerikaa)

Go to the police box first,
then go to Rajprasong Intersection.
(the market)
(the Bank of America)

pay talàat kɔ̀ɔn,
lɛ́ɛw pay bɛ́ŋ ʔameerikaa.
(ráan tàt phǒm sawàt)
(ráan ʔaahǎan ník)

Go to the market first,
then go to the Bank of America.
(Sawat's Barber Shop)
(Nick's Restaurant)

pay ráan tàt phǒm sawàt kɔ̀ɔn,
lɛ́ɛw pay ráan ʔaahǎan ník.
(sathǎanthûut ciin)
(rooŋrɛɛm ʔeerawan)

Go to Sawat's Barber Shop first,
then go to Nick's Restaurant.
(the Chinese Embassy)
(the Erawan Hotel)

pay sathǎanthûut ciin kɔ̀ɔn,
lɛ́ɛw pay rooŋrɛɛm ʔeerawan.

Go to the Chinese Embassy first,
then go to the Erawan Hotel.

d. Response drill.

tɔ̂ŋ khɔɔy naan máy.
    mây naan.
    rawraaw hâa naathii thâwnán.

Will I have to wait long?
    No.
    Only about five minutes.

thîi tham ŋaan yùu klay máy.
    mây klay.
    rawraaw hâa kiloo thâwnán.

Is the office very far?
    No.
    Only about five kilometers.

chûak yaaw máy.
    mây yaaw.
    rawraaw hâa méet thâwnán.

Is the rope very long?
    No.
    Only about five meters.

pay thɛ́ksîi phɛɛŋ máy.
    mây phɛɛŋ.
    rawraaw hâa bàat thâwnán.

Is it very expensive to go by taxi?
    No.
    Only about five baht.

tɔ̂ŋ cháy námman mâak máy.
    mây mâak.
    rawraaw hâa lít thâwnán.

Do you have to use much gas?
    No.
    Only about five liters.

tóʔ nàk máy.
    mây nàk.
    rawraaw hâa kiloo thâwnán.

Is the table heavy?
    No.
    Only about five kilograms.

๒๘.๘ วัน

ถ้าวันนี้วันพฤหัส, พรุ่งนี้วันอะไร	ถ้าพรุ่งนี้วันพุธ วันนี้วันอะไร
วันศุกร์	วันอังคาร
ถ้าเมื่อวานนี้วันอาทิตย์ วันนี้วันอะไร	ถ้าวันนี้วันอาทิตย์ เมื่อวานนี้วันอะไร
วันจันทร์	วันเสาร์

พรุ่งนี้วันอังคาร, วันนี้	....	วันจันทร์
วันนี้วันเสาร์, เมื่อวานนี้	....	วันศุกร์
เมื่อวานนี้วันจันทร์, วันนี้	....	วันอังคาร
พรุ่งนี้วันพฤหัส, วันนี้	....	วันพุธ
วันนี้วันเสาร์, พรุ่งนี้	....	วันอาทิตย์
วันนี้วันศุกร์, เมื่อวานนี้	....	วันพฤหัส
เมื่อวานนี้วันอังคาร, วันนี้	....	วันพุธ
พรุ่งนี้วันอาทิตย์, วันนี้	....	วันเสาร์
วันนี้วันพุธ, เมื่อวานนี้	....	วันอังคาร
วันนี้วันศุกร์, พรุ่งนี้	....	วันเสาร์
วันนี้วันอาทิตย์, พรุ่งนี้	....	วันจันทร์
เมื่อวานนี้วันพุธ, วันนี้	....	วันพฤหัส
วันนี้วันจันทร์, เมื่อวานนี้	....	วันอาทิตย์
พรุ่งนี้วันพฤหัส, วันนี้	....	วันพุธ
เมื่อวานนี้วันพฤหัส, วันนี้	....	วันศุกร์

28.8 Days of the week.

thâa wan níi wan phárɯhàt, phrûŋ níi wan ʔaray. 　wan sùk.	If today were Thursday, what would tomorrow be? 　Friday.
thâa mɯa waan níi wan　ʔathít, wan níi wan ʔaray. 　wan can.	If yesterday were Sunday, what would today be? 　Monday.
thâa phrûŋ níi wan phút, wan níi wan ʔaray. 　wan ʔaŋkhaan.	If tomorrow were Wednesday, what would today be? 　Tuesday.
thâa wan níi wan ʔathít, mɯa waan níi wan ʔaray. 　wan sǎw.	If today were Sunday, what would yesterday have been? 　Saturday.

Practice reading the correct days into the blanks below. Try to get the time under 1 minute and 20 seconds. (Cover the answers with a card, uncovering for confirmation as you proceed.)

phrûŋ níi	wan ʔaŋkhaan, wan níi		....	wan can
wan níi	wan sǎw,	mɯa waan níi	....	wan sùk
mɯa waan níi	wan can,	wan níi	....	wan ʔaŋkhaan
phrûŋ níi	wan phárɯhàt, wan níi		....	wan phút
wan níi	wan sǎw,	phrûŋ níi	....	wan ʔathít
wan níi	wan sùk,	mɯa waan níi	....	wan phárɯhàt
mɯa waan níi	wan ʔaŋkhaan, wan níi		....	wan phút
phrûŋ níi	wan ʔathít,	wan níi	....	wan sǎw
wan níi	wan phút,	mɯa waan níi	....	wan ʔaŋkhaan
wan níi	wan sùk,	phrûŋ níi	....	wan sǎw
wan níi	wan ʔathít,	phrûŋ níi	....	wan can
mɯa waan níi	wan phút,	wan níi	....	wan phárɯhàt
wan níi	wan can,	mɯa waan níi	....	wan ʔathít
phrûŋ níi	wan phárɯhàt, wan níi		....	wan phút
mɯa waan níi	wan phárɯhàt, wan níi		....	wan sùk

28.9 Conversation.

The teacher should read the sentences of lessons 16.9b, 18.9b, and 19.9b (Book 1) to the students and ask them the questions following each.

๒๘.๑๐การเขียน

	เล็ก		เหล็ก
มาก	พบ		คิด
ม่าน	เม็ด		เช็ด
มัก	ไม่		ทุ่ม
มั่ง	พัด		พริก
ขาด	ผัด		ครึ่ง
ข่าง	รับ		ส่ง
ขัด	นั่ง		สิบ
ไข่	สั่ง		ทับ

เล็ก   เหล็ก

lék   lèk
Little   Iron.

There is one exception to the rule that 'dead' syllables (syllables ending abruptly, that is with p, t, k, or ʔ) have a falling tone with low initials and a low tone with mid or high initials. The exception is: When the initial of a dead syllable is *low* and the vowel is *short*, the tone is high —— not falling. The combination of shortness and abruptness cuts the tone off before it can fall. (This last sentence is intended as a mnemonic device only, not as an explanation.)

มาก	*mâak	พบ	*phóp	คิด	*khít
ม่าน	mâan	เม็ด	*mét	เช็ด	*chét
มัก	mák	ไม่	*mây	ทุ่ม	*thûm
มั่ง	mâŋ	พัด	*phát	พริก	*phrík
ขาด	khàat	ผัด	*phàt	ครึ่ง	*khrɛ̂ŋ
ข่าง	khàaŋ	รับ	*ráp	ส่ง	*sòŋ
ขัด	khàt	นั่ง	*nâŋ	สิบ	*sìp
ไข่	*khày	สั่ง	*sàŋ	ทับ	*tháp

111

บทที่ ๒๙

๒๙.๑ คำศัพท์

จวน

เกือบ

จวนถึงแล้ว

ลง
ช้าลง

ขึ้น
เร็วขึ้น

ปั๊ม
ปั๊มน้ำมัน
ปั๊มน้ำมันนั่น

ที่นั่น
ตรงนั่น

ที่นี่
ตรงนี่

ทอน

ซืน
เมื่อวานซืนนี้

รืน
มะรืนนี้

เข้า

ออก

ใน
ข้างใน

LESSON 29

29.1 Vocabulary and expansions.

cuan	Almost, approaching, getting close to.
kừap	Almost, approximately, being close to.
cuan thɐ̌ŋ lɛ́ɛw	Almost there.
loŋ	To descend, go or come down, to 'down'.
cháa loŋ	To slow down.
khɐ̂n	To ascend, go or come up, to 'up'.
rew khɐ̂n	To speed up.
pám	Pump.
pám námman	A gas pump, a gas station.
pám námman nân	That gas station there.
thîi nîi	At here.
troŋ nîi	Precisely here (rare).
thîi níi	This place (rare).
troŋ níi	This exact spot.
thɔɔn	To give change to.
sɐɐn	
mɐ̂a wan sɐɐn níi	The day before yesterday.
rɐɐn	
marɐɐn níi	The day after tomorrow.
khâw	To enter, to go or come in, to 'in'.
ʔɔ̀ɔk	To exit, to go or come out, to 'out'.
nay	In.
khâŋ nay	Inside.

๒๕.๒ โครงสร้างของประโยค

จวนถึงแล้ว

จวนอิ่มแล้ว

จวนเสร็จแล้ว

จวนครึ่งชั่วโมงแล้ว

เลยบ้านไปหน่อย

เลยสี่แยกไปหน่อย

เลยซอยสิบเก้าไปหน่อย

เลยปั๊มน้ำมันไปหน่อย

ช้าลง

ผอมลง

เล็กลง

สั้นลง

ลงไปข้างล่าง

ขึ้นไปข้างบน

เข้าไปข้างใน

ออกไปข้างนอก

เร็วขึ้น

อ้วนขึ้น

ใหญ่ขึ้น

ยาวขึ้น

ลงมาข้างล่าง

ขึ้นมาข้างบน

เข้ามาข้างใน

ออกมาข้างนอก

เห็นบ้านนั่นไหม

เห็นรถนั่นไหม

เห็นร้านอาหารนั่นไหม

เห็นปั๊มน้ำมันนั่นไหม

๒๕.๓ บทสนทนา

ก. ตรงไปหรือเลี้ยวครับ

    ข. ไม่เลี้ยว ตรงไป

       จวนถึงแล้ว

       ขับช้าช้าลงหน่อย

ก. จอดที่ไหนครับ

    ข. เห็นปั๊มน้ำมันนั่นไหม

ก. เห็นครับ

    ข. เลยปั๊มน้ำมันไปหน่อย,

       แล้วเลี้ยวซ้ายที่ซอยหน้า

ก. ตรงนี้ใช่ไหมครับ

    ข. ใช่, นี่ร้อยบาท

       มีทอนไหม

ก. ไม่มีทอนครับ

114

29.2 Patterns.

cuan thǔŋ lέεw.	We're almost there.
cuan ʔìm lέεw.	I'm almost full.
cuan sèt lέεw.	I'm almost finished.
cuan khrûŋ chûamooŋ lέεw.	It's been almost half an hour now.
cháa loŋ.	To slow down.
phɔ̌ɔm loŋ.	To get thinner.
lék loŋ.	To become smaller.
sân loŋ.	To become shorter.
rew khûn.	To speed up.
ʔûan khûn.	To get fatter.
yày khûn.	To become bigger.
yaaw khûn.	To become longer.
hěn bâan nân máy.	Do you see that house there?
hěn rót nân máy.	Do you see that car there?
hěn ráan ʔaahǎan nân máy.	Do you see that restaurant there?
hěn pám námman nân máy.	Do you see that gas station there?
ləəy bâan pay nɔ̀y.	Go a little beyond the house.
ləəy sìiyɛ̂ɛk pay nɔ̀y.	Go a little beyond the intersection.
ləəy sɔɔy sìp kâaw pay nɔ̀y.	Go a little past Soi 19.
ləəy pám námman pay nɔ̀y.	Go a little past the gas station.
loŋ pay khâŋ lâaŋ.	Go downstairs.
khûn pay khâŋ bon.	Go upstairs.
khâw pay khâŋ nay.	Go inside.
ʔɔ̀ɔk pay khâŋ nɔ̂ɔk.	Go outside.
loŋ maa khâŋ lâaŋ.	Come downstairs.
khûn maa khâŋ bon.	Come upstairs.
khâw maa khâŋ nay.	Come inside.
ʔɔ̀ɔk maa khâŋ nɔ̂ɔk.	Come outside.

29.3 Dialog.

A. troŋ pay rɨ́ líaw khráp.

> Shall I go straight or turn?

B. mây líaw. troŋ pay.
cuan thǔŋ lέεw.
khàp chácháa loŋ nɔ̀y.

> Don't turn. Go straight.
> We're almost there now.
> Slow down a little.

A. cɔ̀ɔt thîi nǎy khráp.

> Where should I park?

B. hěn pám námman nân máy.

> Do you see the gas station there?

A. hěn khráp.

> Yes, sir.

B. ləəy pám námman pay nɔ̀y.
lέεw líaw sáay thîi sɔɔy nâa.

> Go a little past the gas station.
> Then turn left at the next Soi.

A. troŋ nǐi chây máy khráp.

> Right here?

B. chây. nîi rɔ́ɔy bàat.
mii thɔɔn máy.

> Yes. Here's a hundred baht.
> Do you have change?

A. mây mii thɔɔn khráp.

> No I don't.

115

๒๕.๔ แบบฝึกหัดการฟังและการออกเสียงสูงต่ำ

ก.

เรียบร้อย   แนะนำ   ถ่ายรูป   เผาศพ   บางแสน

ข.

อาเตือนประชุมใช่ไหม
    ไม่ทราบว่าอาเตือนประชุม
    หรือประชุมเตือนอา

น้าทักประพัทธ์ใช่ไหม
    ไม่ทราบว่าน้าทักประพัทธ์
    หรือประพัทธ์ทักน้า

ปู่บอกประเสริฐใช่ไหม
    ไม่ทราบว่าปู่บอกประเสริฐ
    หรือประเสริฐบอกปู่

ป๋าถามประสงค์ใช่ไหม
    ไม่ทราบว่าป๋าถามประสงค์
    หรือประสงค์ถามป๋า

ป้าพูดกับประภาสใช่ไหม
    ไม่ทราบว่าป้าพูดกับประภาส
    หรือประภาสพูดกับป้า

๒๕.๕ แบบฝึกหัดการสลับเสียงสูงต่ำ

ได้ยาหกเม็ดใช่ไหม
    ไม่ใช่, ได้ห้าเม็ดเท่านั้น

ซื้อกระดาษสามแผ่นใช่ไหม
    ไม่ใช่, ซื้อสองแผ่นเท่านั้น

มีบ้านสี่หลังใช่ไหม
    ไม่ใช่, มีสามหลังเท่านั้น

ขายรถห้าคันใช่ไหม
    ไม่ใช่, ขายสี่คันเท่านั้น

อ่านหนังสือแปดเล่มใช่ไหม
    ไม่ใช่, อ่านเจ็ดเล่มเท่านั้น

29.4 Tone identification and production.

a. Identify the tones and record the number of repetitions required.

In good order.	riap rɔɔy	....	....
To advise.	nɛ ʔnam	....	....
To take a picture.	thaay ruup	....	....
To cremate a corpse.	phaw sop	....	....
Bangsaen.	baaŋsɛɛn	....	....

b. Response drill.

ʔaa tɯan prachum chây máy.
  mây sâap wâa ʔaa tɯan prachum
  rɯ́ prachum tɯan ʔaa.

Ah warned Prachum, didn't he?
  I don't know whether Ah warned
  Prachum or Prachum warned Ah.

pùu bɔ̀ɔk prasə̀ət chây máy.
  mây sâap wâa pùu bɔ̀ɔk prasə̀ət
  rɯ́ prasə̀ət bɔ̀ɔk pùu.

Grandpa told Prasert, didn't he?
  I don't know whether Grandpa told
  Prasert or Prasert told Grandpa.

pâa phûut kàp praphâat chây máy.
  mây sâap wâa pâa phûut kàp praphâat
  rɯ́ praphâat phûut kàp pâa.

Auntie talked to Prapart, didn't she?
  I don't know whether Auntie talked to
  Prapart or Prapart talked to Auntie.

náa thák praphát chây máy.
  mây sâap wâa náa thák praphát
  rɯ́ praphát thák náa.

Nah greeted Prapat, didn't he?
  I don't know whether Nah greeted
  Prapat or Prapat greeted Nah.

păa thăam prasŏŋ chây máy.
  mây sâap wâa păa thăam prasŏŋ
  rɯ́ prasŏŋ thăam păa.

Papa asked Prasong, didn't he?
  I don't know whether Papa asked
  Prasong or Prasong asked Papa.

29.5 Tone manipulation.

a. Response drill.

dây yaa hòk mét chây máy.
  mây chây.
  dây hâa mét thâwnán.

You got six pills, didn't you?
  No.
  I only got five.

mii bâan sìi lăŋ chây máy.
  mây chây.
  mii săam lăŋ thâwnán.

There are four houses, aren't there?
  No.
  There are only three.

ʔàan naŋsɯ̌ɯ pɛ̀ɛt lêm chây máy.
  mây chây.
  ʔàan cèt lêm thâwnán.

You read eight books, didn't you?
  No.
  I only read seven.

sɯ́ɯ kradàat săam phɛ̀n chây máy.
  mây chây.
  sɯ́ɯ sɔ̌ɔŋ phɛ̀n thâwnán.

You bought three sheets of paper, didn't you?
  No.
  I only bought two.

khăay rót hâa khan chây máy.
  mây chây.
  khăay sìi khan thâwnán.

You sold five cars, didn't you?
  No.
  I only sold four.

๒๕.๖ แบบฝึกหัดการออกเสียงสระและพยัญชนะ

ก.

จำหรือยัง	(จาม)	ขุดหรือยัง	(ขูด)
จามหรือยัง	(ใส่)	ขูดหรือยัง	(ใช้)
ใส่หรือยัง	(ส่าย)	ใช้หรือยัง	(ย้าย)
ส่ายหรือยัง	(ไข)	ย้ายหรือยัง	(ตั้ง)
ไขหรือยัง	(ขาย)	ตั้งหรือยัง	(สร้าง)
ขายหรือยัง	(จิบ)	สร้างหรือยัง	
จิบหรือยัง	(จีบ)		
จีบหรือยัง	(ขุด)		

ข.

นวลเหนียม	(ง่วง)
นวลง่วง	(เหงี่ยม)
เหงี่ยมง่วง	(เหนียม)
เหงี่ยมเหนียม	(นวล)

๒๕.๗ แบบฝึกหัดไวยากรณ์

ก.

ขับช้าช้าหน่อย	(พูด)	ทำเร็วเร็วหน่อย	(ขับ)
พูดช้าช้าหน่อย	(กิน)	ขับเร็วเร็วหน่อย	(พูด)
กินช้าช้าหน่อย	(ทำ)	พูดเร็วเร็วหน่อย	(กิน)
ทำช้าช้าหน่อย	(เร็ว)	กินเร็วเร็วหน่อย	

29.6 Vowel and consonant drills.

a. Substitution drill.

Syllables with short vowels are the same length as those with long vowels; the final consonant takes up the extra time. The special spelling used in this drill points this out.

camm rɯ yaŋ.	(caam)	Do you remember it yet? (sneeze)
caam rɯ yaŋ.	(sày)	Have you sneezed yet? (put on)
sàyy rɯ yaŋ.	(sàay)	Have you put it on yet? (sway)
sàay rɯ yaŋ.	(khǎy)	Have you swayed yet? (unlock)
khǎyy rɯ yaŋ.	(khǎay)	Have you unlocked it yet? (sell)
khǎay rɯ yaŋ.	(cìp)	Have you sold it yet? (sip)
cìpp rɯ yaŋ.	(cìip)	Have you sipped it yet? (flirt)
cìip rɯ yaŋ.	(khùt)	Have you flirted with her yet? (dig)
khùtt rɯ yaŋ.	(khùut)	Have you dug it yet? (scrape)
khùut rɯ yaŋ.	(cháy)	Have you scraped it off yet? (use)
cháyy rɯ yaŋ.	(yáay)	Have you used it yet? (move)
yáay rɯ yaŋ.	(tâŋ)	Have you moved (house) yet? (set up)
tâŋŋ rɯ yaŋ.	(sâaŋ)	Have you set it up yet? (build)
sâaŋ rɯ yaŋ.		Have you built it yet?

b. Substitution drill. (ŋ).

nuan nǐam.	(ŋûaŋ)	Nuan's shy. (sleepy)
nuan ŋûaŋ.	(ŋìam)	Nuan's sleepy. (Ngiam)
ŋìam ŋûaŋ.	(nǐam)	Ngiam's sleepy. (shy)
ŋìam nǐam.	(nuan)	Ngiam's shy. (Nuan)

29.7 Grammar drills.

a. Substitution drill.

khàp chácháa nɔ̀y.	(phûut)	Drive a bit slower. (speak)
phûut chácháa nɔ̀y.	(kin)	Speak a bit slower. (eat)
kin chácháa nɔ̀y.	(tham)	Eat a bit slower. (do it)
tham chácháa nɔ̀y.	(rew)	Do it a bit slower. (fast)
tham rewrew nɔ̀y.	(khàp)	Do it a bit faster. (drive)
khàp rewrew nɔ̀y.	(phûut)	Drive a bit faster. (speak)
phûut rewrew nɔ̀y.	(kin)	Speak a bit faster. (eat)
kin rewrew nɔ̀y.		Eat a bit faster.

119

ข.

ลงไป	(มา)	เข้าไป	(มา)
ลงมา	(ขึ้น)	เข้ามา	(ออก)
ขึ้นมา	(ไป)	ออกมา	(ไป)
ขึ้นไป	(เข้า)	ออกไป	(ลง)

ค.

เข้ามา	ออกไป
ลงไป	ขึ้นมา
เข้าไป	ออกมา
ขึ้นไป	ลงมา

ง.

เลยปั๊มน้ำมันไปหน่อย แล้วเลี้ยวซ้าย	(ขวา)
เลยปั๊มน้ำมันไปหน่อยแล้วเลี้ยวขวา	(สี่แยก)
เลยสี่แยกไปหน่อยแล้วเลี้ยวขวา	(สถานีรถไฟ)
เลยสถานีรถไฟไปหน่อย แล้วเลี้ยวขวา	(ซ้าย)
เลยสถานีรถไฟไปหน่อยแล้วเลี้ยวซ้าย	(ตู้ยามตำรวจ)
เลยตู้ยามตำรวจไปหน่อย แล้วเลี้ยวซ้าย	

b. Substitution drill.

loŋ pay. (maa)	Go down. (come)
loŋ maa. (khûn)	Come down. (to up)
khûn maa. (pay)	Come up. (go)
khûn pay. (khâw)	Go up. (to in)
khâw pay. (maa)	Go in. (come)
khâw maa. (ʔɔ̀ɔk)	Come in. (to out)
ʔɔ̀ɔk maa. (pay)	Come out. (go)
ʔɔ̀ɔk pay. (loŋ)	Go out. (to down)

c. Picture response drill.

The teacher should put the following pictures on the board and elicit students' responses by pointing at the pictures in random order. The student should also practice at home to increase his speed of response. To keep the ordering random, he should draw the pictures on cards and shuffle them occasionally as he practices. The asterisk represents the speaker and the arrow his instruction to someone. The viewer's attention should go first to the asterisk and then to the arrow.

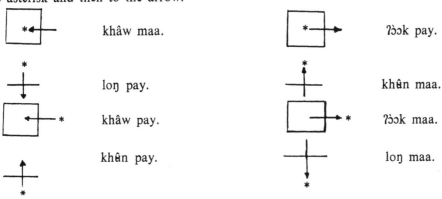

khâw maa.

loŋ pay.

khâw pay.

khûn pay.

ʔɔ̀ɔk pay.

khûn maa.

ʔɔ̀ɔk maa.

loŋ maa.

d. Substitution drill.

lǝǝy pám námman pay nɔ̀y lɛ́ɛw líaw sáay. (khwǎa)	Go a little beyond the gas station and then turn left. (right)
lǝǝy pám námman pay nɔ̀y lɛ́ɛw líaw khwǎa. (sìiyɛ̂ɛk)	Go a little beyond the gas station and then turn right. (intersection)
lǝǝy sìiyɛ̂ɛk pay nɔ̀y lɛ́ɛw líaw khwǎa. (sathǎanii rót fay)	Go a little beyond the intersection and then turn right. (railway station)
lǝǝy sathǎanii rót fay pay nɔ̀y lɛ́ɛw líaw khwǎa. (sáay)	Go a little beyond the railway station and then turn right. (left)
lǝǝy sathǎanii rót fay pay nɔ̀y lɛ́ɛw líaw sáay. (tûu yaam tamrùat)	Go a little beyond the railway station and then turn left. (police box)
lǝǝy tûu yaam tamrùat pay nɔ̀y lɛ́ɛw líaw sáay.	Go a little beyond the police box and then turn left.

121

จ.

จอดตรงหน้าปั๊มน้ำมันใช่ไหม
    ไม่ใช่, เลยปั๊มน้ำมันไปหน่อยแล้วเลี้ยวขวา

จอดตรงหน้าไปรษณีย์ใช่ไหม
    ไม่ใช่, เลยไปรษณีย์ไปหน่อยแล้วเลี้ยวขวา

จอดตรงหน้าตู้ยามตำรวจใช่ไหม
    ไม่ใช่, เลยตู้ยามตำรวจไปหน่อยแล้วเลี้ยวขวา

จอดตรงหน้าสถานีรถไฟใช่ไหม
    ไม่ใช่, เลยสถานีรถไฟไปหน่อยแล้วเลี้ยวขวา

๒๕.๙ วัน

ถ้าเมื่อวานซืนนี้วันจันทร์ เมื่อวานนี้วันอะไร
    วันอังคาร

เมื่อวานนี้วันอาทิตย์	วันนี้.....................	วันจันทร์
มะรืนนี้วันพฤหัส	พรุ่งนี้.....................	วันพุธ
เมื่อวานนี้วันพุธ	เมื่อวันซืนนี้.............	วันอังคาร
พรุ่งนี้วันศุกร์	วันนี้.....................	วันพฤหัส
พรุ่งนี้วันจันทร์	มะรืนนี้..................	วันอังคาร
วันนี้วันอาทิตย์	เมื่อวานนี้................	วันเสาร์
วันนี้วันเสาร์	พรุ่งนี้....................	วันอาทิตย์
เมื่อวานซืนนี้วันอังคาร	เมื่อวานนี้................	วันพุธ
เมื่อวานนี้วันพุธ	วันนี้.....................	วันพฤหัส
มะรืนนี้วันอังคาร	พรุ่งนี้....................	วันจันทร์
พรุ่งนี้วันเสาร์	วันนี้.....................	วันศุกร์
เมื่อวานซืนนี้วันศุกร์	เมื่อวานนี้................	วันเสาร์
พรุ่งนี้วันพฤหัส	มะรืนนี้..................	วันศุกร์
วันนี้วันเสาร์	พรุ่งนี้....................	วันอาทิตย์

e. Response drill.

cɔ̀ɔt troŋ nâa pám námman
chây máy.
  mây chây.
  lɔɔy pám námman pay nɔ̀y
  léɛw líaw khwǎa.

I should park right in front of the
gas station, shouldn't I?
  No.
  Go a little beyond the gas station
  and then turn right.

cɔ̀ɔt troŋ nâa praysanii
chây máy.
  mây chây.
  lɔɔy praysanii pay nɔ̀y
  léɛw líaw khwǎa.

I should park right in front of the
post office, shouldn't I?
  No.
  Go a little beyond the post office
  and then turn right.

cɔ̀ɔt troŋ nâa tûu yaam tamrùat
chây máy.
  mây chây.
  lɔɔy tûu yaam tamrùat pay nɔ̀y
  léɛw líaw khwǎa.

I should park right in front of the
police box, shouldn't I?
  No.
  Go a little beyond the police box
  and then turn right.

cɔ̀ɔt troŋ nâa sathǎanii rót fay
chây máy.
  mây chây.
  lɔɔy sathǎanii rót fay pay nɔ̀y
  léɛw líaw khwǎa.

I should park right in front of the
railway station, shouldn't I?
  No.
  Go a little beyond the railway station
  and then turn right.

29.8 Days of the week.

thâa mûa wan sɯ̆ɯn níi wan can
mûa waan níi wan ʔaray.
  wan ʔaŋkhaan.

If the day before yesterday had been Monday,
what would yesterday have been?
  Tuesday.

Practice reading the correct days into the blanks below. Try to get the time
under 1 minute 30 seconds.

mûa waan níi	wan ʔathít,	wan níi	wan can
marɯɯn níi	wan phárɯhàt,	phrûŋ níi	wan phút
mûa waan níi	wan phút,	mûa wan sɯɯn níi	wan ʔaŋkhaan
phrûŋ níi	wan sùk,	wan níi	wan phárɯhàt
phrûŋ níi	wan can,	marɯɯn níi	wan ʔaŋkhaan
wan níi	wan ʔathít,	mûa waan níi	wan sǎw
wan níi	wan sǎw,	phrûŋ níi	wan ʔathít
mûa wan sɯɯn níi	wan ʔaŋkhaan,	mûa waan níi	wan phút
mûa waan níi	wan phút,	wan níi	wan phárɯhàt
marɯɯn níi	wan ʔaŋkhaan,	phrûŋ níi	wan can
phrûŋ níi	wan sǎw,	wan níi	wan sùk
mûa wan sɯɯn níi	wan sùk,	mûa waan níi	wan sǎw
phrûŋ níi	wan phárɯhàt,	marɯɯn níi	wan sùk
wan níi	wan sǎw,	phrûŋ níi	wan ʔathít

๒๕.๑๐ การเขียน

แซนวิช   เทนนิส   ฟุต

บ	ป	พ	ผ	ฟ	ฝ				ม
ด	ต	ท	ถ	ซ	ส	จ	ช	ฉ	ง
ก	ค	ข							ย
น	ร	ล							ว

29.9 Conversation.

The teacher should write the following on the board, read the narrative of lesson 20 (Book 1) to the students, and ask them the questions.

Mother has a book.   Daughter has some paper.
Father has some matches.   Son has a pencil.

29.10 Writing.

The Thai words for 'sandwich', 'tennis', and 'foot' (the measurement) are *sɛɛnwít*, *thennít*, and *fút*. The English final sounds *ch*, *s*, and *t* are all pronounced the same in Thai. The sounds *ch* and *s* do not occur at the end of Thai words; the abrupt way of closing off syllables does not permit them. But even though the final sounds of these three words are pronounced alike, the Thai spelling shows the English distinctions.

Over the centuries, Thai has borrowed hundreds and hundreds of words from Sanskrit and Pali, and it is still doing so today in order to supply most of its technical vocabulary (as English does from Latin and Greek). These words are, of course, pronounced with Thai sounds, but their spellings reflect the source language. So even though Thai (unlike English) has a regular way of writing all of its sounds, the irregularities arising from borrowings pose a real spelling problem.

Thai syllables can have only nine different consonant endings: p, t, k, m, n, ŋ, y, w, and ʔ; but these nine endings can be spelled in over a hundred different ways. This presents no big problem when reading: all the reader has to do is to cut the ending off short and he will almost always be right. (For example, try to stop the sound after the vowel in the following English words as abruptly as possible: mat, mad, mass, mash, match, Madge. They all sound like *mat*.) But to write irregular words correctly, the spelling must be memorized. (Of course, the English speaker will have no difficulty remembering the endings of *sɛɛnwít* and *thennít;* and the person who knows Sanskrit and Pali will have little trouble with words like *râatprasǒŋ*.)

When a consonant occurring in the source language is not pronounced at all, the symbol called *karan* (see *sapɔ̀ɔt* and *ʔathít* below) is written over it. It is a 'consonant silencer'.

The sounds of the consonant letters when in syllable final position are shown below. The first letter of each group is the regular one.

p ข ป พ ผ ฟ ฝ   m ม

t ด ต ท ถ ช ส จ ซ ฌ   ŋ ง

k ก ค ฆ   y ย

n น ร ล   w ว

พูด	ชอบ
ทูต	รูป
สปอร์ต	กรุงเทพ ฯ
อาทิตย์	มาก
รถ	โรค
บาท	เลข
อาจ	อ่าน
ราช	อาหาร
รถเมล์	น้ำตาล

Practice reading the following words. Then practice writing those that have meanings given. For the first time in this course, following rules alone is not enough. You have to memorize the spelling for each irregularly spelled word.

พูด	phûut To speak.	ชอบ	chɔ̂ɔp To like.
ทูต	thûut Ambassador.	รูป	rûup
สปอร์ต	sapɔ̀ɔt *Sports* Club.	กรุงเทพ ฯ	kruŋthêep Bangkok.
อาทิตย์	ʔaathít Week.	มาก	mâak A lot.
รถ	rót Car.	โรค	rôok
บาท	bàat Baht.	เลข	lêek Number.
อาจ	ʔàat Might.	อ่าน	ʔàan To read.
ราช	râat *Rat*prasong.	อาหาร	ʔaahǎan Food.
รถเมล์	rót mee Bus.	น้ำตาล	námtaan Sugar.

บทที่ ๓๐

๓๐. ข

คุณจอนเป็นคนอเมริกัน เขาทำงานที่ยูซอม และเรียนภาษาไทยที่ เอ ยู เอ
เขาเรียนภาษาไทยสองสามเดือนเท่านั้น และพูดภาษาไทยได้นิดหน่อย

คุณประสงค์เป็นคนไทย และทำงานที่ยูซอมเหมือนกัน เขาเรียนภาษา
อังกฤษที่ เอ ยู เอ มาหลายปีแล้ว และรู้ภาษาอังกฤษมาก แต่พูดภาษาอังกฤษไม่เก่ง

คุณจอนกับคุณประสงค์เป็นเพื่อนกัน คุณประสงค์รู้ภาษาอังกฤษมากกว่า
คุณจอนรู้ภาษาไทย แต่คุณจอนชอบพูดภาษาไทยกับคุณประสงค์เสมอ

วันหนึ่งคุณจอนและคุณประสงค์ไปทานอาหารที่ร้านอาหารใกล้ ๆ ยูซอม
เขาไปรถคุณจอน คุณจอนจอดรถตรงหน้าร้านอาหาร แล้วเข้าไปในร้านและสั่ง
อาหาร คุณจอนสั่งแกงเผ็ดแต่คุณประสงค์สั่งแซนวิชเนยแข็ง ตอนที่เขากำลังกิน
อาหาร ตำรวจคนหนึ่งมาพูดกับคุณจอน แต่คุณจอนไม่เข้าใจ เขาขอให้คุณประสงค์
แปลให้เขา คุณประสงค์บอกคุณจอนว่าตำรวจพูดภาษาอังกฤษ และคุณประสงค์
แปลเป็นภาษาไทยว่า "ตรงนี้จอดรถไม่ได้"

คุณจอนเป็นคนอเมริกันใช่ไหม
เขาพูดภาษาอังกฤษไม่เก่งใช่ไหม
เขามาอยู่กรุงเทพ ฯ สองสามวันเท่านั้นใช่ไหม
เขาทำงานที่สถานทูตใช่ไหม
เขาเรียนภาษาไทยที่ยูซอมใช่ไหม
เขาเรียนภาษาไทยที่ เอ ยู เอ ใช่ไหม
เขาเรียนภาษาไทยสองสามเดือนเท่านั้นใช่ไหม
เขาพูดภาษาไทยได้เก่งใช่ไหม
เขามีเพื่อนชื่อประสงค์ใช่ไหม
เขาชอบพูดภาษาอังกฤษกับคุณประสงค์ใช่ไหม
คุณประสงค์เป็นคนไทยใช่ไหม
เขาทำงานที่ยูซอมใช่ไหม
เขาเรียนภาษาไทยที่ เอ ยู เอ ใช่ไหม

LESSON 30

(Review)

30. a Review sections 3, 5, 7, and 9 of lessons 26–29.

30. b Narrative.

khun cɔɔn pen khon ʔameerikan. kháw tham ŋaan thîi yuusôm (USOM), lέʔ rian phasăa thay thîi ʔee yuu ʔee. kháw rian phasăa thay sɔ̌ɔŋ săam dʉan thâwnán, lέʔ phûut phassăa thay dây nítnɔ̀y.

khun prasŏŋ pen khon thay, lέʔ tham ŋaan thîi yuusôm mʉankan. kháw rian phasăa ʔaŋkrìt thîi ʔee yuu ʔee maa lăay pii (year) lέɛw, lέʔ rúu phassăa ʔaŋkrìt mâak tὲɛ phûut phasăa ʔaŋkrìt mây kèŋ.

khun cɔɔn kàp khun prasŏŋ pen phʉan (friend) kan. khun prasŏŋ rúu phasăa ʔaŋkrìt mâak kwàa khun cɔɔn rúu phasăa thay, tὲɛ khun cɔɔn chɔ̂ɔp phûut phasăa thay kàp khun prasŏŋ samɔ̌ə (always).

wan nʉŋ khun cɔɔn lέʔ khun prasŏŋ pay thaan ʔaahăan thîi ráan ʔaahăan klâyklây yuusôm. kháw pay rót khun cɔɔn. khun cɔɔn cɔ̀ɔt rót troŋ nâa ráan ʔaahăan, lέɛw khâw pay nay ráan lέʔ sàŋ ʔaahăan. khun cɔɔn sàŋ kɛɛŋ phèt, tὲɛ khun prasŏŋ sàŋ sɛɛnwít nɔ̀əykhὲŋ. tɔɔn thîi (while) kháw kamlaŋ (in the process of) kin ʔaahăan, tamrùat khon nʉŋ maa phûut kàp khun cɔɔn, tὲɛ khun cɔɔn mây khâwcay. kháw khɔ̌ɔ hây khun prasŏŋ plɛɛ hây kháw. khun prasŏŋ bɔ̀ɔk khun cɔɔn wâa tamrùat phûut phasăa ʔaŋkrìt, lέʔ khun prasŏŋ plɛɛ pen phasăa thay wâa "troŋ níi cɔ̀ɔt rót mây dây".

Answer the following questions with *chây* or *mây chây.*

khun cɔɔn pen khon ʔameerikan chây máy.
kháw phûut phasăa ʔaŋkrìt mây kèŋ chây máy.
kháw maa yùu kruŋthêep sɔ̌ɔŋ săam wan thâwnán chây máy.
kháw tham ŋaan thîi sathăanthûut chây máy.
kháw rian phasăa thay thîi yuusôm chây máy.
kháw rian phasăa thay thîi ʔee yuu ʔee chây máy.
kháw rian phasăa thay sɔ̌ɔŋ săam dʉan thâwnán chây máy.
kháw phûut phasăa thay dây kèŋ chây máy.
kháw mii phʉan chʉ̂ʉ prasŏŋ chây máy.
kháw chɔ̂ɔp phûut phasăa ʔaŋkrìt kàp khun prasŏŋ chây máy.
khun prasŏŋ pen khon thay chây máy.
kháw tham ŋaan thîi yuusôm chây máy.
kháw rian phasăa thay thîi ʔee yuu ʔee chây máy.
(More.)

129

เขารู้ภาษาไทยมากกว่าคุณจอนใช่ไหม
เขาเรียนภาษาอังกฤษที่ เอ ยู เอ สองสามเดือนเท่านั้นใช่ไหม
เขารู้ภาษาอังกฤษมากใช่ไหม
เขาพูดภาษาอังกฤษเก่งใช่ไหม
เขาพูดภาษาอังกฤษกับคุณจอนเสมอใช่ไหม
เขารู้ภาษาอังกฤษมากกว่าคุณจอนรู้ภาษาไทยใช่ไหม
วันหนึ่งเขาไปทานอาหารด้วยกันใช่ไหม
เขาไปรถคุณประสงค์ใช่ไหม
เขาไปร้านอาหารที่ถนนสุขุมวิทใช่ไหม
คุณจอนขับรถใช่ไหม
เขาจอดรถใกล้ ๆ ร้านอาหารใช่ไหม
เขาทั้งสองสั่งอาหารไทยใช่ไหม
คุณจอนสั่งอาหารไทยใช่ไหม
คุณประสงค์สั่งอาหารฝรั่งใช่ไหม
คุณประสงค์สั่งแซนวิชไข่ใช่ไหม
คุณจอนสั่งข้าวผัดใช่ไหม
ตำรวจเข้ามาพูดกับคุณจอนใช่ไหม
เขาพูดภาษาอังกฤษใช่ไหม
ตำรวจพูดภาษาอังกฤษเก่งใช่ไหม
ตำรวจพูดว่าคุณจอนกินแกงเผ็ดไม่ได้ใช่ไหม
ตรงหน้าร้านอาหารจอดรถไม่ได้ใช่ไหม

คุณจอนเป็นคนอเมริกันหรือคนไทย
เขาทำงานที่ เอ ยู เอ หรือที่ยูซอม
เขาเรียนภาษาไทยหรือภาษาอังกฤษ
เขาทำงานที่สถานีรถไฟหรือที่ยูซอม
คุณจอนกับคุณประสงค์พูดภาษาไทยหรือภาษาอังกฤษกัน
เขาทั้งสองไปทานอาหารที่ร้านใกล้แบงค์อเมริกาหรือใกล้ยูซอม
เขาไปร้านอาหาร ไปรถคุณจอนหรือรถคุณประสงค์
เขาจอดรถใกล้ร้านอาหารหรือไกลร้านอาหาร
คุณจอนสั่งอาหารไทยหรืออาหารฝรั่ง
คุณประสงค์สั่งแซนวิชไข่หรือแซนวิชเนยแข็ง
ตำรวจพูดกับคุณจอนหรือคุณประสงค์
เขาพูดภาษาอังกฤษหรือภาษาไทย
เขาบอกว่าตรงหน้าร้านอาหารจอดรถได้หรือไม่ได้

kháw rúu phasǎa thay mâak kwàa khun cɔɔn chây máy.

kháw rian phasǎa ʔaŋkrìt thîi ʔee yuu ʔee sɔ̌ɔŋ sǎam dʉan thâwnán chây máy.

kháw rúu phasǎa ʔaŋkrìt mâak chây máy.

kháw phûut phasǎa ʔaŋkrìt kèŋ chây máy.

kháw phûut phasǎa ʔaŋkrìt kàp khun cɔɔn samɔ̌ə chây máy.

kháw rúu phasǎa ʔaŋkrìt mâak kwàa khun cɔɔn rúu phasǎa thay chây máy.

wan nʉŋ kháw pay thaan ʔaahǎan dûaykan chây máy.

kháw pay rót khun prasǒŋ chây máy.

kháw pay ráan ʔaahǎan thîi thanǒn sùkhǔmwít chây máy.

khun cɔɔn khàp rót chây máy.

kháw cɔ̀ɔt rót klâyklây ráan ʔaahǎan chây máy.

kháw tháŋ sɔ̌ɔŋ sàŋ ʔaahǎan thay chây máy.

khun cɔɔn sàŋ ʔaahǎan thay chây máy.

khun prasǒŋ sàŋ ʔaahǎan faràŋ chây máy.

khun prasǒŋ sàŋ sɛɛnwít khày chây máy.

khun cɔɔn sàŋ khâaw phàt chây máy.

tamrùat khâw maa phûut kàp khun cɔɔn chây máy.

kháw phûut phasǎa ʔaŋkrìt chây máy.

tamrùat phûut phasǎa ʔaŋkrìt kèŋ chây máy.

tamrùat phûut wâa khun cɔɔn kin kɛɛŋ phèt mây dây chây máy.

troŋ nâa ráan ʔaahǎan cɔ̀ɔt rót mây dây chây máy.

Answer the following questions with the correct alternative.

khun cɔɔn pen khon ʔameerikan rʉ́ khon thay.

kháw tham ŋaan thîi ʔee yuu ʔec rʉ́ thîi yuusôm.

kháw rian phasǎa thay rʉ́ phasǎa ʔaŋkrìt.

kháw tham ŋaan thîi sathǎanii rót fay rʉ́ thîi yuusôm.

khun cɔɔn kàp khun prasǒŋ phûut phasǎa thay rʉ́ phasǎa ʔaŋkrìt kan.

kháw tháŋ sɔ̌ɔŋ pay thaan ʔaahǎan thîi ráan klây bέŋ ʔameerikaa rʉ́ klây yuusôm.

kháw pay ráan ʔaahǎan pay rót khun cɔɔn rʉ́ rót khun prasǒŋ.

kháw cɔ̀ɔt rót klây ráan ʔaahǎan rʉ́ klay ráan ʔaahǎan.

khun cɔɔn sàŋ ʔaahǎan thay rʉ́ ʔaahǎan faràŋ.

khun prasǒŋ sàŋ sɛɛnwít khày rʉ́ sɛɛnwít nəəykhɛ̌ŋ.

tamrùat phûut kàp khun cɔɔn rʉ́ khun prasǒŋ.

kháw phûut phasǎa ʔaŋkrìt rʉ́ phasǎa thay.

kháw bɔ̀ɔk wâa troŋ nâa ráan ʔaahǎan cɔ̀ɔt rót dây rʉ́ mây dây.

131

คุณจอนเป็นคนชาติอะไร
เขาทำงานที่ไหน
เขาเรียนที่ไหน
เขาเรียนอะไร
เขาเรียนภาษาไทยนานเท่าไหร่
คุณประสงค์เป็นคนชาติอะไร
เขาทำงานที่ไหน
เขาเรียนที่ไหน
เขาเรียนอะไร
เขาเรียนภาษาอังกฤษนานเท่าไหร่
คุณจอนกับคุณประสงค์พูดภาษาอะไรกัน
เขาไปทานอาหารที่ไหน

เขาไปยังไง
รถใคร
คุณจอนจอดรถที่ไหน
คุณจอนสั่งอะไร
คุณประสงค์สั่งอะไร
ใครสั่งแกงเผ็ด
ใครสั่งแซนวิชเนยแข็ง
ตอนที่เขากำลังกินอาหาร
   ใครเข้ามาพูดกับเขา
ตำรวจพูดกับใคร
ตำรวจพูดภาษาอะไร
เขาพูดว่าอะไร

คุณจอนเป็นคนอังกฤษใช่ไหม
      ไม่ใช่, เป็นคนอเมริกัน

เขาทำงานที่ เอ ยู เอ ใช่ไหม
      ไม่ใช่, ทำงานที่ยูซอม

เขาเรียนภาษาเวียดนามใช่ไหม
      ไม่ใช่, เรียนภาษาไทย

เขาเรียนที่ วาย เอ็ม ซี เอ ใช่ไหม
      ไม่ใช่, เรียนที่ เอ ยู เอ

เขาเรียนภาษาไทยหลายปีแล้วใช่ไหม
      ไม่ใช่, เรียนสองสามเดือนเท่านั้น

Answer the following questions with the shortest possible answers.

khun cɔɔn pen khon châat ʔaray.

kháw tham ŋaan thîi nǎy.

kháw rian thîi nǎy.

kháw rian ʔaray.

kháw rian phasǎa thay naan thâwrày.

khun prasǒŋ pen khon châat ʔaray.

kháw tham ŋaan thîi nǎy.

kháw rian thîi nǎy.

kháw rian ʔaray.

kháw rian phasǎa ʔaŋkrìt naan thâwrày.

khun cɔɔn kàp khun prasǒŋ phûut phasǎa ʔaray kan.

kháw pay thaan ʔaahǎan thîi nǎy.

kháw pay yaŋŋay.

rót khray.

khun cɔɔn cɔ̀ɔt rót thîi nǎy.

khun cɔɔn sàŋ ʔaray.

khun prasǒŋ sàŋ ʔaray.

khray sàŋ kɛɛŋ phèt.

khray sàŋ sɛɛnwít nɔ́əykhě̌ŋ.

tɔɔn thîi kháw kamlaŋ kin ʔaahǎan khray khâw maa phûut kàp kháw.

tamrùat phûut kàp khray.

tamrùat phûut phasǎa ʔaray.

kháw phûut wâa ʔaray.

After practicing reading and listening to the following questions and answers, try answering the questions without books.

khun cɔɔn pen khon ʔaŋkrìt chây máy.
    mây chây. pen khon ʔameerikan.

kháw tham ŋaan thîi ʔee yuu ʔee chây máy.
    mây chây. tham ŋaan thîi yuusôm.

kháw rian phasǎa wîatnaam chây máy.
    mây chây. rian phasǎa thay.

kháw rian thîi waay ʔem sii ʔee chây máy.
    mây chây. rian thîi ʔee yuu ʔee.

kháw rian phasǎa thay lǎay pii lɛ́ɛw chây máy.
    mây chây. rian sɔ̌ɔŋ sǎam dɯan thâwnan.
(More.)

133

เพื่อนเขาชื่อประเสริฐใช่ไหม
    ไม่ใช่, ชื่อประสงค์

คุณประสงค์เป็นคนพม่าใช่ไหม
    ไม่ใช่, เป็นคนไทย

คุณประสงค์ทำงานที่แบงค์อเมริกา
ใช่ไหม
    ไม่ใช่, ทำงานที่ยูซอม

เขาเรียนภาษาไทยใช่ไหม
    ไม่ใช่, เรียนภาษาอังกฤษ

เขาเรียนที่ยูซอมใช่ไหม
    ไม่ใช่, เรียนที่ เอ ยู เอ

เขาเรียนภาษาอังกฤษสองสามเดือน
เท่านั้น ใช่ไหม
    ไม่ใช่, เรียนหลายปีแล้ว

เขาพูดภาษาอังกฤษเก่งมากใช่ไหม
    ไม่ใช่, พูดไม่เก่ง

เพื่อนเขาชื่อจิมใช่ไหม
    ไม่ใช่, ชื่อจอน

คุณจอนกับคุณประสงค์
พูดภาษาอังกฤษกันใช่ไหม
    ไม่ใช่, พูดภาษาไทย

เขาไปปั๊มน้ำมันใกล้ ๆ ยูซอมใช่ไหม
    ไม่ใช่, ไปร้านอาหาร

เขาไปรถคุณประสงค์ใช่ไหม
    ไม่ใช่, ไปรถคุณจอน

เขาจอดรถตรงหน้ายูซอมใช่ไหม
    ไม่ใช่, จอดตรงหน้าร้านอาหาร

คุณจอนสั่งอาหารฝรั่งใช่ไหม
    ไม่ใช่, สั่งอาหารไทย

ข้าวผัดใช่ไหม
    ไม่ใช่, แกงเผ็ด

คนขายของมาพูดกับเขาใช่ไหม
    ไม่ใช่, ตำรวจ

ตำรวจพูดกับคุณประสงค์ใช่ไหม
    ไม่ใช่, พูดกับคุณจอน

ตำรวจพูดภาษาไทยใช่ไหม
    ไม่ใช่, พูดภาษาอังกฤษ

คุณจอนแปลให้คุณประสงค์ใช่ไหม
    ไม่ใช่, คุณประสงค์แปลให้คุณจอน

ตำรวจพูดว่าหน้าร้านอาหาร
จอดรถได้ใช่ไหม
    ไม่ใช่, พูดว่าหน้าร้านอาหาร
จอดรถไม่ได้

phûan kháw chûu prasə̀ət chây máy.
    mây chây. chûu prasǒŋ.

khun prasǒŋ pen khon phamâa chây máy.
    mây chây. pen khon thay.

khun prasǒŋ tham ŋaan thîi bέŋ ʔameeríkaa chây máy.
    mây chây. tham ŋaan thîi yuusôm.

kháw rian phasǎa thay chây máy.
    mây chây. rian phasǎa ʔaŋkrìt.

kháw rian thîi yuusôm chây máy.
    mây chây. rian thîi ʔee yuu ʔee.

kháw rian phasǎa ʔaŋkrìt sɔ̌ɔŋ sǎam dʉan thâwnán chây máy.
    mây chây. rian lǎay pii lέεw.

kháw phûut phasǎa ʔaŋkrìt kèŋ mâak chây máy.
    mây chây. phûut mây kèŋ.

phûan kháw chûu cim chây máy.
    mây chây. chûu cɔɔn.

khun cɔɔn kàp khun prasǒŋ phûut phasǎa ʔaŋkrìt kan chây máy.
    mây chây. phûut phasǎa thay.

kháw pay pám námman klâyklây yuusôm chây máy.
    mây chây. pay ráan ʔaahǎan.

kháw pay rót khun prasǒŋ chây máy.
    mây chây. pay rót khun cɔɔn.

khaw cɔ̀ɔt rót troŋ nâa yuusôm chây máy.
    mây chây. cɔ̀ɔt troŋ nâa ráan ʔaahǎan.

khun cɔɔn sàŋ ʔaahǎan faràŋ chây máy.
    mây chây. sàŋ ʔaahǎan thay.

khâaw phàt chây máy.
    mây chây. kεεŋ phèt.

khon khǎay khɔ̌ɔŋ maa phûut kàp kháw chây máy.
    mây chây. tamrùat.

tamrùat phûut kàp khun prasǒŋ chây máy.
    mây chây. phûut kàp khun cɔɔn.

tamrùat phûut phasǎa thay chây máy.
    mây chây. phûut phasǎa ʔaŋkrìt.

khun cɔɔn plεε hây khun prasǒŋ chây máy.
    mây chây. khun prasǒŋ plεε hây khun cɔɔn.

tamrùat phûut wâa nâa ráan ʔaahǎan cɔ̀ɔt rót dây chây máy.
    mây chây. phûut wâa nâa ráan ʔaahǎan cɔ̀ɔt rót mây dây.

๓๐ **ค.**

ก. แท๊กซี่

 ข. ไปไหนครับ

ก. ไปแบงค์อเมริกาก่อน แล้วไปสถานีรถไฟ รู้จักไหม

 ข. รู้จักครับ

ก. เอาเท่าไหร่

 ข. ต้องคอยนานไหมครับ

ก. ไม่นาน ห้านาทีเท่านั้น

 ข. ขอสิบสองบาทครับ

ก. แพงไป, สิบบาทได้ไหม

 ข. ไม่ได้ครับ, อยู่ไกลมาก สิบสองบาทดีแล้วครับ

ก. ตกลง, ขับดี ๆ นะ อย่าขับเร็ว

 ข. ถึงแล้วครับ

ก. จอดตรงหน้าแบงค์

 ข. หน้าแบงค์จอดรถไม่ได้ครับ

ก. งั้นจะคอยได้ที่ไหน

 ข. ต้องเลยแบงค์ไปหน่อยแล้วจอดทางซ้ายครับ

ก. อีกห้านาทีจะกลับมานะ

 ข. ครับ

30. c Dialog.   (Taking a taxi.)

A. thɛ́ksîi.

   B. pay nǎy khráp.

A. pay bɛ́ŋ ʔameerikaa kɔ̀ɔn, lɛ́ɛw pay sathǎanii rót fay.   rúucàk máy.

   B. rúucàk khráp.

A. ʔaw thâwrày.

   B. tôŋ khɔɔy naan máy khráp.

A. mây naan.   hâa naathii thâwnán.

   B. khɔ̌ɔ sìp sɔ̌ɔŋ bàat khráp.

A. phɛɛŋ pay.   sìp bàat dây máy.

   B. mây dây khráp.   yùu klay mâak.   sìp sɔ̌ɔŋ bàat dii lɛ́ɛw khráp.

A. tòkloŋ.   khàp didii ná.   yàa khàp rew.   (Don't drive fast. *yàa* is the negative imperative.)

   B. thǔŋ lɛ́ɛw khráp.

A. cɔ̀ɔt troŋ nâa bɛ́ŋ.

   B. ñâa bɛ́ŋ cɔ̀ɔt rót mây dây khráp.

A. ŋán ca khɔɔy dây thîi nǎy.   (*ŋán* is short for *thâa yaŋŋán*.)

   B. tôŋ ləəy bɛ́ŋ pay nɔ̀y lɛ́ɛw cɔ̀ɔt thaaŋ sáay khráp.

A. ʔìik hâa naathii ca klàp maa ná.

   B. khráp.

137

บทที่ ๓๑

๓๑.๑ คำศัพท์

ตัด	ซัก
รอง	คู่
เท้า	สักคู่หนึ่ง
รองเท้า	
ตัดรองเท้า	พอใช้ได้
เสื้อ	ราคา
ฮะ	ล้าง
ฮะ (ฮ่ะ)	ดัน
กำลัง	ดึง
	คืน

LESSON 31

31.1 Vocabulary and expansions.

tàt	To cut.
rɔɔŋ	To underlay, place underneath.
tháaw	Feet.
rɔŋtháaw	Shoes.
tàt rɔŋtháaw	To have shoes made (cut).
sûa	Upper garment, shirt, blouse, coat, sweater.
há?	Short form of *khráp*.
há (hâ)	Short form of *khá (khâ)*.
kamlaŋ	To be in the process of.
sák	At least, or so, anyway, and maybe more later.
khûu	A pair (classifier).
sák khûu nɯŋ	One pair, anyway.
phɔɔ cháy dây	Good enough to use, passable.
rakhaa	Price, cost.
láaŋ	To wash.
dan	To push.
dɯŋ	To pull.
khɯɯn	Night.

๓๑.๒ โครงสร้างของประโยค

ตัดรองเท้า	รองเท้าคู่นี้
ตัดเสื้อ	เสื้อตัวนั้น
ตัดกางเกง	เบียร์ขวดโน้น
กำลังกินข้าว	ตัดกี่วันเสร็จ
กำลังพูดโทรศัพท์	ทำกี่เดือนเสร็จ
กำลังอยากได้รองเท้า	อ่านกี่ชั่วโมงเสร็จ
รองเท้าสักคู่หนึ่ง	ไม่ถึงชั่วโมงหนึ่ง
เสื้อสักสองตัว	ไม่ถึงสองอาทิตย์
เบียร์สักสามขวด	ไม่ถึงสามเดือน

ตัดดี
ตัดพอใช้ได้
ตัดไม่ดี

๓๑.๓ บทสนทนา

ก. คุณตัดรองเท้าที่ไหนฮะ, สวยดี

   ข. ที่ร้านเล็ก ๆ ใกล้ ๆ ที่ทำงาน
      คุณชอบหรือฮะ

ก. ครับ, ผมกำลังอยากได้สักคู่หนึ่ง

   ข. ที่ร้านนี้ตัดพอใช้ได้ ราคาก็ไม่แพง

ก. คู่นี้ตัดเท่าไหร่ฮะ

   ข. สองร้อยห้าสิบบาท

ก. ตัดกี่วันเสร็จฮะ

   ข. ไม่ถึงอาทิตย์ฮะ

31.2 Patterns.

tàt rɔŋtháaw.	To have shoes made.
tàt sûa.	To have a shirt made.
tàt kaŋkeeŋ.	To have trousers made.
kamlaŋ kin khâaw.	He is (was) eating just now (then).
kamlaŋ phûut thoorasàp.	He's speaking on the phone.
kamlaŋ yàak dây rɔŋtháaw.	He was just thinking of getting some shoes.
rɔŋtháaw sák khûu nɯŋ.	One pair of shoes, anyway (maybe more).
sûa sák sɔ̌ɔŋ tua.	A couple of shirts (or so).
bia sák sǎam khùat.	At least three bottles of beer.
tàt dii.	To cut well.
tàt phɔɔ cháy dây.	To cut passably well, good enough.
tàt mây dii.	To cut poorly.
rɔŋtháaw khûu níi.	This pair of shoes.
sûa tua nán.	That shirt.
bia khùat nóon.	That bottle of beer (over there).
tàt kìi wan sèt.	'Cut, how many days finish?'. How long will it take?
tham kìi dɯan sèt.	How many months will it take to finish it?
ʔàan kìi chûamooŋ sèt.	How many hours will it take to read it?
mây thɯ̌ŋ chûamooŋ nɯŋ.	'Not reach one hour', in less than an hour.
mây thɯ̌ŋ sɔ̌ɔŋ ʔathít.	In less than two weeks.
mây thɯ̌ŋ sǎam dɯan.	In less than three months.

31.3 Dialog.

A. khun tàt rɔŋtháaw thîi nǎy há?.	Where did you have your shoes made?
sǔay dii.	They're nice looking.
B. thîi ráan léklék	At a small shop
klâyklây thîi tham ŋaan.	near my office.
khun chɔ̂ɔp lɔ̌ə há?.	Do you like them?
A. khráp.	Yes.
phǒm kamlaŋ yàak dây sák khûu nɯŋ.	I was just wanting to get a pair.
B. thîi ráan níi tàt phɔɔ cháy dây.	This shop does a pretty good job.
rakhaa kɔ̂ mây phɛɛŋ.	And the price isn't high.
A. khûu níi tàt thâwrày há?.	How much was this pair?
B. sɔ̌ɔŋ rɔ́ɔy hâa sìp bàat.	250 baht.
A. tàt kìi wan sèt há?.	How long does it take to make them?
B. mây thɯ̌ŋ ʔathít há?.	Less than a week.

141

๓๑.๔ แบบฝึกหัดการฟังและการออกเสียงสูงต่ำ

ก.

ถุงสี่พัน   นายห้าง   เยอะแยะ   อุดหนุน   ขี้เกียจ

ข.

ปิดหน้าต่างทำไม
 ไม่ได้ปิด, เปิด

เช็ดรถทำไม
 ไม่ได้เช็ด, ล้าง

ทอดกุ้งทำไม
 ไม่ได้ทอด, ต้ม

ดันประตูทำไม
 ไม่ได้ดัน, ดึง

เผาหนังสือทำไม
 ไม่ได้เผา, ขาย

๓๑.๕ แบบฝึกหัดการสลับเสียงสูงต่ำ

ก.

ทำไมไม่อ่านหนังสือ
 ไม่มีหนังสือจะอ่าน

ทำไมไม่ทำงาน
 ไม่มีงานจะทำ

ทำไมไม่ขายรถ
 ไม่มีรถจะขาย

ทำไมไม่กินข้าว
 ไม่มีข้าวจะกิน

ทำไมไม่ใช้ช้อน
 ไม่มีช้อนจะใช้

ทำไมไม่พูดโทรศัพท์
 ไม่มีโทรศัพท์จะพูด

31.4 Tone identification and production.

a. Identify the tones and record the number of repetitions required.

To brush the teeth.	sii fan	....	....
The boss of a firm.	naay haaŋ	....	....
Plenty.	yə ʔyɛ ʔ	....	....
To patronize.	ʔutnun	....	....
To be lazy.	khiikiat	....	....

b. Response . drill.

pìt nâatàaŋ thammay.
  mây dây pìt. pə̀ət.

Why did you close the window?
  I didn't close it. I opened it.

chét rót thammay.
  mây dây chét. láaŋ.

Why did you wipe the car?
  I didn't wipe it. I washed it.

thɔ̂ɔt kûŋ thammay.
  mây dây thɔ̂ɔt. tôm.

Why did you fry the shrimps?
  I didn't fry them. I boiled them.

dan pratuu thammay.
  mây dây dan. dɯŋ.

Why did you push the door?
  I didn't push it. I pulled it.

phǎw naŋsɯ̌ɯ thammay.
  mây dây phǎw. khǎay.

Why did you burn the books?
  I didn't burn them. I sold them.

31.5 Tone manipulation.

a. Response drill.

thammay mây ʔàan naŋsɯ̌ɯ.
  mây mii naŋsɯ̌ɯ ca ʔàan.

Why don't you read a book?
  I don't have a book to read.

thammay mây tham ŋaan.
  mây mii ŋaan ca tham.

Why don't you work?
  I don't have any work to do.

thammay mây khǎay rót.
  mây mii rót ca khǎay.

Why don't you sell your car?
  I don't have a car to sell.

thammay mây kin khâaw.
  mây mii khâaw ca kin.

Why don't you eat?
  I don't have anything to eat.

thammay mây cháy chɔ́ɔn.
  mây mii chɔ́ɔn ca cháy.

Why don't you use a spoon?
  I don't have a spoon to use.

thammay mây phûut thoorasàp.
  mây mii thoorasàp ca phûut.

Why don't you use a phone?
  I don't have a phone to use.

๓๑.๖ แบบฝึกหัดการออกเสียงสระและพยัญชนะ

ก.

สีสิว	สิว	คิ้ว
เสียเสียว	เสียว	เคี้ยว

ข.

บิ๋มบอกปู่ใช่ไหม
  ไม่ใช่, ปู่บอกบิ๋ม

พ่อแพ้ปู่ใช่ไหม
  ไม่ใช่, ปู่แพ้พ่อ

ปู่ป้อนบิ๋มใช่ไหม
  ไม่ใช่, บิ๋มป้อนปู่

ปู่ป้อนพ่อใช่ไหม
  ไม่ใช่, พ่อป้อนปู่

เบิ๋มป้อนบ้าใช่ไหม
  ไม่ใช่, บ้าป้อนเบิ๋ม

พี่ป้อนบ้าใช่ไหม
  ไม่ใช่, บ้าป้อนพี่

บ้าบอกเบิ๋มใช่ไหม
  ไม่ใช่, เบิ๋มบอกบ้า

บ้าแพ้พี่ใช่ไหม
  ไม่ใช่, พี่แพ้บ้า

๓๑.๗ แบบฝึกหัดไวยากรณ์

ก.

ที่ร้านเล็ก ๆ ใกล้ ๆ บ้าน	(ใหญ่)
ที่ร้านใหญ่ ๆ ใกล้ ๆ บ้าน	(ใกล้ที่ทำงาน)
ที่ร้านใหญ่ ๆ ใกล้ ๆ ที่ทำงาน	(เล็ก)
ที่ร้านเล็ก ๆ ใกล้ ๆ ที่ทำงาน	(ที่โรงเรียน)
ที่โรงเรียนเล็ก ๆ ใกล้ ๆ ที่ทำงาน	(ใหญ่)
ที่โรงเรียนใหญ่ ๆ ใกล้ ๆ ที่ทำงาน	(ใกล้สถานทูต)
ที่โรงเรียนใหญ่ ๆ ใกล้ ๆ สถานทูต	

144

31.6 Vowel and consonant drills.

a. iw-iaw contrast drills.

sǐisǐw	sǐw	khíw
sǐasǐaw	sǐaw	khíaw

b. Response drill. (b, p, and ph).

bǐm bɔ̀ɔk pùu chây máy.   Bim told Grandpa, didn't he?
    mây chây. pùu bɔ̀ɔk bǐm.   No. Grandpa told Bim.

pùu pɔ̂ɔn bǐm chây máy.   Grandpa fed Bim, didn't he?
    mây chây. bǐm pɔ̂ɔn pùu.   No. Bim fed Grandpa.

bɘ̂m pɔ̂ɔn pâa chây máy.   Berm fed Auntie, didn't he?
    mây chây. pâa pɔ̂ɔn bɘ̂m.   No. Auntie fed Berm.

pâa bɔ̀ɔk bɘ̂m chây máy.   Auntie told Berm, didn't she?
    mây chây. bɘ̂m bɔ̀ɔk pâa.   No. Berm told Auntie.

phɔ̂ɔ phɛ́ɛ pùu chây máy.   Father lost to Grandpa, didn't he?
    mây chây. pùu phɛ́ɛ phɔ̂ɔ.   No. Grandpa lost to Father.

pùu pɔ̂ɔn phɔ̂ɔ chây máy.   Grandpa fed Father, didn't he?
    mây chây. phɔ̂ɔ pɔ̂ɔn pùu.   No. Father fed Grandpa.

phîi pɔ̂ɔn pâa chây máy.   Older One fed Auntie, didn't he?
    mây chây. pâa pɔ̂ɔn phîi.   No. Auntie fed Older One.

pâa phɛ́ɛ phîi chây máy.   Auntie lost to Older One, didn't she?
    mây chây. phîi phɛ́ɛ pâa.   No. Older One lost to Auntie.

31.7 Grammar drills.

a. Substitution drill.

thîi ráan léklék klâyklây bâan. (yày)   At a small shop near my house. (large)

thîi ráan yàyyày klâyklây bâan.
(kɨ̂ay thîi tham ŋaan)   At a large store near my house.
(near my office)

thîi ráan yàyyày klâyklây
thîi tham ŋaan. (lék)   At a large store near my office.
(small)

thîi ráan léklék klâyklây
thîi tham ŋaan. (thîi rooŋrian)   At a small shop near my office.
(at a school)

thîi rooŋrian léklék klâyklây
thîi tham ŋaan. (yày)   At a small school near my office.
(large)

thîi rooŋrian yàyyày klâyklây
thîi tham ŋaan. (klây sathǎanthûut)   At a large school near my office.
(near the Embassy)

thîi rooŋrian yàyyày klâyklây sathǎanthûut.   At a large school near the Embassy.

ข.

กี่คน	กี่แผ่น
สองคน	สามแผ่น
สองคนไหน	สามแผ่นไหน
สองคนนั้น	สามแผ่นนั้น
กี่ชิ้น	กี่หลัง
ชิ้นเดียว	หลังเดียว
ชิ้นไหน	หลังไหน
ชิ้นนั้น	หลังนั้น
กี่ตัว	
ห้าตัว	
ห้าตัวไหน	
ห้าตัวนั้น	

ค.

เด็กสองคนนี้	(เสื้อ)	กระดาษห้าแผ่นนั้น	(โน้น)
เสื้อสองตัวนี้	(นั้น)	กระดาษห้าแผ่นโน้น	(ไข่)
เสื้อสองตัวนั้น	(ห้า)	ไข่ห้าลูกโน้น	
เสื้อห้าตัวนั้น	(กระดาษ)		

ง.

สักคู่หนึ่ง	(สอง)	สักห้าหลัง	(หนึ่ง)
สักสองคู่	(คน)	สักหลังหนึ่ง	(อีก)
สักสองคน	(หนึ่ง)	อีกสักหลังหนึ่ง	(เล่ม)
สักคนหนึ่ง	(ชิ้น)	อีกสักเล่มหนึ่ง	(แปด)
สักชิ้นหนึ่ง	(ห้า)	อีกสักแปดเล่ม	
สักห้าชิ้น	(หลัง)		

b. Response drill.

kìi khon.	How many people?
sɔ̌ɔŋ khon.	Two people.
sɔ̌ɔŋ khon nǎy.	Which two people?
sɔ̌ɔŋ khon nán.	Those two people.
kìi chín.	How many pieces?
chín diaw.	One piece.
chín nǎy.	Which piece?
chín nán.	That piece.
kìi tua.	How many articles of clothing?
hâa tua.	Five articles of clothing.
hâa tua nǎy.	Which five articles of clothing?
hâa tua nán.	Those five articles of clothing.
kìi phèn.	How many sheets?
sǎam phèn.	Three sheets.
sǎam phèn nǎy.	Which three sheets?
sǎam phèn nán.	Those three sheets.
kìi lǎŋ.	How many houses?
lǎŋ diaw.	One house.
lǎŋ nǎy.	Which house?
lǎŋ nán.	That house.

c. Substitution drill.

dèk sɔ̌ɔŋ khon níi. (sɨ̂a)	These two children. (shirts)
sɨ̂a sɔ̌ɔŋ tua níi. (nán)	These two shirts. (those)
sɨ̂a sɔ̌ɔŋ tua nán. (hâa)	Those two shirts. (five)
sɨ̂a hâa tua nán. (kradàat)	Those five shirts. (paper)
kradàat hâa phèn nán. (nóon)	Those five sheets of paper. (yonder)
kradàat hâa phèn nóon. (khày)	Yonder five sheets of paper. (eggs)
khày hâa lûuk nóon.	Yonder five eggs.

d. Substitution drill.

sák khûu nɨŋ. (sɔ̌ɔŋ)	At least one pair. (two)
sák sɔ̌ɔŋ khûu. (khon)	At least two pairs. (people)
sák sɔ̌ɔŋ khon. (nɨŋ)	At least two people. (one)
sák khon nɨŋ. (chín)	At least one person. (piece)
sák chín nɨŋ (hâa)	At least one piece. (five)
sák hâa chín. (lǎŋ)	At least five pieces. (houses)
sák hâa lǎŋ. (nɨŋ)	At least five houses. (one)
sák lǎŋ nɨŋ. (ʔìik)	At least one house. (more)
ʔìik sák lǎŋ nɨŋ. (lêm)	At least one more house. (book)
ʔìik sák lêm nɨŋ. (pὲεt)	At least one more book. (eight)
ʔìik sák pὲεt lêm.	At least eight more books.

147

๓๑.๘ เวลา

เช้านี้   เย็นนี้
เมื่อเช้านี้   เมื่อเย็นนี้
พรุ่งนี้เช้า   คืนนี้
                          เมื่อคืนนี้

๓๑.๙ การสนทนาโต้ตอบ

แท๊กซี่

   ไปไหนครับ

ไป............ก............รู้จักไหม

   ไม่รู้จักครับ

รู้จัก........ข........ไหม

   รู้จักครับ

ไป............ข............ ....ก............ อยู่ใกล้ ๆ ....ข............ เอาเท่าไหร่

   แปดบาทครับ

หกบาทได้ไหม

   เจ็ดบาทครับ

ตกลง, ไม่ต้องขับเร็วนะ

   ถึง............ข............แล้วครับ

ตรงไปอีกหน่อย (เลี้ยวขวาที่ซอยหน้า ฯลฯ)

............ก............อยู่ที่โน่น จอดที่........................

31.8 Periods of the day.

cháaw níi	This morning (present).
mûa cháaw níi	This morning (past).
phrûŋ níi cháaw	Tomorrow morning.
yen níi	This evening (future or present).
mûa yen níi	This evening (past).
khɯɯn níi	Tonight (future or present).
mûa khɯɯn níi	Last night.

Practice referring to the following periods at the stated times.

At noon.	**At 10:00 p.m.**	**At 8:00 a.m.**
This morning.	Last night.	Tomorrow.
Tonight.	This evening.	Last night.
Tomorrow morning.	Yesterday.	This evening.
Yesterday.	Tonight.	Today.
Last night.	Tomorrow morning.	Yesterday.
Today.	This morning.	This morning.
This evening.	Today.	Tomorrow morning.
Tomorrow.	Tomorrow.	Tonight.

31.9 Conversation.

Use the following framework to practice getting a taxi.

thɛ́ksîi.

   pay nǎy khráp.

pay.........A........ .   rúucàk máy.

   mây rúucàk khráp.

rúucàk.........B.........máy.

   rúucàk khráp.

pay ....B........ .   ...A.......... yùu klâyklây ....B........ .   ʔaw thâwrày.

   pɛ̀ɛt bàat khráp.

hòk bàat dây máy.

   cèt bàat khráp.

tòkloŋ.   mây tôŋ khàp rew nâ.

   thǎŋ ....B......... lɛ́ɛw khráp.

troŋ pay ʔìik nòy (líaw khwǎa thîi sɔ̌ɔy nâa, etc.).

.........A......... yùu thîi nôon.   cɔ̀ɔt thîi ....

149

๓๑.๑๐ การเขียน

ซื้อกุ้งแห้ง

ให้	เตี้ย	ใช้
เก้าอี้	ล้าน	หน้าต่าง
นี้	ผู้	บ้าน
ขึ้น	อ้วน	ร้าน
ได้	น้อง	ถ้า
ร้อน	สั้น	แก้
ถ้วย	ใกล้	นั้น

แล้วเลี้ยวซ้าย   ป้าเข้าส้วม

31.10 Writing.

ซื้อกุ้งแห้ง

sɯ́ɯ kûŋ hɛ̂ɛŋ

Buy dried shrimps.

The second tone marker (máy thoo) gives a high tone to syllables with low initials and a falling tone to syllables with mid and high initials.

The student should recognize all of the following words.

ให้	hây	เตี้ย	tîa	ใช้	cháy
เก้าอี้	kâw ʔîi	ล้าน	láan	หน้าต่าง	nâatàaŋ
นี้	níi	ผู้	phûu	บ้าน	bâan
ขึ้น	khɯ̂n	อ้วน	ʔûan	ร้าน	ráan
ได้	dây	น้อง	nɔ́ɔŋ	ถ้ำ	thâa
ร้อน	rɔ́ɔn	สั้น	sân	แก้	kɛ̂ɛ
ถ้วย	thûay	ใกล้	klây	นั้น	nán

แล้วเลี้ยวซ้าย   บ้าเข้าส้วม

151

บทที่ ๓๒

๓๒.๑ คำศัพท์

กำลังจะ	คับ
ธุระ	หลวม
มีธุระอะไร	
ทั้ง	หมด
ทั้งวัน	เสื้อหมดแล้ว
	เสื้อคับหมด
งั้น	
	หมอ
พา	ไปหาหมอ
ร้านตัดเสื้อ	ดู
	หนัง
เสื้อผ้า	ดูหนัง

LESSON 32

32.1 Vocabulary and expansions.

kamlaŋ ca	To be about to, on the point of.
thúrá?	An item of business, an errand.
mii thúrá? ?aray	(Said to someone who calls at your office or on the phone.) What do you want? What can I do for you? What's on your mind? State your business.
tháŋ	All, the whole of.
tháŋ wan	All day.
ŋán	Short for *thâa yaŋŋán*.
phaa	To take someone somewhere.
ráan tàt sûa	Tailor shop.
sûa phâa	Clothing.
kháp	Tight.
lŭam	Loose.
mòt	To be all gone, to the last one.
sûa mòt léɛw	All the shirts are gone. We're all out of shirts.
sûa kháp mòt	All of my shirts are tight (they are tight down to the last one).
mɔ̆ɔ	Doctor.
pay hăa mɔ̆ɔ	To go see a doctor.
duu	To look at.
năŋ	Moving pictures.
duu năŋ	To see a movie.

153

๓๒.๒ โครงสร้างของประโยค

กำลังจะไปซื้อของ

กำลังจะไปดูหนัง

กำลังจะไปหาหมอ

กำลังจะกินข้าว

พาฉันไปร้านตัดเสื้อ

พาเพื่อนไปเที่ยว

พาลูกไปดูหนัง

พาน้องไปหาหมอ

มีธุระที่ไหนอีกไหม

เอาอะไรอีกไหม

จะไปไหนอีกไหม

เสื้อผ้าคับหมด

อาหารเสียหมด

รองเท้าหลวมหมด

ทั้งวัน

ทั้งคืน

ทั้งอาทิตย์

ทั้งเดือน

ทั้งปี

ทั้งสอง

ทั้งสาม

๓๒.๓ บทสนทนา

ก. กำลังทำอะไรอยู่หรือเปล่าฮะ

ข. เปล่าฮะ

ก. ไปซื้อของกันไหมฮะ

ข. ไปซิฮะ กำลังจะออกไปซื้อบุหรี่

ก. แล้วมีธุระที่ไหนอีกไหมฮะ

ข. ไม่มีฮะ ผมว่างทั้งวัน

ก. งั้น, ช่วยพาผมไปร้านตัดเสื้อหน่อยนะฮะ
ผมอ้วนขึ้นมาก เสื้อผ้าคับหมด

ข. ได้ฮะ ผมก็อยากจะตัดกางเกงสัก
ตัวหนึ่งเหมือนกัน

154

32.2 Patterns.

kamlaŋ ca pay sǔu khɔ̌oŋ.	I'm just about to go shopping.
kamlaŋ ca pay duu nǎŋ.	I'm just leaving for the movies.
kamlaŋ ca pay hǎa mɔ̌ɔ.	I'm going to see the doctor.
kamlaŋ ca kin khâaw.	I'm just getting ready to eat.

mii thúráʔ thîi nǎy ʔìik máy.	Do you have any business anywhere else?
ʔaw ʔaray ʔìik máy.	Do you want anything else?
ca pay nǎy ʔìik máy.	Are you going anywhere else?

tháŋ wan.	All day.
tháŋ khʉʉn.	All night.
tháŋ ʔathít.	All week.
tháŋ dʉan.	All month.
tháŋ pii.	All year.
tháŋ sɔ̌ɔŋ.	Both.
tháŋ sǎam.	All three.

phaa chán pay ráan tàt sʉ̂a.	Take me to a tailor shop.
phaa phʉan pay thîaw.	Take your friend out.
phaa lûuk pay duu nǎŋ.	Take your child to a show.
phaa nɔ́ɔŋ pay hǎa mɔ̌ɔ.	Take younger brother to the doctor.

sʉ̂a phâa kháp mòt.	All my clothes are tight.
ʔaahǎan sǐa mòt.	All the food is spoiled.
rɔŋtháaw lǔam mòt.	All my shoes are too loose.

32.3 Dialog.

A. kamlaŋ tham ʔaray yùu rʉ́ plàaw há?.   Are you doing anything right now?

B. plàaw há?.   No.

A. pay sǔu khɔ̌oŋ kan máy há?.   How about going shopping with me?

B. pay si há?.   Yes, indeed.
kamlaŋ ca ʔɔ̀ɔk pay sǔu burìi.   I was just going out to get some cigarets.

A. lɛ́ɛw mii thúráʔ thîi nǎy ʔìik máy há?.   Do you have business anywhere else?

B. mây mii há?.   No.
phǒm wâaŋ tháŋ wan.   I'm free all day.

A. ŋán, chûay phaa phǒm pay
ráan tàt sʉ̂a nɔ̀y ná há?.   Could you take me to a tailor shop,
then?
phǒm ʔûan khʉ̂n mâak.   I've gained a lot of weight.
sʉ̂a phâa kháp mòt.   All my clothes are too tight.

B. dây há?.   Yes, I can.
phǒm kɔ̂ yàak ca tàt kaŋkeeŋ   I'd like to get a pair of trousers
sák tua nʉŋ mʉ́ankan.   made, too.

155

๓๒.๔ แบบฝึกหัดการฟังและการออกเสียงสูงต่ำ

ก.

ร้องไห้   โกนหนวด   ศึกษา   หัวเราะ   แม่แรง

ข.

ถามศรีทำไม
    ไม่ได้ถามศรี ถามประสงค์

พูดกับต้อยทำไม
    ไม่ได้พูดกับต้อย พูดกับประภาส

เตือนแดงทำไม
    ไม่ได้เตือนแดง เตือนประชุม

ทักแอ๊ดทำไม
    ไม่ได้ทักแอ๊ด ทักประพัทธ์

บอกหน่อยทำไม
    ไม่ได้บอกหน่อย บอกประเสริฐ

๓๒.๕. แบบฝึกหัดการสลับเสียงสูงต่ำ

ทำไมไม่อ่านหนังสือ
    อยากจะอ่านหนังสือเหมือนกัน,
    แต่ไม่มีหนังสือจะอ่าน

ทำไมไม่กินข้าว
    อยากจะกินข้าวเหมือนกัน,
    แต่ไม่มีข้าวจะกิน

ทำไมไม่ทำงาน
    อยากจะทำงานเหมือนกัน,
    แต่ไม่มีงานจะทำ

ทำไมไม่ใช้ช้อน
    อยากจะใช้ช้อนเหมือนกัน
    แต่ไม่มีช้อนจะใช้

ทำไมไม่ขายรถ
    อยากจะขายรถเหมือนกัน,
    แต่ไม่มีรถจะขาย

ทำไมไม่พูดโทรศัพท์
    อยากจะพูดโทรศัพท์เหมือนกัน
    แต่ไม่มีโทรศัพท์จะพูด

32.4 Tone identification and production.

a. Identify the tones and record the number of repetitions required.

To cry.	rɔɔŋ haay	....	....
To shave.	koon nuat	....	....
To educate.	sɯksaa	....	....
To laugh.	huarɔʔ	....	....
A car jack.	mɛɛ rɛɛŋ	....	....

b. Response drill.

thǎam sǐi thammay.
  mây dây thǎam sǐi. thǎam prasǒŋ.

Why did you ask Sri?
  I didn't ask Sri. I asked Prasong.

tɯan dɛɛŋ thammay.
  mây dây tɯan dɛɛŋ. tɯan prachum.

Why did you warn Daeng?
  I didn't warn Daeng. I warned Prachum.

bɔ̀ɔk nɔ̀y thammay.
  mây dây bɔ̀ɔk nɔ̀y. bɔ̀ɔk prasə̀ət.

Why did you tell Noy?
  I didn't tell Noy. I told Prasert.

phûut kàp tɔ̂y thammay.
  mây dây phûut kàp tɔ̂y.
  phûut kàp praphâat.

Why did you speak to Toy?
  I didn't speak to Toy.
  I spoke to Prapart.

thák ʔɛ́ɛt thammay.
  mây dây thák ʔɛ́ɛt. thák praphát.

Why did you greet At?
  I didn't greet At. I greeted Prapat.

32.5 Tone manipulation.

thammay mây ʔàan naŋsɯ̌ɯ.
  yàak ca ʔàan naŋsɯ̌ɯ mɯ̌ankan,
  tɛ̀ɛ mây mii naŋsɯ̌ɯ ca ʔàan.

Why don't you read a book?
  I'd like to read a book (now that you mention it),
  but I haven't got one to read.

thammay mây tham ŋaan.
  yàak ca tham ŋaan mɯ̌ankan,
  tɛ̀ɛ mây mii ŋaan ca tham.

Why don't you work?
  I'd like to work,
  but I haven't got any work to do.

thammay mây khǎay rót.
  yàak ca khǎay rót mɯ̌ankan,
  tɛ̀ɛ mây mii rót ca khǎay.

Why don't you sell your car?
  I'd like to sell my car,
  but I haven't got one to sell.

thammay mây kin khâaw.
  yàak ca kin khâaw mɯ̌ankan,
  tɛ̀ɛ mây mii khâaw ca kin.

Why don't you eat?
  I'd like to eat,
  but there isn't any rice.

thammay mây cháy chɔ́ɔn.
  yàak ca cháy chɔ́ɔn mɯ̌ankan,
  tɛ̀ɛ mây mii chɔ́ɔn ca cháy.

Why don't you use a spoon?
  I'd like to use a spoon,
  but there isn't one to use.

thammay mây phûut thoorasàp.
  yàak ca phûut thoorasàp mɯ̌ankan,
  tɛ̀ɛ mây mii thoorasàp ca phûut.

Why don't you use the phone?
  I'd like to use the phone,
  but there isn't one to use.

๓๒.๖ แบบฝึกหัดการอ่านออกเสียงสระและพยัญชนะ

ก.

ชู่ชุ่ย	ชุ่ย	กรุย
ชั่วช่วย	ช่วย	กรวย

ข.

แดงด่าติ๋มใช่ไหม

  ไม่ใช่, ติ๋มด่าแดง

ติ๋มตีแดงใช่ไหม

  ไม่ใช่, แดงตีติ๋ม

ดำตีต้อยใช่ไหม

  ไม่ใช่, ต้อยตีดำ

ต้อยด่าดำใช่ไหม

  ไม่ใช่, ดำด่าต้อย

แถมแทงติ๋มใช่ไหม

  ไม่ใช่, ติ๋มแทงแถม

ติ๋มตีแถมใช่ไหม

  ไม่ใช่, แถมตีติ๋ม

ทอมตีต้อยใช่ไหม

  ไม่ใช่, ต้อยตีทอม

ต้อยแทงทอมใช่ไหม

  ไม่ใช่, ทอมแทงต้อย

๓๒.๗ แบบฝึกหัดไวยากรณ์

ก.

ฉันว่างทั้งวัน	(มีธุระ)
ฉันมีธุระทั้งวัน	(อาทิตย์)
ฉันมีธุระทั้งอาทิตย์	(ว่าง)
ฉันว่างทั้งอาทิตย์	(วัน)

ข.

อ้วนขึ้นมาก เสื้อผ้าคับหมด (ผอม)

ผอมลงมาก เสื้อผ้าหลวมหมด (อ้วน)

158

32.6 Vowel and consonant drills.

a. uy-uay contrast drills.

chûuchûy   chûy   kruy
chûachûay   chûay   kruay

b. Response drill. (d. t, and th).

dɛɛŋ dàa tím chây máy.
  mây chây. tím dàa dɛɛŋ.

Daeng cursed Tim, didn't she?
  No. Tim cursed Daeng.

tím tii dɛɛŋ chây máy.
  mây chây. dɛɛŋ tii tím.

Tim beat Daeng, didn't she?
  No. Daeng beat Tim.

dam tii tɔ̂y chây máy.
  mây chây. tɔ̂y tii dam.

Dum beat Toy, didn't he?
  No. Toy beat Dum.

tɔ̂y dàa dam chây máy.
  mây chây. dam dàa tɔ̂y.

Toy cursed Dum, didn't she?
  No. Dum cursed Toy.

thěɛm theeŋ tím chây máy.
  mây chây. tím theeŋ thěɛm.

Tam stabbed Tim, didn't she?
  No. Tim stabbed Tam.

tím tii thěɛm chây máy.
  mây chây. thěɛm tii tím.

Tim beat Tam, didn't she?
  No. Tam beat Tim.

thɔɔm tii tɔ̂y chây máy.
  mây chây. tɔ̂y tii thɔɔm.

Tom beat Toy, didn't he?
  No. Toy beat Tom.

tɔ̂y theeŋ thɔɔm chây máy.
  mây chây. thɔɔm theeŋ tɔ̂y.

Toy stabbed Tom, didn't she?
  No. Tom stabbed Toy.

32.7 Grammar drills.

a. Substitution drill.

chán wâaŋ tháŋ wan. (mii thúrá?)
chán mii thúrá? tháŋ wan. (?athít)
chán mii thúrá? tháŋ ?athít. (wâaŋ)
chán wâaŋ tháŋ ?athít. (wan)

I'm free all day. (busy)
I'm busy all day. (week)
I'm busy all week. (free)
I'm free all week. (day)

b. Substitution drill.

?ûan khûn mâak.
sûa phâa kháp mòt. (phɔ̌ɔm)

I'm getting very fat.
My clothes are all too tight. (thin)

phɔ̌ɔm loŋ mâak.
sûa phâa lǔam mòt. (?ûan)

I'm getting very thin.
My clothes are all too loose. (fat)

ค.

จะนั่งที่ไหน
    นั่งที่ไหนก็ได้

จะไปเมื่อไหร่
    ไปเมื่อไหร่ก็ได้

จะเอาเสื้อตัวไหน
    เอาตัวไหนก็ได้

จะอ่านหนังสือเล่มไหน
    อ่านเล่มไหนก็ได้

จะพูดกับใคร
    พูดกับใครก็ได้

จะใส่รองเท้าคู่ไหน
    ใส่คู่ไหนก็ได้

จะซื้อบ้านหลังไหน
    ซื้อหลังไหนก็ได้

จะเอาถ้วยกี่ใบ
    เอากี่ใบก็ได้

ง.

จะเอากางเกงตัวไหน
    ตัวนี้ก็ได้, ตัวโน้นก็ได้

จะอ่านหนังสือเล่มไหน
    เล่มนี้ก็ได้, เล่มโน้นก็ได้

จะซื้อรถคันไหน
    คันนี้ก็ได้, คันโน้นก็ได้

จะใส่ถุงเท้าคู่ไหน
    คู่นี้ก็ได้, คู่โน้นก็ได้

c. Response drill.

ca nâŋ thîi nǎy.
    nâŋ thîi nǎy kɔ̂ dây.

    Where are you going to sit?
    Anywhere. It doesn't matter.

ca ʔaw sɯ̂a tua nǎy.
    ʔaw tua nǎy kɔ̂ dây.

    Which shirt do you want?
    Any one. It doesn't matter.

ca phûut kàp khray.
    phûut kàp khray kɔ̂ dây.

    Who do you want to talk to?
    Anyone. It doesn't matter.

ca sɯ́ɯ bâan lǎŋ nǎy.
    sɯ́ɯ lǎŋ nǎy kɔ̂ dây.

    Which house are you going to buy?
    Any one. It doesn't matter.

ca pay mɯ̂arày.
    pay mɯ̂arày kɔ̂ dây.

    When do you want to go?
    Any time. It doesn't matter.

ca ʔàan naŋsɯ̌ɯ lêm nǎy.
    ʔàan lêm nǎy kɔ̂ dây.

    Which book do you want to read?
    Any one. It doesn't matter.

ca sày rɔŋtháaw khûu nǎy.
    sày khûu nǎy kɔ̂ dây.

    Which pair of shoes do you want to wear?
    Any pair. It doesn't matter.

ca ʔaw thûay kìi bay.
    ʔaw kìi bay kɔ̂ dây.

    How many cups do you want?
    Any number. It doesn't matter.

d. Response drill.

ca ʔaw kaŋkeeŋ tua nǎy.
    tua níi kɔ̂ dây,
    tua nóon kɔ̂ dây.

    Which pair of trousers do you want?
    This pair is all right.
    And so is that one. (Either one.)

ca sɯ́ɯ rót khan nǎy.
    khan níi kɔ̂ dây,
    khan nóon kɔ̂ dây.

    Which car do you want to buy?
    This one is all right.
    And so is that one.

ca ʔàan naŋsɯ̌ɯ lêm nǎy.
    lêm níi kɔ̂ dây,
    lêm nóon kɔ̂ dây.

    Which book do you want to read?
    This one is all right.
    And so is that one.

ca sày thǔŋtháaw khûu nǎy.
    khûu níi kɔ̂ dây,
    khûu nóon kɔ̂ dây.

    Which pair of socks do you want to wear?
    This pair is all right.
    And so is that one.

จ.

ไม่ไปหรือ
    ฮึ, ไปไม่ได้

คืนนี้ไม่ไปดูหนังหรือ
    ฮึ, คืนนี้ไปดูหนังไม่ได้

ไม่กินเบียร์หรือ
    ฮึ, กินเบียร์ไม่ได้

วันนี้ไม่ไปทำงานหรือ
    ฮึ, วันนี้ไปทำงานไม่ได้

วันนี้ไม่ไปหาหมอหรือ
    ฮึ, วันนี้ไปหาหมอไม่ได้

คืนนี้ไม่เรียนภาษาไทยหรือ
    ฮึ, คืนนี้เรียนภาษาไทยไม่ได้

๓๒.๘ เวลา

เมื่อวานนี้	วันนี้	พรุ่งนี้
เมื่ออาทิตย์ที่แล้ว	อาทิตย์นี้	อาทิตย์หน้า
เมื่อวันจันทร์ที่แล้ว	วันอังคารนี้	วันพุธหน้า
เมื่อเดือนที่แล้ว	เดือนนี้	เดือนหน้า
เมื่อปีที่แล้ว	ปีนี้	ปีหน้า

เมื่อวานซืนนี้	มะรืนนี้
สองอาทิตย์มาแล้ว	อีกสองอาทิตย์
วันอาทิตย์ก่อนโน้น	วันเสาร์โน้น
สองเดือนมาแล้ว	อีกสองเดือน
สองปีมาแล้ว	อีกสองปี

e. Response drill.

mây pay lɔ̌ə.   Aren't you going?
   hm̂m. pay mây dây.   No, I can't go.

mây kin bia lɔ̌ə.   Aren't you going to have some beer?
   hm̂m. kin bia mây dây.   No, I can't drink beer.

wan níi mây pay hǎa mɔ̌ɔ lɔ̌ə.   Aren't you going to see the doctor today?
   hm̂m. wan níi pay hǎa mɔ̌ɔ mây dây.   No, I can't go see him today.

khɯɯn níi mây pay duu nǎŋ lɔ̌ə.   Aren't you going to a show tonight?
   hm̂m. khɯɯn níi pay duu nǎŋ mây dây.   No, I can't go to a show tonight.

wan níi mây pay tham ŋaan lɔ̌ə.   Aren't you going to work today?
   hm̂m. wan níi pay tham ŋaan mây dây.   No, I can't go to work today.

khɯɯn níi mây rian phasǎa thay lɔ̌ə.   Aren't you going to study Thai tonight?
   hm̂m. khɯɯn níi rian phasǎa thay mây dây.   No, I can't study Thai tonight.

32.8 Time periods.

mɯ̂a waan níi	wan níi	phrûŋ níi
mɯ̂a ʔathít thîi lɛ́ɛw	ʔathít níi	ʔathít nâa
mɯ̂a wan can thîi lɛ́ɛw ←	wan ʔaŋkhaan níi →	wan phút nâa
mɯ̂a dɯan thîi lɛ́ɛw	dɯan níi	dɯan nâa
mɯ̂a pii thîi lɛ́ɛw	pii níi	pii nâa
↓		↓
mɯ̂a wan sɯɯn níi		marɯɯn níi
sɔ̌ɔŋ ʔathít maa lɛ́ɛw		ʔìik sɔ̌ɔŋ ʔathít
wan ʔathít kɔ̀ɔn nóon		wan sǎw nóon
sɔ̌ɔŋ dɯan maa lɛ́ɛw		ʔìik sɔ̌ɔŋ dɯan
sɔ̌ɔŋ pii maa lɛ́ɛw		ʔìik sɔ̌ɔŋ pii

Practice translating the following time periods for speed.

Day before yesterday.	This week.	Tuesday after next.
Last week.	Next Thursday.	Two months ago.
This Friday.	In two more months.	Last year.
Next month.	Two years ago.	Today.
In two more years.	Yesterday.	Next week.
Last month.	Next year.	Day before yesterday.
This year.	Day after tomorrow.	Last week.
Tomorrow.	Last Saturday.	This Sunday.
In two more weeks.	Two weeks ago.	Next month.
Monday before last.	This month.	In two more years.

163

๓๒.๕ การสนทนาโต้ตอบ

สวนลุมฯ อยู่ที่ไหนคะ

คุณรู้จักวงเวียนศาลาแดงไหมฮะ

ไม่รู้จักฮ่ะ

รู้จักโรงแรมเอราวัณไหมฮะ

ไม่รู้จักฮ่ะ

รู้จักสถานทูตอังกฤษไหมฮะ

รู้จักฮ่ะ ดิฉันทำงานที่นั่น

เอ้า........

นี่สถานทูตอังกฤษ...........นะฮะ

แล้วนี่ถนนเพลินจิต...........นะฮะ

นี่สี่แยกราชประสงค์...........นะฮะ

โรงแรมเอราวัณอยู่ที่นี่...........นะฮะ

แล้วนี่ถนนราชดำริห์...........นะฮะ

สปอร์ตคลับอยู่ที่นี่...........นะฮะ

แล้วก็วงเวียนศาลาแดงอยู่ที่นี่...........นะฮะ

ที่นี่สวนลุมฯ

ขับรถออกจากสถานทูตอังกฤษไปตามถนนเพลินจิต........นะฮะ

พอถึงสี่แยกราชประสงค์เลี้ยวซ้าย........นะฮะ

แล้วก็ไปตามถนนราชดำริห์........นะฮะ

พอเลยสปอร์ตคลับ........นะฮะ........จะเห็นวงเวียนศาลาแดง

ก่อนถึงวงเวียนศาลาแดงจะมีทางแยกทางซ้าย

เลี้ยวซ้ายไปตามถนนนี้

32.9 Conversation.

In the following example, instructions are given for going from the British Embassy to Lumpini Park (sǔan lum). The teacher should go through the example many times while the students listen especially to the particles (náhá or náhá?) noticing especially the pauses, rhythm, and the tone of voice. Only after the student has a feeling for the matching of rhythm and tone of voice to the meaning should he attempt to repeat after the teacher. The purpose in this lesson is *to get a feeling for* the particles used in giving instructions. The teacher does most of the work. The students will get their chance in the next lesson.

sǔan lum yùu thîi nǎy khá.

khun rúucàk woŋwian sǎaladɛɛŋ máy há?.

  mây rúucàk hâ.

rúucàk rooŋrɛɛm ʔeerawan máy há?.

  mây rúucàk hâ.

rúucàk sathǎanthûut ʔaŋkrìt máy há?.

  rúucàk hâ. dichán tham ŋaan thîi nân.

ʔâw (We're ready to start.) (Teacher proceeds to draw or point to a map.)
nîi sathǎanthûut ʔaŋkrìt......náhá?.
lɛ́ɛw nîi thanǒn phlɔɔncìt......náha?.
nîi sìiyɛ̂ɛk râatprasǒŋ......náhá?.
rooŋrɛɛm ʔeerawan yùu thîi nîi......náhá?.
lɛ́ɛw nîi thanǒn râatdamrì?......náhá?.
sapɔ̀ɔt khláp (Sports Club) yùu thîi nîi......náhá?.
lɛ́ɛw kɔ̂ woŋwian sǎaladɛɛŋ yùu thîi nîi......náhá?.
thîi nîi sǔan lum.

khàp rót ʔɔ̀ɔk càak (from) sathǎanthûut ʔaŋkrìt pay taam thanǒn phlɔɔncìt......náhá?.
phɔɔ (as soon as) thǔŋ sìiyɛ̂ɛk râatprasǒŋ líaw sáay......náhá?.
lɛ́ɛw kɔ̂ pay taam thanǒn râatdamrì?......náhá?.
phɔɔ ləəy sapɔ̀ɔt khláp......náhá?......ca hěn woŋwian sǎaladɛɛŋ.
kɔ̀ɔn thǔŋ woŋwian sǎaladɛɛŋ ca mii thaaŋ yɛ̂ɛk (branching off) thaaŋ sáay.
líaw sáay pay taam thanǒn nîi.

165

ไม้ไหม้

	ขา		ข่า		ข้า
			ค่า		ค้า	คา

แพ	แผ่	แพ่	แผ้	แพ้	แผ		เท่	เถ้	เถ	เท	เท้	เถ่
ฉา	ฉ่า	ช้า	ช่า	ฉ้า	ชา		ส่อ	ซ่อ	ส้อ	สอ	ซอ	ซ้อ
พี	ฟี	ผี่	ผี	ฟี่	ผี้		หมู่	มู่	หมู้	หมู	มู	มู้
เหนอ	เน่อ	เหน้อ	เนอ	เน้อ	เหน่อ		โง่	โหง้	โง้	โหง่	โหง	โง
เวีย	เว่ย	เหวย้	เหว่ย	เว้ย	เหวย		รั้ว	รั่ว	หรั้ว	รัว	หรั่ว	หรัว
เหลือ	เลื่อ	เลือ	เลื่อ	เหลือ	เหลื่อ		หยอ	ย้อ	หยือ	ย่อ	ยอ	หยอ

166

ไม่ไหม้

mây mây
Doesn't burn.

The combinations of high and low initials with no tonal marker, *máy ʔèek*, and *máy thoo* are used to write the five tones in live syllables as shown below.

khǎa	khàa	khâa	kháa	khaa
ขา	ข่า	ข้า		
		ค่า	ค้า	คา

Since the falling tone can be written in two different ways, the spellings of particular words must be memorized (see *mây mây* above).

Practice writing the following nonsense syllables. All falling tones should be written in two ways.

phɛ̀ɛ	phɛ̂ɛ	phɛ̂ɛ	phɛ́ɛ	phɛ̌ɛ	thêe	thěe	thee	thée	thèe
chǎa	chàa	cháa	châa	chaa	sɔ̀ɔ	sɔ̂ɔ	sɔ̌ɔ	sɔɔ	sɔ́ɔ
fíi	fii	fìi	fïi	fǐi	mùu	mûu	mǔu	muu	múu
nǒ̂ə	nɔ̂ə	nəə	nɔ́ə	nɔ̀ə	ŋôo	ŋóo	ŋòo	ŋǒo	ŋoo
wia	wîa	wìa	wía	wǐa	rúa	rûa	rua	rùa	rǔa
lǔa	lʉa	lʉ́a	lʉ̂a	lʉ̀a	yʉ̀ʉ	yʉ́ʉ	yʉ̌ʉ	yʉʉ	yʉ̂ʉ

บทที่ ๓๓

๓๓.๑ คำศัพท์

สี	แปรง
พัน	แปรงสีฟัน
สีฟัน	
ยาสีฟัน	หวี
	มีด
สบู่	
	คีม
อย่าง	
	เขียง
หลอด	
	ครก
ก้อน	
	เงิน
กลาง	
	เหล็ก
ผ่าน	
	ไม้
หนา	
	หิน
บาง	
	ทำด้วย
สูบ	ทำด้วยอะไร
สูบบุหรี่	

LESSON 33

33.1 Vocabulary and expansions.

sǐi	To rub, scrub.
fan	Teeth.
sǐi fan	To brush the teeth.
yaa sǐi fan	Toothpaste (medicine for scrubbing the teeth).
sabùu	Soap.
yàaŋ	Kind, sort, variety (used as a classifier).
lɔ̀ɔt	A tube. Classifier for things in tubes.
kɔ̂ɔn	A lump. Classifier for things in lumps.
klaaŋ	Medium, center.
phàan	To pass a fixed object.
nǎa	To be thick.
baaŋ	To be thin.
sùup	To draw on, pump, smoke.
sùup burìi	To smoke a cigarette.
prɛɛŋ	A brush, to brush.
prɛɛŋ sǐi fan	A tooth brush.
wǐi	A comb, to comb.
mîit	Knife.
khiim	Pliers.
khǐaŋ	A chopping board.
khrók	A mortar.
ŋən	Silver.
lèk	Iron.
máay	Wood.
hǐn	Stone.
tham dûay	To be made of.
tham dûay ʔaray	What is it made of.

๓๓.๒ โครงสร้างของประโยค

อย่างใหญ่

อย่างกลาง

อย่างเล็ก

สบู่อย่างไหน

สบู่อย่างนี้

สบู่อย่างใหญ่

ยาอย่างเดียว

ยาสองอย่าง

ยาหลายอย่าง

ร้านขายผ้า

ร้านขายหนังสือ

ร้านขายกระดาษ

ร้านขายรองเท้า

ร้านตัดรองเท้า

ร้านตัดเสื้อ

ร้านตัดผม

ผ้าขาวหนา ๆ

ผ้าดำบาง ๆ

กระดาษขาวบาง ๆ

ทำด้วยเงิน

ทำด้วยเหล็ก

ทำด้วยแก้ว

ทำด้วยไม้

ทำด้วยหิน

๓๓.๓ บทสนทนา

ก. วันนี้ฉันจะไปซื้อของ คุณต้องการ
อะไรบ้างไหมฮะ จะช่วยซื้อให้

ข. ขอบคุณฮ่ะ ฉันอยากได้ยาสีฟัน
กับสบู่ ยาสีฟันอย่างกลางหลอด
หนึ่ง แล้วก็สบู่อย่างใหญ่สอง
ก้อน

ก. เอาอะไรอีกไหมฮะ

ข. ถ้าผ่านร้านขายผ้าช่วยซื้อผ้า
ให้ด้วยนะฮะ

ก. ผ้าอะไรฮะ

ข. ผ้าขาวหนา ๆ สักสองเมตร

170

33.2 Patterns.

yàaŋ yày.	The large kind.
yàaŋ klaaŋ.	The medium-sized kind.
yàaŋ lék.	The small kind.
sabùu yàaŋ nǎy.	What kind of soap?
sabùu yàaŋ níi.	This kind of soap.
sabùu yàaŋ yày.	The large kind of soap.
yaa yàaŋ diaw.	One kind of medicine.
yaa sɔ̌ɔŋ yàaŋ.	Two kinds of medicine.
yaa lǎay yàaŋ.	Several kinds of medicine.
ráan khǎay phâa.	A cloth store.
ráan khǎay naŋsɰ̌ɰ.	A bookstore.
ráan khǎay kradàat.	A paper store.
ráan khǎay rɔŋtháaw.	A shoe shop.
ráan tàt rɔŋtháaw.	A shoemaker's shop.
ráan tàt sɰ̂a.	A tailor shop.
ráan tàt phǒm.	A barbershop.
phâa khǎaw nǎnǎa.	Thick, white cloth
phâa dam baŋbaaŋ.	Thin, black cloth.
kradàat khǎaw baŋbaaŋ.	Thin, white paper.
tham dûay ŋən.	It's made of silver.
tham dûay lèk.	It's made of iron.
tham dûay kɛ̂ɛw.	It's made of glass.
tham dûay máay.	It's made of wood.
tham dûay hǐn.	It's made of stone.

33.3 Dialog.

A.	wan níi chán ca pay sɰ́ɰ khɔ̌ɔŋ.	I'm going shopping today.
	khun tôŋkaan ʔaray bâaŋ máy há.	Do you want anything?
	ca chûay sɰ́ɰ hây.	I'll buy it for you.
B.	khɔ̀ɔpkhun hâ.	Thanks.
	chán yàak dây yaa sǐi fan ka sabùu.	I want some toothpaste and soap.
	yaa sǐi fan yàaŋ klaaŋ lɔ̀ɔt nɰŋ.	A medium-sized tube of toothpaste,
	lɛ́ɛw kɔ̂ sabùu yàaŋ yày sɔ̌ɔŋ kɔ̂n.	and two large bars of soap.
A.	ʔaw ʔaray ʔìik máy há.	Do you want anything else?
B.	thâa phàan ráan khǎay phâa,	If you pass a cloth shop,
	chûay sɰ́ɰ phâa hây dûay ná há.	could you buy some cloth for me?
A.	phâa ʔaray há.	What kind of cloth?
B.	phâa khǎaw nǎnǎa sák sɔ̌ɔŋ méet.	Two meters of thick, white cloth.

๓๓.๔ แบบฝึกหัดการฟังและการออกเสียงสูงต่ำ

ก.

รบกวน หน่อไม้ เข็มขัด ยี่ห้อ ภูเขา

ข.

ศรีทำไมใส่เสื้อต้อย
    นั่นเสื้อศรี, ไม่ใช่เสื้อต้อย

แอ๊ดทำไมใช้แปรงแดง
    นั่นแปรงแอ๊ด, ไม่ใช่แปรงแดง

ต้อยทำไมสูบบุหรี่หน่อย
    นั่นบุหรี่ต้อย, ไม่ใช่บุหรี่หน่อย

แดงทำไมใช้หวีศรี
    นั่นหวีแดง, ไม่ใช่หวีศรี

หน่อยทำไมขับรถแอ๊ด
    นั่นรถหน่อย, ไม่ใช่รถแอ๊ด

๓๓.๕ แบบฝึกหัดการสลับเสียงสูงต่ำ

ก.

มีดนี่ทำด้วยอะไร
    มีดนั่นทำด้วยเงิน

เขียงนี่ทำด้วยอะไร
    เขียงนั่นทำด้วยไม้

ขวดนี่ทำด้วยอะไร
    ขวดนั่นทำด้วยแก้ว

ครกนี่ทำด้วยอะไร
    ครกนั่นทำด้วยหิน

คีมนี่ทำด้วยอะไร
    คีมนั่นทำด้วยเหล็ก

33.4 Tone identification and production.

a. Identify the tones and record the number of repetitions required.

To bother.   ropkuan   ....

Bamboo shoots.   nɔɔmaay   ....

A belt.   khemkhat   ....

A brand or make.   yiihɔɔ   ....

Mountains.   phuukhaw   ....

b. Response drill.

sǐi thammay sày sûa tôy.   Why is Sri wearing Toy's blouse?
  nân sûa sǐi, mây chây sûa tôy.   That's Sri's blouse, not Toy's.

tôy thammay sùup burìi nɔ̀y.   Why is Toy smoking Noy's cigarets?
  nân burìi tôy, mây chây burìi nɔ̀y.   They're Toy's cigarets, not Noy's.

nɔ̀y thammay khàp rót ʔέɛt.   Why is Noy driving At's car?
  nân rót nɔ̀y, mây chây rót ʔέɛt.   That's Noy's car, not At's.

ʔέɛt thammay cháy prɛɛŋ dɛɛŋ.   Why is At using Daeng's brush?
  nân prɛɛŋ ʔέɛt, mây chây prɛɛŋ dɛɛŋ.   That's At's brush, not Daeng's.

dɛɛŋ thammay cháy wǐi sǐi.   Why is Daeng using Sri's comb?
  nân wǐi dɛɛŋ, mây chây wǐi sǐi.   That's Daeng's comb, not Sri's.

33.5 Tone manipulation.

a. Response drill.

mîit níi tham dûay ʔaray.   What is this knife made of?
  mîit nân tham dûay ŋən.   That knife is made of silver.

khùat níi tham dûay ʔaray.   What is this bottle made of?
  khùat nân tham dûay kɛ̂ɛw.   That bottle is made of glass.

khiim níi tham dûay ʔaray.   What are these pliers made of?
  khiim nân tham dûay lèk.   Those pliers are made of iron.

khǐaŋ níi tham dûay ʔaray.   What is this chopping board made of?
  khǐaŋ nân tham dûay máay.   That chopping board is made of wood.

khrók níi tham dûay ʔaray.   What is this mortar made of?
  khrók nân tham dûay hǐn.   That mortar is made of stone.

173

๓๓.๖ แบบฝึกหัดการออกเสียงสระและพยัญชนะ

ก.

โดย   โหย

ดอย   หอย

ข.

ชมช่วยจอนใช่ไหม

     ไม่ใช่, จอนช่วยชม

แจ๋วจับชดใช่ไหม

     ไม่ใช่, ชดจับแจ๋ว

ชดจับจอนใช่ไหม

     ไม่ใช่, จอนจับชด

แจ๋วช่วยชมใช่ไหม

     ไม่ใช่, ชมช่วยแจ๋ว

แขกคอยโกใช่ไหม

     ไม่ใช่, โกคอยแขก

เกียรติเกาเข็มใช่ไหม

     ไม่ใช่, เข็มเกาเกียรติ

เข็มเกาโกใช่ไหม

     ไม่ใช่, โกเกาเข็ม

เกียรติคอยแขกใช่ไหม

     ไม่ใช่, แขกคอยเกียรติ

๓๓.๗ แบบฝึกหัดไวยากรณ์

ก.

ฉันจะไปร้านขายผ้า

     งั้นช่วยซื้อผ้าให้ด้วย

ฉันจะไปร้านขายยา

     งั้นช่วยซื้อยาให้ด้วย

ฉันจะไปร้านขายกระดาษ

     งั้นช่วยซื้อกระดาษให้ด้วย

ฉันจะไปร้านขายหนังสือ

     งั้นช่วยซื้อหนังสือให้ด้วย

ฉันจะไปร้านขายรองเท้า

     งั้นช่วยซื้อรองเท้าให้ด้วย

ฉันจะไปร้านขายวิทยุ

     งั้นช่วยซื้อวิทยุให้ด้วย

33.6 Vowel and consonant drills.

a. ooy-ɔɔy contrast drills.

dooy   hǒoy

dɔɔy   hɔ̌ɔy

b. Response drill. (c, ch, and k, kh).

chom chûay cɔɔn chây máy.   Chom helped John, didn't he?
  mây chây. cɔɔn chûay chom.   No. John helped Chom.

cɛ̌w càp chót chây máy.   Jaeo grabbed Chote, didn't she?
  mây chây. chót càp cɛ̌w.   No. Chote grabbed Jaeo.

chót càp cɔɔn chây máy.   Chote grabbed John, didn't he?
  mây chây. cɔɔn càp chót.   No. John grabbed Chote.

cɛ̌w chûay chom chây máy.   Jaeo helped Chom, didn't she?
  mây chây. chom chûay cɛ̌w.   No. Chom helped Jaeo.

khὲɛk khɔɔy koo chây máy.   Kaek waited for Ko, didn't she?
  mây chây. koo khɔɔy khὲɛk.   No. Ko waited for Kaek.

kìat kaw khɛ̌m chây máy.   Kiat scratched Kem, didn't he?
  mây chây. khɛ̌m kaw kìat.   No. Kem scratched Kiat.

khɛ̌m kaw koo chây máy.   Kem scratched Ko, didn't she?
  mây chây. koo kaw khɛ̌m.   No. Ko scratched Kem.

kìat khɔɔy khὲɛk chây máy.   Kiat waited for Kaek, didn't he?
  mây chây. khὲɛk khɔɔy kìat.   No. Kaek waited for Kiat.

33.7 Grammar drills.

a. Response drill.

chán ca pay ráan khǎay phâa.   I'm going to a cloth shop.
  ŋán chûay sɯ́ɯ phâa hây dûay.   Then please buy me some cloth.

chán ca pay ráan khǎay yaa.   I'm going to a drug store.
  ŋán chûay sɯ́ɯ yaa hây dûay.   Then please buy me some medicine.

chán ca pay ráan khǎay kradàat.   I'm going to a stationery shop.
  ŋán chûay sɯ́ɯ kradàat hây dûay.   Then please buy me some paper.

chán ca pay ráan khǎay naŋsɯ̌ɯ.   I'm going to a bookstore.
  ŋán chûay sɯ́ɯ naŋsɯ̌ɯ hây dûay.   Then please buy me some books.

chán ca pay ráan khǎay rɔŋtháaw.   I'm going to a shoe shop.
  ŋán chûay sɯ́ɯ rɔŋtháaw hây dûay.   Then please buy me some shoes.

chán ca pay ráan khǎay wítthayúʔ.   I'm going to a radio shop.
  ŋán chûay sɯ́ɯ wítthayúʔ hây dûay.   Then please buy me a radio.

ข.

ถ้าผ่านร้านขายยา,
ช่วยซื้อยาให้ด้วย   (รองเท้า)

ถ้าผ่านร้านขายรองเท้า,
ช่วยซื้อรองเท้าให้ด้วย (ผ้า)

ถ้าผ่านร้านขายผ้า
ช่วยซื้อผ้าให้ด้วย   (กระดาษ)

ถ้าผ่านร้านขายกระดาษ
ช่วยซื้อกระดาษให้ด้วย   (หนังสือ)

ถ้าผ่านร้านขายหนังสือ
ช่วยซื้อหนังสือให้ด้วย   (วิทยุ)

ถ้าผ่านร้านขายวิทยุ
ช่วยซื้อวิทยุให้ด้วย

ค.

สบู่อย่างใหญ่สองก้อน   (กลาง)

สบู่อย่างกลางสองก้อน   (ยาสีฟัน)

ยาสีฟันอย่างกลางสองหลอด   (สี่)

ยาสีฟันอย่างกลางสี่หลอด   (เล็ก)

ยาสีฟันอย่างเล็กสี่หลอด   (น้ำมันใส่ผม)

น้ำมันใส่ผมอย่างเล็กสี่ขวด   (ใหญ่)

น้ำมันใส่ผมอย่างใหญ่สี่ขวด

ง.

ผู้ชายสูง ๆ โน่น
     ผู้ชายสูง ๆ คนโน้น

คู่สีดำนี่
     คู่สีดำคู่นี้

หนังสือหนา ๆ นั่น
     หนังสือหนา ๆ เล่มนั้น

ตัวสีขาวนี่
     ตัวสีขาวตัวนี้

คนอ้วน ๆ โน่น
     คนอ้วน ๆ คนโน้น

บ้านสีเขียวนั่น
     บ้านสีเขียวหลังนั้น

b. Substitution drill.

thâa phàan ráan khăay yaa,
chûay sɨɨ yaa hây dûay. (rɔŋtháaw)

If you pass a drug store,
please buy me some medicine. (shoe)

thâa phàan ráan khăay rɔŋtháaw,
chûay sɨɨ rɔŋtháaw hây dûay. (phâa)

If you pass a shoe shop,
please buy me some shoes. (cloth)

thâa phàan ráan khăay phâa,
chûay sɨɨ phâa hây dûay. (kradàat)

If you pass a cloth shop,
please buy me some cloth. (paper)

thâa phàan ráan khăay kradàat,
chûay sɨɨ kradàat hây dûay. (naŋsɨɨ)

If you pass a stationery shop,
please buy me some paper. (book)

thâa phàan ráan khăay naŋsɨɨ,
chûay sɨɨ naŋsɨɨ hây dûay. (wítthayú?)

If you pass a bookstore,
please buy me some books. (radio)

thâa phàan ráan khăay wítthayú?,
chûay sɨɨ wítthayú? hây dûay.

If you pass a radio shop,
please buy me a radio.

c. Substitution drill.

sabùu yàaŋ yày sɔ̌ɔŋ kɔ̂ɔn.
(klaaŋ)

Two large bars of soap.
(medium-sized)

sabùu yàaŋ klaaŋ sɔ̌ɔŋ kɔ̂ɔn.
(yaa sǐi fan)

Two medium-sized bars of soap.
(toothpaste)

yaa sǐi fan yàaŋ klaaŋ sɔ̌ɔŋ lɔ̀ɔt.
(sìi)

Two medium-sized tubes of toothpaste.
(four)

yaa sǐi fan yàaŋ klaaŋ sìi lɔ̀ɔt.
(lék)

Four medium-sized tubes of toothpaste.
(small)

yaa sǐi fan yàaŋ lék sìi lɔ̀ɔt.
(námman sày phǒm)

Four small tubes of toothpaste.
(hair oil)

námman sày phǒm yàaŋ lék sìi khùat.
(yày)

Four small bottles of hair oil.
(large)

námman sày phǒm yàaŋ yày sìi khùat.

Four large bottles of hair oil.

d. Transformation drill.

phûu chaay sǔŋsǔuŋ nôon.
   phûu chaay sǔŋsǔuŋ khon nóon.
khûu sǐi dam nîi.
   khûu sǐi dam khûu níi.
naŋsɨɨ nǎnǎa nân.
   naŋsɨɨ nǎnǎa lêm nán.
tua sǐi khǎaw nîi.
   tua sǐi khǎaw tua níi.
khon ?ûan?ûan nôon.
   khon ?ûan?ûan khon nóon.
bâan sǐi khǐaw nân.
   bâan sǐi khǐaw lǎŋ nán.

The tall man over there.
   That tall man.
The black pair here.
   This black pair.
The thick book there.
   That thick book.
The white one here.
   This white one.
The fat person over there.
   That fat person.
The green house there.
   That green house.

177

๓๓.๙ **เดือน**

พฤศจิกายน

ธันวาคม

มกราคม

กุมภาพันธ์

๓๓.๑๐ **การเขียน**

อ่านได้   ใส่ถ้วย   ว่างแล้ว

33.8 Months.

The four coldest months of the year are listed below. The student should practice saying them in class until he is sure of the pronunciation (especially the rhythm). Then he should practice reading them for increased speed at home.

phrútsacìkaayon	November.
thanwaakhom	December.
mókkaraakhom	January.
kumphaaphan	February.

33.9 Conversation.

Review section 32.9.

The teacher should ask each student where his house (or some other place) is. The student should ask whether the teacher knows some nearby place. When he finds a place known to the teacher, he should draw a map showing how to get from the latter place to the former.

33.10 Writing.

ʔàan dây	sày thûay	wâaŋ lέɛw
He can read.	Put it in a cup.	I'm free now.

The fact that tonal markers stand for different tones depending on the initial consonant presents one of the biggest problems in reading and writing Thai. The student should practice until he can make an instantaneous association between each combination of initial consonant plus tone marker and the tone that combination represents.

The student should be familiar with all of the following words.

179

ก่อน	อิ่ม	ยี่
กุ้ง	อ้วน	ย้าย
นั่ง	ใหม่	บ่าย
เนื้อ	ไหม้	บ้าน
ผ่าน	ล่าง	หนึ่ง
ผู้	แล้ว	หน้า
ซื้อ	ปู่	เมื่อ
ใช้	ปิ้ง	มุ้ง
ด่า	พรุ่ง	ไข่
ด้วย	พื้น	ขึ้น
เที่ยว	สั่ง	แต่
ทิ้ง	เสื้อ	ต้ม

ก่อน	kɔ̀ɔn	อิ่ม	ʔìm	ยี่	yîi
กุ้ง	kûŋ	อ้วน	ʔûan	ย้าย	yáay
นั่ง	nâŋ	ใหม่	mày	บ่าย	bàay
เนื้อ	nɨ́a	ไหม้	mây	บ้าน	bâan
ผ่าน	phàan	ล่าง	lâaŋ	หนึ่ง	nɨ̀ŋ
ผู้	phûu	แล้ว	lέεw	หน้า	nâa
ชื่อ	chɨ̂ɨ	ปู่	pùu	เมื่อ	mɨ̂a
ใช้	cháy	บิ้ง	pîŋ	มุ้ง	múŋ
ด่า	dàa	พรุ่ง	phrûŋ	ไข่	khày
ด้วย	dûay	พื้น	phɨ́ɨn	ขึ้น	khɨ̂n
เที่ยว	thîaw	สั่ง	sàŋ	แต่	tὲε
ทิ้ง	thíŋ	เสื้อ	sɨ̂a	ต้ม	tôm

บทที่ ๓๔

๓๔.๑ คำศัพท์

รับ

ถุง

ถุงเท้า

ไหนดูซิ

สุด

ที่สุด

บางที่สุด

ละ

คู่ละเท่าไหร่

น้ำเงิน

สีน้ำเงิน

นาย

ห้าง

นายห้าง

เมือง

เมืองไทย

ชัด

ยิ้ม

ทั้งหมด

เพื่อน

ครู

ซิ

ขา

แขน

มวน

ซอง

182

LESSON 34

34.1 Vocabulary and expansions.

ráp	To receive. When someone wants and gets something, four steps are passed through: wanting, taking, receiving, and having. In English we ask about a person's intentions by using either the first (What do you want?) or the last (What will you have?). Thai uses either the second (ʔaw ʔaray) or the third (ráp ʔaray). The latter is more polite.
thǔŋ	A sack, bag.
thǔŋ tháaw	Stockings.
nǎy duu sí	Let me have a look. Let me see it.
sùt	The end, extreme, utmost.
thîisùt	The most, extremely.
baaŋ thîisùt	The thinnest.
lá	Per.
khûu la thâwràay	How much per pair?
námŋən	
sǐi námŋən	Blue (medium and dark, not sky blue).
naay	Mr., master, boss.
hâaŋ	A business firm, commercial establishment, store.
naay hâaŋ	The owner of a store or firm. The term is commonly used as the second person pronoun (you) by Thais when speaking to foreign men.
mɯaŋ	Town, city, country.
mɯaŋ thay	Thailand.
chát	To be plain, clear, distinct.
yím	To smile.
tháŋmòt	Altogether.
phɯ̂an	Friend.
khruu	Teacher.
sî	A particle used to request or urge an action (compare sí, 18.1). 'Please ...' 'Come on and ...'
khǎa	Leg.
khɛ̌ɛn	Arm, sleeve.
muan	Classifier for single cigarets.
sɔɔŋ	An envelope. A pack of cigarets.

๓๔.๒ โครงสร้างของประโยค

รองเท้า

ถุงเท้า

ถุงมือ

ไหนดูซิ

ไหนดูมือซิ

ไหนดูคู่นั้นซิ

คู่นี้หรือ

สีดำนี่หรือ

คู่สีดำนี่หรือ

ถุงเท้านี่หรือ

ถุงเท้าสีดำนี่หรือ

ถุงเท้าคู่สีดำนี่หรือ

ถุงเท้าสีดำคู่นี้หรือ

อย่างบางกว่านี้

อย่างหนากว่านี้

อย่างใหญ่กว่านี้

บางที่สุด

หนาที่สุด

เล็กที่สุด

คู่ละเท่าไหร่

ตัวละร้อยบาท

ขวดละสิบสามบาท

๓๔.๓ บทสนทนา

ก. รับอะไรคะ

  ข. ถุงเท้าอยู่ที่ไหน

ก. อยู่นี่ฮะ

  ข. ไหนดูคู่นั้นซิ

ก. คู่สีดำนี่หรือฮะ

  ข. ใช่

ก. นี่ฮะ

  ข. หนาไปหน่อย
     อย่างบางกว่านี้มีไหม

ก. มีฮะ, นี่ฮะ อย่างบางที่สุด

  ข. คู่ละเท่าไหร่

ก. สิบห้าบาทฮะ

  ข. เอาสีดำสองคู่ สีน้ำเงินคู่หนึ่ง

ก. นายห้างอยู่เมืองไทยนานแล้วหรือยังฮะ

  ข. สองปีแล้ว

ก. พูดไทยชัดดี

  ข. (ยิ้ม) ทั้งหมดเท่าไหร่

ก. สี่สิบห้าบาทฮะ

184

34.2 Patterns.

rɔŋtháaw.	Shoes.
thŭŋtháaw.	Stockings.
thŭŋmʉʉ.	Gloves.
nǎy duu sí.	Let me see it.
nǎy duu mʉʉ sí.	Let me see your hands.
nǎy duu khûu nán sí.	Let me see that pair.
khûu níi lɔ̌ə.	This pair?
sǐi dam níi lɔ̌ə.	The black ones here?
khûu sǐi dam níi lɔ̌ə.	The black pair here?
thŭŋtháaw níi lɔ̌ə.	The stockings here?
thŭŋtháaw sǐi dam níi lɔ̌ə.	The black stockings here?
thŭŋtháaw khûu sǐi dam níi lɔ̌ə.	The black pair of stockings here?
thŭŋtháaw sǐi dam khûu níi lɔ̌ə.	This pair of black stockings?
yàaŋ baaŋ kwàa níi.	Thinner than this.
yàaŋ nǎa kwàa níi.	Thicker than this.
yàaŋ yày kwàa níi.	Bigger than this.
baaŋ thîisùt.	The thinnest.
nǎa thîisùt.	The thickest.
lék thîisùt.	The smallest.
khûu la thâwrày.	How much a pair?
tua la rɔ́ɔy bàat.	100 baht each.
khùat la sìp sǎam bàat.	Thirteen baht a bottle.

34.3 Dialog.

A. ráp ʔaray khá.	What do you want?
B. thŭŋtháaw yùu thîi nǎy.	Where are the stockings?
A. yùu nîi hâ.	Here.
B. nǎy duu khûu nán sí.	Let me see that pair.
A. khûu sǐi dam níi lɔ̌ə há.	This black pair here?
B. chây.	Yes.
A. nîi hâ.	Here you are.
B. nǎa pay nɔ̀y.	They are a bit too thick.
yàaŋ baaŋ kwàa níi mii máy.	Do you have any thinner ones?
A. mii hâ.	Yes.
nîi hâ. yàaŋ baaŋ thîisùt.	Here. These are the very thinnest.
B. khûu la thâwrày.	How much are they a pair?
A. sìp hâa bàat hâ.	Fifteen baht.
B. ʔaw sǐi dam sɔ̌ɔŋ khûu.	I'll have two pairs of black ones,
sǐi námŋən khûu nʉŋ.	and one pair of blue ones.
A. naay hâaŋ yùu mʉaŋ thay	Have you been in Thailand
naan lɛ́ɛw rʉ́ yaŋ há.	very long?
B. sɔ̌ɔŋ pii lɛ́ɛw.	Two years.
A. phûut thay chát dii.	You speak very clearly.
B. (yím) tháŋmòt thâwrày.	(Smiles.) How much altogether?
A. sǐi sìp hâa bàat hâ.	Forty-five baht.

185

๓๔.๔ แบบฝึกหัดการฟังและการออกเสียงสูงต่ำ

ก. รักษา   หลีกเลี่ยง   หลังคา   บังคับ   ต้นเหตุ

ข.

พูดกับเพื่อนไหม, พ่อ   ทักน้องไหม, น้า
พูดกับเพื่อนซี่, พ่อ   ทักน้องซี่, น้า

บอกปู่ไหม, หน่อย   ถามหมอไหม, ป้า
บอกปู่ซี่, หน่อย   ถามหมอซี่, ป้า

เตือนครูไหม, ลุง
เตือนครูซี่, ลุง

๓๔.๕ แบบฝึกหัดการสลับเสียงสูงต่ำ

ก.

มีดทำด้วยหินใช่ไหม   เขียงทำด้วยเหล็กใช่ไหม
   ไม่ใช่, มีดทำด้วยเงิน   ไม่ใช่, เขียงทำด้วยไม้

คีมทำด้วยแก้วใช่ไหม   ครกทำด้วยเงินใช่ไหม
   ไม่ใช่, คีมทำด้วยเหล็ก   ไม่ใช่, ครกทำด้วยหิน

ขวดทำด้วยไม้ใช่ไหม
   ไม่ใช่, ขวดทำด้วยแก้ว

186

34.4 Tone identification and production.

a. Identify the tones and record the number of repetitions required.

To take care of, treat.	raksaa	....
To avoid.	liik lian	....
Roof.	lankhaa	....
To force.	bankhap	....
The cause.	ton heet	....

b. Comparison drill.

Notice especially the different intonations on the final word of each pair.

phûut kàp phɨ̂an máy, phɔ̂ɔ.	Are you going to speak to my friend, father?
phûut kàp phɨ̂an sî, phɔ̂ɔ.	Please speak to my friend, father.
bɔ̀ɔk pùu máy, nɔ̀y.	Are you going to tell Grandpa, Noy?
bɔ̀ɔk pùu sî, nɔ̀y.	Please tell Grandpa, Noy.
tɨan khruu máy, luŋ.	Are you going to remind the teacher, Uncle?
tɨan khruu sî, luŋ.	Please remind the teacher, Uncle.
thák nɔ́ɔŋ máy, náa.	Are you going to greet Younger One, Nah?
thák nɔ́ɔŋ sî, náa.	Please greet Younger One, Nah.
thăam mɔ̌ɔ máy, păa.	Are you going to ask the doctor, Papa?
thăam mɔ̌ɔ sî, păa.	Please ask the doctor, Papa.

34.5 Tone manipulation.

a. Response drill.

mîit tham dûay hǐn chây máy.	The knife is made of stone, isn't it?
mây chây.	No.
mîit tham dûay ŋɔn.	The knife is made of silver.
khiim tham dûay kɛ̂ɛw chây máy.	The pliers are made of glass, aren't they?
mây chây.	No.
khiim tham dûay lèk.	The pliers are made of iron.
khùat tham dûay máay chây máy.	The bottle is made of wood, isn't it?
mây chây.	No.
khùat tham dûay kɛ̂ɛw.	The bottle is made of glass.
khǐaŋ tham dûay lèk chây máy.	The chopping board is made of iron, isn't it?
mây chây.	No.
khǐaŋ tham dûay máay.	The chopping board is made of wood.
khrók tham dûay ŋɔn chây máy.	The mortar is made of silver, isn't it?
mây chây.	No.
khrók tham dûay hǐn.	The mortar is made of stone.

๓๔.๖ แบบฝึกหัดการออกเสียงสระและพยัญชนะ

ก.

เป๋ว	เอว
แป๋ว	แอว
เป๋า	อาว

ข.

เนื้องเหนื้อย	(เงี๊ยบ)
เนื้องเงี๊ยบ	(หงวน)
หงวนเงี๊ยบ	(เหนื้อย)
หงวนเหนื้อย	(เนื้อง)

๓๔.๗ แบบฝึกหัดไวยากรณ์

ก.

ไหนดูคู่นั้นซิ
   คู่สีดำนี่หรือ

ไหนดูตัวนั้นซิ
   ตัวสีดำนี่หรือ

ไหนดูขวดนั้นซิ
   ขวดสีดำนี่หรือ

ไหนดูเล่มนั้นซิ
   เล่มสีดำนี่หรือ

ไหนดูแผ่นนั้นซิ
   แผ่นสีดำนี่หรือ

ข.

ผ้าหนาไปหน่อย อย่างบางกว่านี้มีไหม
(กระดาษบาง)

กระดาษบางไปหน่อย อย่างหนากว่านี้
มีไหม
(ถุงเท้าเล็ก)

ถุงเท้าเล็กไปหน่อย อย่างใหญ่กว่านี้มีไหม
(เสื้อใหญ่)

เสื้อใหญ่ไปหน่อย อย่างเล็กกว่านี้มีไหม
(ราคาแพง)

ราคาแพงไปหน่อย อย่างถูกกว่านี้มีไหม

188

34.6 Vowel and consonant drills.

a. ew-εw-aw and eew-εεw-aaw contrast drills.

pěw	ʔeew
pɛ́w	ʔεεw
păw	ʔaaw

b. Substitution drill.   (ŋ).

nɨaŋ nɨay. (ŋîap)	Nueang's tired. (quiet)
nɨaŋ ŋîap. (ŋŭan)	Nueang's quiet. (Nguan)
ŋŭan ŋîap. (nɨay)	Nguan's quiet. (tired)
ŋŭan nɨay. (nɨaŋ)	Nguan's tired. (Nueang)

34.7 Grammar drills.

a. Response drill.

nǎy duu khûu nán sí.	Let me see that pair.
khûu sǐi dam nîi lɔ̌ə.	This black pair here?
nǎy duu tua nán sí.	Let me see that one.
tua sǐi dam nîi lɔ̌ə.	This black one here?
nǎy duu khùat nán sí.	Let me see that bottle.
khùat sǐi dam nîi lɔ̌ə.	This black one here?
nǎy duu lêm nán sí.	Let me see that book.
lêm sǐi dam nîi lɔ̌ə.	This black one here?
nǎy duu phɛ̀n nán sí.	Let me see that sheet.
phɛ̀n sǐi dam nîi lɔ̌ə.	This black one here?

b. Substitution drill.

phâa nǎa pay nɔ̀y.	The cloth is a bit too thick.
yàaŋ baaŋ kwàa níi mii máy.	Do you have any that's thinner than this?
(kradàat baaŋ)	(the paper is thin)
kradàat baaŋ pay nɔ̀y.	The paper is a bit too thin.
yàaŋ nǎa kwàa níi mii máy.	Do you have any that's thicker than this?
(thǔŋtháaw lék)	(the stockings are small)
thǔŋtháaw lék pay nɔ̀y.	The stockings are a bit too small.
yàaŋ yày kwàa níi mii máy.	Do you have any that are bigger than these?
(sɨa yày)	(the shirt is big)
sɨa yày pay nɔ̀y.	The shirt is too big.
yàaŋ lék kwàa níi mii máy.	Do you have any that are smaller than this?
(rakhaa phɛɛŋ)	(the price is expensive)
rakhaa phɛɛŋ pay nɔ̀y.	The price is too expensive.
yàaŋ thùuk kwàa níi mii máy.	Do you have any that are cheaper than this?

189

ก.

หลอดนี้ (หก)
หกหลอดนี้ (อย่างใหญ่)
อย่างใหญ่หกหลอดนี้ (ยาสีฟัน)
ยาสีฟันอย่างใหญ่หกหลอดนี้

ตัวนี้ (ห้า)
ห้าตัวนี้ (แขนสั้น)
แขนสั้นห้าตัวนี้ (เสื้อ)
เสื้อแขนสั้นห้าตัวนี้

หลังโน้น (สอง)
สองหลังโน้น (สีเขียว)
สีเขียวสองหลังโน้น (บ้าน)
บ้านสีเขียวสองหลังโน้น

คู่โน้น (เก้า)
เก้าคู่โน้น (สีดำ)
สีดำเก้าคู่โน้น (ถุงเท้า)
ถุงเท้าสีดำเก้าคู่โน้น

ก้อนนั้น (แปด)
แปดก้อนนั้น (อย่างเล็ก)
อย่างเล็กแปดก้อนนั้น (สบู่)
สบู่อย่างเล็กแปดก้อนนั้น

เม็ดนี้ (สิบ)
สิบเม็ดนี้ (เม็ดเล็ก ๆ)
เม็ดเล็ก ๆ สิบเม็ดนี้ (ยา)
ยาเม็ดเล็ก ๆ สิบเม็ดนี้

ง.

เอาข้าวผัดไหม
  ข้าวผัดจานละเท่าไหร่

เอาน้ำมะนาวไหม
  น้ำมะนาวแก้วละเท่าไหร่

เอาขนมปังไหม
  ขนมปังแผ่นละเท่าไหร่

เอาไข่ดาวไหม
  ไข่ดาวลูกละเท่าไหร่

เอากาแฟไหม
  กาแฟถ้วยละเท่าไหร่

เอาเบียร์ไหม
  เบียร์ขวดละเท่าไหร่

เอาบุหรี่ไหม
  บุหรี่มวนละเท่าไหร่
  บุหรี่ซองละเท่าไหร่

c. Expansion drill.

lɔ̀ɔt níi   (hòk)
hòk lɔ̀ɔt níi   (yàaŋ yày)
yàaŋ yày hòk lɔ̀ɔt níi   (yaa sǐi fan)
yaa sǐi fan yàaŋ yày hòk lɔ̀ɔt níi.

This tube. (six)
These six tubes. (large)
These six large tubes. (toothpaste)
These six large tubes of toothpaste.

lǎŋ nóon   (sɔ̌ɔŋ)
sɔ̌ɔŋ lǎŋ nóon   (sǐi khǐaw)
sǐi khǐaw sɔ̌ɔŋ lǎŋ nóon   (bâan)
bâan sǐi khǐaw sɔ̌ɔŋ lǎŋ nóon.

That one (house) over there. (two)
Those two (houses). (green)
Those two green ones. (house)
Those two green houses over there.

kɔ̂ɔn nán   (pɛ̀ɛt)
pɛ̀ɛt kɔ̂ɔn nán   (yàaŋ lék)
yàaŋ lék pɛ̀ɛt kɔ̂ɔn nán   (sabùu)
sabùu yàaŋ lék pɛ̀ɛt kɔ̂ɔn nán.

That bar. (eight)
Those eight bars. (small)
Those eight small bars. (soap)
Those eight small bars of soap.

tua níi   (hâa)
hâa tua níi   (khɛ̌ɛn sân)
khɛ̌ɛn sân hâa tua níi   (sɯ̂a)
sɯ̂a khɛ̌ɛn sân hâa tua níi.

This one (shirt). (five)
These five (shirts). (short-sleeved)
These five short-sleeved ones. (shirt)
These five short-sleeved shirts.

khûu nóon   (kâaw)
kâaw khûu nóon   (sǐi dam)
sǐi dam kâaw khûu nóon   (thǔŋtháaw)
thǔŋtháaw sǐi dam kâaw khûu nóon.

That pair. (nine)
Those nine pairs. (black)
Those nine black pairs. (stockings)
Those nine black pairs of stockings.

mét níi   (sìp)
sìp mét níi   (mét léklék)
mét léklék sìp mét níi   (yaa)
yaa mét léklék sìp mét níi.

This one (pill). (ten)
These ten. (little)
These ten little ones. (medicine)
These ten little pills.

d. Response drill.

ʔaw khâaw phàt máy.
   khâaw phàt caan la thâwrày.

Do you want some fried rice?
   How much is it a plate?

ʔaw nám manaaw máy.
   nám manaaw kɛ̂ɛw la thâwrày.

Do you want some limeade?
   How much is it a glass?

ʔaw khanǒmpaŋ máy.
   khanǒmpaŋ phɛ̀n la thâwrày.

Do you want some bread?
   How much is it a slice?

ʔaw khày daaw máy.
   khày daaw lûuk la thâwrày.

Do you want some fried eggs?
   How much are they apiece?

ʔaw kaafɛɛ máy.
   kaafɛɛ thûay la thâwrày.

Do you want some coffee?
   How much is it a cup?

ʔaw bia máy.
   bia khùat la thâwrày.

Do you want some beer?
   How much is it a bottle?

ʔaw burìi máy.
   burìi muan la thâwrày.
   burìi sɔɔŋ la thâwrày.

Do you want some cigarets?
   How much are they apiece?
   How much are they a pack?

191

จ.

คู่นี้ (สีดำ)
คู่สีดำนี่

แผ่นนี้ (บาง ๆ)
แผ่นบาง ๆ นี่

ตัวโน้น (ใหญ่ ๆ)
ตัวใหญ่ ๆ โน่น

ก้อนนั้น (สีเขียว)
ก้อนสีเขียวนั่น

เล่มนั้น (สีแดง)
เล่มสีแดงนั่น

เม็ดโน้น (เล็ก ๆ)
เม็ดเล็ก ๆ โน่น

๓๔.๘ เดือน

มีนาคม

เมษายน

พฤษภาคม

e. Expansion drill.

khûu níi (sǐi dam)	This pair. (black)
khûu sǐi dam nîi.	The black pair here.
tua nóon (yàyyày)	That shirt. (large)
tua yàyyày nôon.	The large shirt over there.
lêm nán (sǐi dɛɛŋ)	That book. (red)
lêm sǐi dɛɛŋ nân.	The red book there.
phɛ̀n níi (baŋbaaŋ)	This sheet. (thin)
phɛ̀n baŋbaaŋ nîi.	The thin sheet here.
kɔ̌ɔn nán (sǐi khǐaw)	That bar. (green)
kɔ̌ɔn sǐi khǐaw nân.	The green bar there.
mét nóon (léklék)	That pill. (little)
mét léklék nôon.	The little pill over there.

34.8 Months.

The three hottest months of the year are listed below. The student should practice them in class until he can say them rapidly without the slightest hesitation.

miinaakhom	March.
meesǎayon	April.
phrɨ́tsaphaakhom	May.

Practice translating the following English month names into Thai for increased speed.

January.	February.	March.	April.
November.	March.	May.	December.
May.	November.	December.	February.
February.	December.	April.	November.
March.	April.	November.	January.
April.	January.	February.	March.
December.	May.	January.	May.

34.9 Conversation.

The teacher should read the narrative of lesson 25 to the students and ask them the questions.

๓๔.๑๐ การเขียน

ชอบขับรถคันไหน

แดง	แสด	เรียก
ผัด	หา	พริก
มาก	ไฟ	ถึง
ทับ	รับ	เกลือ
หวี	ชอบ	บีบ
หลอด	เป็น	ฉาย
ขอ	มืด	ซุบ
จวน	หนัก	แยก
ลูก	ชัด	เนย
คิด	ฝน	อบ

ชอบขับรถคันไหน

chɔ̂ɔp khàp rót khan nǎy

Which car do you like to drive?

An even bigger problem than the one mentioned in 33.10 is that all five tones can be written with no tone marker at all. The initial (high, mid, or low), the vowel (long or short), and the final (live or dead) must all be considered in determining the tone of the syllable. Notice as you practice reading and writing the following that all five tones are represented in each group. All of the words should be recognized as words known to the student.

แดง	dɛɛŋ	แสด	sὲɛt	เรียก	rîak
ผัด	phàt	หา	hǎa	พริก	phrík
มาก	mâak	ไฟ	fay	ถึง	thǔŋ
ทับ	tháp	รับ	ráp	เกลือ	klɰa
หวี	wǐi	ชอบ	chɔ̂ɔp	บีบ	bìip
หลอด	lɔ̀ɔt	เป็น	pen	ฉาย	chǎay
ขอ	khɔ̌ɔ	มีด	mɰ̂ɰt	ซุบ	súp
จวน	cuan	หนัก	nàk	แยก	yɛ̂ɛk
ลูก	lûuk	ชัด	chát	เนย	nəəy
คิด	khít	ฝน	fǒn	อบ	ʔòp

บทที่ ๓๕

๓๕. ข

คุณจอนมาอยู่เมืองไทยยังไม่นาน   แต่เขาอ้วนขึ้นมากเพราะเขาชอบทาน
อาหารไทย เดี๋ยวนี้เสื้อผ้าเขาคับหมด เขาอยากไปตัดใหม่ที่ร้านตัดเสื้อกางเกง และ
ต้องการซื้อของอีกหลายอย่าง แต่เขายังพูดภาษาไทยไม่เก่ง และไม่รู้จักต่อราคาเลย
เขาเลยชวนคุณประเสริฐเพื่อนเขาไปด้วย ประเสริฐกำลังว่างและเขาอยากจะตัดกาง
เกงใหม่ด้วย เขาเลยออกไปกับจอน

คุณจอนมาอยู่เมืองไทยนานแล้วใช่ไหม
คุณจอนอ้วนขึ้นใช่ไหม
เสื้อผ้าเขาหลวมใช่ไหม
เขาอยากจะไปตัดใหม่ใช่ไหม
และเขาอยากจะซื้อของอีกหลายอย่างด้วยใช่ไหม
คุณจอนไม่ชอบอาหารไทยใช่ไหม
เขาพูดภาษาไทยเก่งแล้วใช่ไหม
เขาไม่รู้จักต่อราคาใช่ไหม
เขาชวนคุณประสิทธิ์ไปด้วยใช่ไหม
คุณประเสริฐอยากจะตัดกางเกงเหมือนกันใช่ไหม

คุณจอนมาอยู่เมืองไทยนานแล้วหรือยัง
เขาอ้วนขึ้นหรือผอมลง
เสื้อผ้าเขาคับหรือหลวม
คุณประเสริฐว่างหรือเปล่า
คุณประเสริฐไปกับคุณจอนหรือเปล่า
คุณจอนอยากจะตัดเสื้อผ้าอย่างเดียวหรืออยากจะซื้อของอีกหลายอย่างด้วย
เพื่อนคุณจอนชื่อประเสริฐหรือประสิทธิ์
คุณประเสริฐอยากตัดเสื้อหรือกางเกง
คุณประเสริฐชวนคุณจอนหรือคุณจอนชวนคุณประเสริฐ
คุณจอนรู้จักต่อราคาหรือเปล่า

196

LESSON 35

(Review)

35.a Review sections 3, 5, 7, and 9 of lessons 31 – 34.

35.b Narrative.

khun cɔɔn maa yùu mɯaŋ thay yaŋ mây naan, tɛ̀ɛ kháw ʔûan khɯ̂n mâak phrɔ́ʔ kháw chɔ̂ɔp thaan ʔaahǎan thay. dǐawníi (now) sɯ̂a phâa kháw kháp mòt. kháw yàak pay tàt mày thîi ráan tàt sɯ̂a kaŋkeeŋ, lɛ́ʔ tôŋkaan sɯ́ɯ khɔ̌ɔŋ ʔìik lǎay yàaŋ. tɛ̀ɛ kháw yaŋ phûut phasǎa thay mây kèŋ lɛ́ʔ mây rúucàk tɔ̀ɔ rakhaa (to bargain) ləəy, kháw ləəy (therefore) chuan (invite) khun prasɤ̀ɤt, phɯ̂an kháw, pay dûay. prasɤ̀ɤt kamlaŋ wâaŋ lɛ́ʔ kháw yàak ca tàt kaŋkeeŋ mày dûay, kháw ləəy ʔɔ̀ɔk pay kàp cɔɔn.

Answer the following questions with *chây* or *mây chây*.

khun cɔɔn maa yùu mɯaŋ thay naan lɛ́ɛw chây máy.
khun cɔɔn ʔûan khɯ̂n chây máy.
sɯ̂a phâa kháw lǔam chây máy.
kháw yàak ca pay tàt mày chây máy.
lɛ́ʔ kháw yàak ca sɯ́ɯ khɔ̌ɔŋ ʔìik lǎay yàaŋ dûay chây máy.
khun cɔɔn mây chɔ̂ɔp ʔaahǎan thay chây máy.
kháw phûut phasǎa thay kèŋ lɛ́ɛw chây máy.
kháw mây rúucàk tɔ̀ɔ rakhaa chây máy.
kháw chuan khun prasìt pay dûay chây máy.
khun prasɤ̀ɤt yàak ca tàt kaŋkeeŋ mǔankan chây máy.

Answer the following questions with the correct alternative.

khun cɔɔn maa yùu mɯaŋ thay naan lɛ́ɛw rɯ́ yaŋ.
kháw ʔûan khɯ̂n rɯ́ phɔ̌ɔm loŋ.
sɯ̂a phâa kháw kháp rɯ́ lǔam.
khun prasɤ̀ɤt wâaŋ rɯ́ plàaw.
khun prasɤ̀ɤt pay kàp khun cɔɔn rɯ́ plàaw.
khun cɔɔn yàak ca tàt sɯ̂a phâa yàaŋ diaw rɯ́ yàak ca sɯ́ɯ khɔ̌ɔŋ ʔìik lǎay yàaŋ dûay.
phɯ̂an khun cɔɔn chɯ̂ɯ prasɤ̀ɤt rɯ́ prasìt.
khun prasɤ̀ɤt yàak tàt sɯ̂a rɯ́ kaŋkeeŋ.
khun prasɤ̀ɤt chuan khun cɔɔn rɯ́ khun cɔɔn chuan khun prasɤ̀ɤt.
khun cɔɔn rúucàk tɔ̀ɔ rakhaa rɯ́ plàaw.

คุณจอนอยู่เมืองไทยนานแล้วใช่ไหม
    ไม่ใช่, ยังไม่นาน

เขาผอมลงใช่ไหม
    ไม่ใช่, เขาอ้วนขึ้น

เสื้อผ้าเขาหลวมใช่ไหม
    ไม่ใช่, เสื้อผ้าคับ

ทำไมคุณประเสริฐไปกับคุณจอน
    เพราะคุณจอนชวน

ทำไมคุณจอนชวนคุณประเสริฐ
    เพราะเขาต่อราคาไม่เป็น

ทำไมเขาต่อราคาไม่เป็น
    เพราะเขาพูดไทยไม่เก่ง

ทำไมเขาพูดไทยไม่เก่ง
    เพราะเขามาอยู่เมืองไทยยังไม่นาน

คุณจอนอยากจะไปไหน
    อยากจะไปร้านตัดเสื้อกางเกง

ทำไมเขาอยากจะไปร้านตัดเสื้อกางเกง
    เพราะเขาอยากจะตัดเสื้อผ้าใหม่

เขาอยากจะไปตัดเสื้อผ้าอย่างเดียวใช่ไหม
    ไม่ใช่
    เขาอยากจะซื้อของอีกหลายอย่างด้วย

เขาไปคนเดียวใช่ไหม
    ไม่ใช่, เขาไปกับคุณประเสริฐ

ทำไมเขาอยากจะตัดเสื้อผ้าใหม่
    เพราะเสื้อผ้าเขาคับหมด

ทำไมเสื้อผ้าเขาคับหมด
    เพราะเขาอ้วนขึ้นมาก

ทำไมเขาอ้วนขึ้นมาก
    เพราะเขาทานอาหารไทยมาก

ทำไมเขาทานอาหารไทยมาก
    เพราะเขาชอบอาหารไทย

ทำไมเขาชอบอาหารไทย
    เพราะอาหารไทยอร่อย

After practicing reading and listening to the following questions and answers, try answering the questions without books.

khun cɔɔn yùu mʉaŋ thay naan lɛɛ́w chây máy.
   mây chây. yaŋ mây naan.

kháw phɔ̌ɔm loŋ chây máy.
   mây chây. kháw ʔûan khʉ̂n.

sʉ̂a phâa kháw lǔam chây máy.
   mây chây. sʉ̂a phâa kháp.

kháw yàak ca pay tàt sʉ̂a phâa yàaŋ diaw chây máy.
   mây chây. kháw yàak ca sʉ́ʉ khɔ̌ɔŋ ʔìik lǎay yàaŋ dûay.

kháw pay khon diaw chây máy.
   mây chây. kháw pay kàp khun prasə̀ət.

thammay khun prasə̀ət pay kàp khun cɔɔn.
   phrɔ́ʔ khun cɔɔn chuan.

thammay khun cɔɔn chuan khun prasə̀ət.
   phrɔ́ʔ kháw tɔ̀ɔ rakhaa mây pen.

thammay kháw tɔ̀ɔ rakhaa mây pen.
   phrɔ́ʔ kháw phûut thay mây kèŋ.

thammay kháw phûut thay mây kèŋ.
   phrɔ́ʔ kháw maa yùu mʉaŋ thay yaŋ mây naan.

khun cɔɔn yàak ca pay nǎy.
   yàak ca pay ráan tàt sʉ̂a kaŋkeeŋ.

thammay kháw yàak ca pay ráan tàt sʉ̂a kaŋkeeŋ.
   phrɔ́ʔ kháw yàak ca tàt sʉ̂a phâa mày.

thammay kháw yàak ca tàt sʉ̂a phâa mày.
   phrɔ́ʔ sʉ̂a phâa kháw kháp mòt.

thammay sʉ̂a phâa kháw kháp mòt.
   phrɔ́ʔ kháw ʔûan khʉ̂n mâak.

thammay kháw ʔûan khʉ̂n mâak.
   phrɔ́ʔ kháw thaan ʔaahǎan thay mâak.

thammay kháw thaan ʔaahǎan thay mâak.
   phrɔ́ʔ kháw chɔ̂ɔp ʔaahǎan thay.

thammay kháw chɔ̂ɔp ʔaahǎan thay.
   phrɔ́ʔ ʔaahǎan thay ʔarɔ̀y.

บทที่ ๓๖

๓๖.๑ คำศัพท์

นาย

แหม่ม

สั่ง

อย่า

จาก
หลังจาก

ของ

ยุง

จิ้งจก

ต่างหาก

ที่

ทุก

๓๖.๒ โครงสร้างของประโยค

มีใครอยู่
มีใครอยู่ไหม
มีใครมาหาฉัน
มีใครมาหาฉันไหม

มีผู้ชายโทรมา
มีคนมาหา
มีคนคอยข้างนอก

ก่อนนายมาถึงนี่
ก่อนนายไปถึงโน่น
หลังจากนายไปถึงโน่น
หลังจากนายมาถึงนี่

เขาสั่งอะไรบ้าง
เขาสั่งอะไรบ้างไหม

สั่งว่าอย่าไปไหน
บอกว่าอย่าไปไหน
พูดว่าอย่าไปไหน
ถามว่าจะไปไหน

ทำยังไงดี
นั่งที่ไหนดี
ไปเมื่อไหร่ดี
กินอะไรดี

บ้านของเขา
เพื่อนของคุณ
เบอร์โทรศัพท์ของฉัน

LESSON 36

36.1 Vocabulary and expansions.

naay	Mr., master, boss. The usual term used by servants when speaking to or about the male head of the house.
mὲm	Ma'am. The usual term used by servants when speaking to or about a Farang lady.
sàŋ	To leave word, to leave a message. In this use there is no suggestion of ordering.
yàa	Don't. The negative imperative.
càak	Away from, to separate from.
lǎŋ càak	After.
khɔ̌ɔŋ, khɔ́ŋ	Of (possessive).
yuŋ	Mosquito.
cîŋcòk	House lizard.
taŋhàak	On the contrary, contrary to what you think.
thîi	The relative pronoun. Who, that, which.
thúk	Every.

36.2 Patterns.

mii khray yùu.	Who is here?
mii khray yùu máy.	Is anybody here?
mii khray maa hǎa chán.	Who came to see me?
mii khray maa hǎa chán máy.	Did anybody come to see me?
mii phûu chaay thoo maa.	A man phoned.
mii khon maa hǎa.	Someone came to see you.
mii khon khɔɔy khâŋ nɔ̂ɔk.	There's somebody waiting outside.
kɔ̀ɔn naay maa thǔŋ nîi.	Before you got here, Master.
kɔ̀ɔn naay pay thǔŋ nôon.	Before you got there, Master.
lǎŋcàak naay pay thǔŋ nôon.	After you got there. Master.
lǎŋcàak naay maa thǔŋ nîi.	After you got here, Master.
kháw sàŋ ʔaray bâaŋ.	What did he say (for me to do)?
kháw sàŋ ʔaray bâaŋ máy.	Did he leave a message?
sàŋ wâa yàa pay nǎy.	He said for you not to go anywhere.
bɔ̀ɔk wâa yàa pay nǎy.	He told me not to go anywhere.
phûut wâa yàa pay nǎy.	He said not to go anywhere.
thǎam wâa ca pay nǎy.	He asked where you were going.
tham yaŋŋay dii.	What should I do?
nâŋ thîi nǎy dii.	Where shall we sit?
pay mûarày dii.	When is the best time to go?
kin ʔaray dii.	What would be good to eat?
bâan khɔ́ŋ kháw.	His house.
phûan khɔ́ŋ khun.	Your friend.
bəə thoorasàp khɔ́ŋ chán.	My telephone number.

201

๓๖.๓ **บทสนทนา**

ก. มีใครโทรมาหาฉันบ้างไหม

    ข. มีค่ะ, มีผู้ชายโทรมา

ก. ชื่ออะไร

    ข. ชื่อคุณประสงค์ฮะ

ก. โทรมานานแล้วหรือยัง

    ข. ไม่นานฮะ, ก่อนนายมาถึงนี่
       ห้านาทีเท่านั้น

ก. เขาสั่งอะไรบ้าง

    ข. สั่งว่าเย็นนี้อย่าไปไหน
       เขาจะมาหานายที่บ้าน

ก. เย็นนี้ฉันไม่ว่าง   ต้องไปหาหมอ
  ทำยังไงดี

    ข. โทรไปบอกเขาที่บ้านซิฮะ

ก. ที่บ้านเขาไม่มีโทรศัพท์

    ข. ที่ที่ทำงานล่ะฮะ มีไหม

ก. มี แต่ไม่ทราบว่าเบอร์อะไร

    ข. เขาทำงานที่ไหนฮะ
       จะหาเบอร์โทรศัพท์ให้

ก. ทำที่สถานทูตอเมริกัน

    ข. นี่ เบอร์ ๕๕๔๑๐ ฮะ

๓๖.๔ **แบบฝึกหัดการฟังและการออกเสียงสูงต่ำ**

ก.

   ยกเว้น   ตอบแทน   หมอนวด   ตำแหน่ง   ขี้เหนียว

36.3 Dialog.

A. mii khray thoo maa hǎa chán bâaŋ máy.   Did anyone phone me?

  B. mii khâ.   Yes.
     mii phûuchaay thoo maa.   A man phoned.

A. chɨ̂ɨ ʔaray.   What was his name?

  B. chɨ̂ɨ khun prasǒŋ hâ.   Khun Prasong.

A. thoo maa naan lɛ́ɛw rɨ́ yaŋ.   Did he phone long ago?

  B. mây naan hâ.   Not long.
     kɔ̀ɔn naay maa thɨ̌ŋ nîi   Only five minutes before you
     hâa naathii thâwnán.   got here.

A. kháw sàŋ ʔaray bâaŋ.   What did he say?

  B. sàŋ wâa yen níi yàa pay nǎy.   He said for you not to go anywhere this
         evening.
     kháw ca maa hǎa naay thîi bâan.   He's going to come see you at your house.

A. yen níi chán mây wâaŋ.   I won't be free this evening.
   tôŋ pay hǎa mɔ̌ɔ.   I have to go see a doctor.
   tham yaŋŋay dii.   What should I do?

  B. thoo pay bɔ̀ɔk kháw thîi bâan si há.   Phone him at his house.

A. thîi bâan kháw mây mii thoorasàp.   There isn't a phone at his house.

  B. thîi thîi tham ŋaan la há.   How about at his office?
     mii máy.   Is there one there?

A. mii. tɛ̀ɛ mây sâap wâa bəə ʔaray.   Yes, but I don't know the number.

  B. kháw tham ŋaan thîi nǎy há.   Where does he work?
     ca hǎa bəə thoorasàp hây.   I'll look up his number for you.

A. tham thîi sathǎanthûut ʔameerikan.   He works at the American Embassy.

  B. nîi. bəə 59800 hâ.   Here it is. 59800.

36.4 Tone identification and production.

a. Identify the tones and record the number of repetitions required.

To except.	yokwen	....
To pay back.	tɔɔp thɛɛn	....
Masseur, masseuse.	mɔɔ nuat	....
Rank, position.	tamnɛŋ	....
To be stingy.	khii niaw	....

ข.

แดงมาแล้ว
   มานี่แดง จะบอกอะไรให้

ศรีมาแล้ว
   มานี่ศรี จะบอกอะไรให้

หน่อยมาแล้ว
   มานี่หน่อย จะบอกอะไรให้

แอ๊ดมาแล้ว
   มานี่แอ๊ด จะบอกอะไรให้

ต้อยมาแล้ว
   มานี่ต้อย จะบอกอะไรให้

๓๖.๕ แบบฝึกหัดการสลับเสียงสูงต่ำ

ก.

ยุงกินจิ้งจกใช่ไหม
   ไม่ใช่, จิ้งจกกินยุงต่างหาก

ประสงค์ถามจอนใช่ไหม
   ไม่ใช่, จอนถามประสงค์ต่างหาก

ฝรั่งสอนคนไทยใช่ไหม
   ไม่ใช่, คนไทยสอนฝรั่งต่างหาก

ผู้หญิงช่วยผู้ชายใช่ไหม
   ไม่ใช่, ผู้ชายช่วยผู้หญิงต่างหาก

คนใช้เรียกนายใช่ไหม
   ไม่ใช่, นายเรียกคนใช้ต่างหาก

หมอไปหาตำรวจใช่ไหม
   ไม่ใช่, ตำรวจไปหาหมอต่างหาก

ต้อยอยู่ที่บ้านต๋อยใช่ไหม
   ไม่ใช่, ต๋อยอยู่ที่บ้านต้อยต่างหาก

b. Response drill.

The main purpose of this drill is to maintain tonal accuracy at high speed.

dɛɛŋ maa lɛ́ɛw.	Here comes Daeng.
maa nîi dɛɛŋ.	Come here, Daeng.
ca bɔ̀ɔk ʔaray hây.	I've got something to tell you.
sǐi maa lɛ́ɛw.	Here comes Sri.
maa nîi sǐi.	Come here, Sri.
ca bɔ̀ɔk ʔaray hây.	I've got something to tell you.
nɔ̀y maa lɛ́ɛw.	Here comes Noy.
maa nîi nɔ̀y.	Come here, Noy.
ca bɔ̀ɔk ʔaray hây.	I've got something to tell you.
ʔɛ́ɛt maa lɛ́ɛw.	Here comes At.
maa nîi ʔɛ́ɛt.	Come here, At.
ca bɔ̀ɔk ʔaray hây.	I've got something to tell you.
tôy maa lɛ́ɛw.	Here comes Toy.
maa nîi tôy.	Come here, Toy.
ca bɔ̀ɔk ʔaray hây.	I've got something to tell you.

36.5 Tone manipulation.

a. Response drill.

yuŋ kin cîŋcòk chây máy.	Mosquitoes eat chingchoks, don't they?
mây chây.	No.
cîŋcòk kin yuŋ taŋhàak.	Chingchoks eat mosquitoes.
prasǒŋ thǎam cɔɔn chây máy.	Prasong asked John, didn't he?
mây chây.	No.
cɔɔn thǎam prasǒŋ taŋhàak.	John asked Prasong.
faràŋ sɔ̌ɔn khon thay chây máy.	The Farang taught the Thai, didn't he?
mây chây.	No.
khon thay sɔ̌ɔn faràŋ taŋhàak.	The Thai taught the Farang.
phûuyǐŋ chûay phûuchaay chây máy.	The girl is helping the boy, isn't she?
mây chây.	No.
phûuchaay chûay phûuyǐŋ taŋhàak.	The boy is helping the girl.
khon cháay rîak naay chây máy.	The servant called the master, didn't he?
mây chây.	No.
naay rîak khon cháay taŋhàak.	The master called the servant.
mɔ̌ɔ pay hǎa tamrùat chây máy.	The doctor went to see the policeman, didn't he?
mây chây.	No.
tamrùat pay hǎa mɔ̌ɔ taŋhàak.	The policeman went to see the doctor.
tôy yùu thîi bâan tǒy chây máy.	Toy Fall lives with Toy Rise, doesn't she?
mây chây.	No.
tǒy yùu thîi bâan tôy taŋhàak.	Toy Rise lives with Toy Fall.

๓๖.๖ แบบฝึกหัดการออกเสียงสระและพยัญชนะ

ก.

อีอิว   เอียเอี๋ยว   เอเอว   แอแอว   อาอาว

ข.

บอกบิ๋มทำไม
    ไม่ได้บอกบิ๋ม บอกบ้า

บอกบ้าทำไม
    ไม่ได้บอกบ้า บอกบิ๋ม

ป้อนบิ๋มทำไม
    ไม่ได้ป้อนบิ๋ม ป้อนบ้า

ป้อนบ้าทำไม
    ไม่ได้ป้อนบ้า ป้อนบิ๋ม

๓๖.๗ แบบฝึกหัดไวยากรณ์

ก.

คุณประสงค์สั่งแกงเผ็ด (โอเลี้ยง)
    เขาสั่งโอเลี้ยงด้วย

คุณประชุมเรียนภาษาอังกฤษ
(ภาษาเวียดนาม)
    เขาเรียนภาษาเวียดนามด้วย

คุณประภาสไปไปรษณีย์ (ธนาคาร)
    เขาไปธนาคารด้วย

คุณพ่อต้องไปทำงาน (หาหมอ)
    เขาต้องไปหาหมอด้วย

คุณประเสริฐชอบไปสามล้อ (แท๊กซี่)
    เขาชอบไปแท๊กซี่ด้วย

คุณแม่ทานอาหารกลางวันที่โรงแรม
(อาหารเย็น)
    เขาทานอาหารเย็นที่โรงแรมด้วย

คุณประพัทธ์กำลังกินเบียร์ (สูบบุหรี่)
    เขากำลังสูบบุหรี่ด้วย

36.6 Vowel and cosonant drills.

a. Vowels with final w.

ʔii ʔiw   ʔia ʔiaw   ʔee ʔeew   ʔɛɛ ʔɛɛw   ʔaa ʔaaw

b. Response drill. (p and b).

bɔ̀ɔk bǐm thammay.	Why did you tell Bim?
mây dây bɔ̀ɔk bǐm. bɔ̀ɔk pâa.	I didn't tell Bim. I told Auntie.
pɔ̂ɔn bǐm thammay.	Why did you feed Bim?
mây dây pɔ̂ɔn bǐm. pɔ̂ɔn pâa.	I didn't feed Bim. I fed Auntie.
bɔ̀ɔk pâa thammay.	Why did you tell Auntie?
mây dây bɔ̀ɔk pâa. bɔ̀ɔk bǐm.	I didn't tell Auntie. I told Bim.
pɔ̂ɔn pâa thammay.	Why did you feed Auntie?
mây dây pɔ̂ɔn pâa. pɔ̂ɔn bǐm.	I didn't feed Auntie. I fed Bim.

36.7 Grammar drills.

a. Response drill.

khun prasǒŋ sàŋ kɛɛŋ phèt.	Prasong ordered hot curry.
(ʔoolíaŋ)	(iced coffee)
kháw sàŋ ʔoolíaŋ dûay.	He ordered iced coffee, too.
khun praphâat pay praysanii.	Prapart went to the post office.
(thanaakhaan)	(bank)
kháw pay thanaakhaan dûay.	He went to the bank, too.
khun prasə̀ət chɔ̂ɔp pay sǎamlɔ́ɔ.	Prasert likes to go by samlor.
(thɛ́ksîi)	(taxi)
kháw chɔ̂ɔp pay thɛ́ksîi dûay.	He likes to go by taxi, too.
khun praphát kamlaŋ kin bia.	Prapat is drinking beer.
(sùup burìi)	(smoke a cagaret)
kháw kamlaŋ sùup burìi dûay.	He's smoking a cigaret, too.
khun prachum rian phasǎa ʔaŋkrìt.	Prachum is studying English.
(phasǎa wîatnaam)	(Vietnamese)
kháw rian phasǎa wîatnaam dûay.	He's studying Vietnamese, too.
khun phɔ̂ɔ tɔ̂ŋ pay tham ŋaan.	Father has to go to work.
(hǎa mɔ̌ɔ)	(go see a doctor)
kháw tɔ̂ŋ pay hǎa mɔ̌ɔ dûay.	He has to go see a doctor, too.
khun mɛ̂ɛ thaan ʔaahǎan klaaŋwan thîi roonreem. (ʔaahǎan yen)	Mother ate lunch at the hotel. (dinner)
kháw thaan ʔaahǎan yen thîi rooŋrɛɛm dûay. She ate dinner at the hotel, too.	

ข.

มีคนมาหาจอน
    คนที่มาหาจอนชื่ออะไร

มีคนคอยข้างนอก
    คนที่คอยข้างนอกชื่ออะไร

มีฝรั่งกำลังพูดโทรศัพท์
    ฝรั่งที่กำลังพูดโทรศัพท์ชื่ออะไร

มีตำรวจยืนตรงหน้าบ้าน
    ตำรวจที่ยืนตรงหน้าบ้านชื่ออะไร

มีคนไทยเรียนภาษาเวียดนาม
    คนไทยที่เรียนภาษาเวียดนามชื่ออะไร

มีผู้หญิงอยากจะพูดกับคุณ
    ผู้หญิงที่อยากจะพูดกับฉันชื่ออะไร

ก.

    (สั่งอะไร)
เขาสั่งอะไรหรือเปล่า
    สั่ง
เขาสั่งอะไรบ้างล่ะ

    (ไปไหน)
เขาไปไหนหรือเปล่า
    ไป
เขาไปไหนบ้างล่ะ

    (พูดกับใคร)
เขาพูดกับใครหรือเปล่า
    พูด
เขาพูดกับใครบ้างล่ะ

    (ซื้ออะไร)
เขาซื้ออะไรหรือเปล่า
    ซื้อ
เขาซื้ออะไรบ้างล่ะ

    (บอกใคร)
เขาบอกใครหรือเปล่า
    บอก
เขาบอกใครบ้างล่ะ

    (ถามอะไร)
เขาถามอะไรหรือเปล่า
    ถาม
เขาถามอะไรบ้างล่ะ

b. Response drill.

mii khon maa hǎa cɔɔn.
  khon thîi maa hǎa cɔɔn
  chɯ̂ɯ ʔaray.

Someone has come to see John.
What's the name of the person
who has come to see John?

mii khon khɔɔy khân nôɔk.
  khon thîi khɔɔy khân nôɔk
  chɯ̂ɯ ʔaray.

Someone is waiting outside.
What's the name of the person
who is waiting outside?

mii faràŋ kamlaŋ phûut thoorasàp.
  faràŋ thîi kamlaŋ phûut thoorasàp
  chɯ̂ɯ ʔaray.

A Farang is making a phone call.
What's the name of the Farang
who is making a phone call?

mii tamrùat yɯɯn troŋ nâa bâan.
  tamrùat thîi yɯɯn troŋ nâa bâan
  chɯ̂ɯ ʔaray.

A policeman is standing in front of the house.
What's the name of the policeman
who is standing in front of the house?

mii khon thay rian phasǎa wîatnaam.
  khon thay thîi rian phasǎa wîatnaam
  chɯ̂ɯ ʔaray.

A Thai is studying Vietnamese.
What's the name of the Thai
who is studying Vietnamese?

mii phûuyǐŋ yàak ca phûut kàp khun.
  phûuyǐŋ thîi yàak ca phûut kàp chán
  chɯ̂ɯ ʔaray.

A girl wants to talk to you.
What's the name of the girl
who wants to talk to me?

c. Response drill.

  (sàŋ ʔaray)
kháw sàŋ ʔaray rɯ́ plàaw.
  sàŋ.
kháw sàŋ ʔaray bâaŋ lâ.

  (leave word)
Did he leave any word?
  Yes.
What did he say?

  (pay nǎy)
kháw pay nǎy rɯ́ plàaw.
  pay.
kháw pay nǎy bâaŋ lâ.

  (go somewhere)
Did he go anywhere?
  Yes.
Where all did he go?

  (phûut kàp khray)
kháw phûut kàp khray rɯ́ plàaw.
  phûut.
kháw phûut kàp khray bâaŋ lâ.

  (talk to someone)
Did he talk to anybody?
  Yes.
Who all did he talk to?

  (sɯ́ɯ ʔaray)
kháw sɯ́ɯ ʔaray rɯ́ plàaw.
  sɯ́ɯ.
kháw sɯ́ɯ ʔaray bâaŋ lâ.

  (buy something)
Did he buy anything?
  Yes.
What all did he buy?

  (bɔ̀ɔk khray)
kháw bɔ̀ɔk khray rɯ́ plàaw.
  bɔ̀ɔk.
kháw bɔ̀ɔk khray bâaŋ lâ.

  (tell someone)
Did he tell anybody?
  Yes.
Who all did he tell?

  (thǎam ʔaray)
kháw thǎam ʔaray rɯ́ plàaw.
  thǎam.
kháw thǎam ʔaray bâaŋ lâ.

  (ask something)
Did he ask you something?
  Yes.
What did he ask you?

๓๖.๘ เดือน

กรกฎาคม
สิงหาคม
กันยายน

๓๖.๙ การสนทนาโต้ตอบ

(คุณประภาสไปหาหมอเมื่อเช้านี้เพราะว่าไม่สบายนะฮะ)

ใครไปหาหมอเมื่อเช้านี้ฮะ	คุณประภาสฮะ
เขาไปเมื่อไหร่ฮะ	ไปเมื่อเช้านี้ฮะ
เขาไปทำไมฮะ	เพราะว่าไม่สบายฮะ
เขาไปไหนฮะ	ไปหาหมอฮะ

คุณประสงค์ไปหาหมอใช่ไหมฮะ	ไม่ใช่ฮะ, คุณประภาสต่างหากไปหาหมอ
เขาไปดูหนังใช่ไหมฮะ	ไม่ใช่ฮะ, เขาไปหาหมอ
เขาไปเมื่อคืนนี้ใช่ไหมฮะ	ไม่ใช่ฮะ, เขาไปเมื่อเช้านี้
เขาไปหาเพื่อนใช่ไหมฮะ	ไม่ใช่ฮะ, เขาไปหาหมอ

(เมื่อวานนี้คุณประสงค์ให้หนังสือคุณประภาสสามเล่มนะฮะ)

ใครให้หนังสือฮะ	คุณประสงค์ฮะ
ให้ใครฮะ	ให้คุณประภาสฮะ
ให้อะไรฮะ	ให้หนังสือฮะ
หนังสือกี่เล่มฮะ	สามเล่มฮะ
เมื่อไหร่ฮะ	เมื่อวานนี้ฮะ

ประภาสให้ประสงค์ใช่ไหมฮะ	ไม่ใช่ฮะ, ประสงค์ต่างหากให้ประภาส
ให้เก้าอี้ใช่ไหมฮะ	ไม่ใช่ฮะ, ให้หนังสือต่างหาก
หนังสือสี่เล่มใช่ไหมฮะ	ไม่ใช่ฮะ, สามเล่มเท่านั้น
ให้วันนี้ใช่ไหมฮะ	ไม่ใช่ฮะ, ให้เมื่อวานนี้ต่างหาก
ให้ทำไมฮะ	ไม่ทราบฮะ

36.8 Months.

The three rainiest months of the year are listed below. The student should practice them in class until he can say them rapidly without the slightest hesitation.

karákkadaakhom	July.
sĭŋhǎakhom	August.
kanyaayon	September.

Practice translating the following English month names into Thai for increased speed.

September.	July.	November.	August.
January.	February.	September.	May.
August.	September.	March.	July.
April.	December.	August.	January.
July.	August.	February.	September.
March.	April.	July.	December.
September.	July.	September.	August.
November.	May.	January.	February.

36.9 Conversation.

(khun praphâat pay hǎa mɔ̌ɔ mɨa cháaw níi phrɔ́ʔ wâa mây sabaay ná há.)

khray pay hǎa mɔ̌ɔ mɨa cháaw níi há.	khun praphâat há?.
kháw pay mɨarày há.	pay mɨa cháaw níi há?.
kháw pay thammay há.	phrɔ́ʔ wâa mây sabaay há?.
kháw pay nǎy há.	pay hǎa mɔ̌ɔ há?.

khun prasŏŋ pay hǎa mɔ̌ɔ chây máy há.	mây chây há?. khun praphâat taŋhàak pay hǎa mɔ̌ɔ.
kháw pay duu nǎŋ chây máy há.	mây chây há?. kháw pay hǎa mɔ̌ɔ.
kháw pay mɨa khɨɨn níi chây máy há.	mây chây há?. kháw pay mɨa cháaw níi.
kháw pay hǎa phɨan chây máy há.	mây chây há?. kháw pay hǎa mɔ̌ɔ.

(mɨa waan níi khun prasŏŋ hây naŋsɨɨ khun praphâat sǎam lêm ná há.)

khray hây naŋsɨɨ há.	khun prasŏŋ há?.
hây khray há.	hây khun praphâat há?.
hây ʔaray há.	hây naŋsɨɨ há?.
naŋsɨɨ kìi lêm há.	sǎam lêm há?.
mɨarày há.	mɨa waan níi há?.

praphâat hây prasŏŋ chây máy há.	mây chây há?. prasŏŋ taŋhàak hây praphâat.
hây kâwʔîi chây máy há.	mây chây há?. hây naŋsɨɨ taŋhàak.
naŋsɨɨ sìi lêm chây máy há.	mây chây há?. sǎam lêm thâwnán.
hây wan níi chây máy há.	mây chây há?. hây mɨa waan níi taŋhàak.
hây thammay há.	mây sâap há?.

211

(ลูกคุณจอนไปเรียนภาษาไทยที่ เอ ยู เอ ตอนเช้า ทุกวันจันทร์ พุธ ศุกร์นะฮะ)

ใครไปเรียนฮะ	ลูกคุณจอนฮะ
เรียนอะไรฮะ	เรียนภาษาไทยฮะ
เรียนที่ไหนฮะ	ที่ เอ ยู เอฮะ
เรียนตอนไหนฮะ	เรียนตอนเช้าฮะ
ลูกของใครไป เอ ยู เอฮะ	ลูกคุณจอนฮะ
เขาไปทำอะไรที่นั่นฮะ	ไปเรียนภาษาไทยฮะ
เขาเรียนวันไหนบ้างฮะ	เรียนวันจันทร์ พุธ ศุกร์ฮะ

คุณพ่อคุณจอนเรียนใช่ไหมฮะ	ไม่ใช่ฮะ, ลูกเขาต่างหากเรียน
เรียนภาษาจีนใช่ไหมฮะ	ไม่ใช่ฮะ, เรียนภาษาไทยต่างหาก
เรียนทุกวันใช่ไหมฮะ	ไม่ใช่ฮะ, เรียนวันจันทร์ พุธ ศุกร์
เรียนตอนบ่ายใช่ไหมฮะ	ไม่ใช่ฮะ, เรียนตอนเช้า

(คุณสุจินต์ไปส่งลูกชายเขาที่ที่ทำงานทุกเช้านะฮะ)

ใครไปส่งฮะ	คุณสุจินต์ฮะ
ไปส่งใครฮะ	ลูกเขาฮะ
ลูกชายหรือลูกสาวฮะ	ลูกชายฮะ
ส่งที่ไหนฮะ	ส่งที่ที่ทำงานฮะ
ส่งเมื่อไหร่ฮะ	ทุกเช้าฮะ
ลูกชายคุณสุจินต์ไปไหนทุกเช้าฮะ	ไปทำงานฮะ
เขาไปยังไงฮะ	คุณพ่อไปส่งเขาฮะ

คุณสุจินต์ส่งคุณพ่อใช่ไหมฮะ	ไม่ใช่ฮะ, ส่งลูกต่างหาก
ลูกสาวใช่ไหมฮะ	ไม่ใช่ฮะ, ลูกชาย
ลูกส่งพ่อใช่ไหมฮะ	ไม่ใช่ฮะ, พ่อส่งลูกต่างหาก
ส่งที่โรงเรียนใช่ไหมฮะ	ไม่ใช่ฮะ, ส่งที่ที่ทำงาน
ส่งทุกวันจันทร์ พุธ ศุกร์ใช่ไหมฮะ	ไม่ใช่ฮะ, ส่งทุกวัน

(lûuk khun cɔɔn pay rian phasăa thay thîi ʔee yuu ʔee tɔɔn cháaw thúk wan can phút sùk ná há.)

khray pay rian há.
rian ʔaráy há.
rian thîi năy há.
rian tɔɔn năy há.
lûuk khɔ́ŋ khray pay ʔee yuu ʔee há.
kháw pay tham ʔaráy thîi nân há.
kháw rian wan năy bâaŋ há.

lûuk khun cɔɔn há?.
rian phasăa thay há?.
thîi ʔee yuu ʔee há?.
rian tɔɔn cháaw há?.
lûuk khun cɔɔn há?.
pay rian phasăa thay há?.
rian wan can phút sùk há?.

khun phɔ̂ɔ khun cɔɔn rian chây máy há.
rian phasăa ciin chây máy há.
rian thúk wan chây máy há.
rian tɔɔn bàay chây máy há.

mây chây há?. lûuk kháw taŋhàak rian.
mây chây há?. rian phasăa thay taŋhàak.
mây chây há?. rian wan can phút sùk.
mây chây há?. rian tɔɔn cháaw.

(khun sucin pay sòŋ lûuk chaay kháw thîi thîi tham ŋaan thúk cháaw ná há.)

khray pay sòŋ há.
pay sòŋ khray há.
lûuk chaay rɯ́ lûuk săaw há.
sòŋ thîi năy há.
sòŋ mɯ̂arày há.
lûuk chaay khun sucin pay năy thúk cháaw há.
kháw pay yaŋŋay há.

khun sucin há?.
lûuk kháw há?.
lûuk chaay há?.
sòŋ thîi thîi tham ŋaan há?.
thúk cháaw há?.
pay tham ŋaan há?.
khun phɔ̂ɔ pay sòŋ kháw há?.

khun sucin sòŋ khun phɔ̂ɔ chây máy há.
lûuk săaw chây máy há.
lûuk sòŋ phɔ̂ɔ chây máy há.
sòŋ thîi rooŋrian chây máy há.
sòŋ thúk wan can phút sùk chây máy há.

mây chây há?. sòŋ lûuk taŋhàak.
mây chây há?. lûuk chaay.
mây chây há?. phɔ̂ɔ sòŋ lûuk taŋhàak.
mây chây há?. sòŋ thîi thîi tham ŋaan.
mây chây há?. sòŋ thúk wan.

๓๖.๑๐ **การเขียน**

กางเกงของเพื่อนแดงอยู่ที่โรงเรียน

เลี้ยวซ้ายที่สี่แยก โรงเรียนอยู่ทางขวา

เลี้ยวขวาที่ซอยหน้า โรงเรียนอยู่ทางซ้าย

หน้าต่างเสียมาหลายเดือนแล้ว

เพื่อนของน้องชายเรียนที่เอ ยู เอ มาหลายปีแล้ว

กางเกง ของ เพื่อน แดง อยู่ที่ โรงเรียน

kaaŋkeeŋ   khɔ̌ɔŋ   phâan   dɛɛŋ   yùu thîi   rooŋrian

Of the twelve long vowels, nine are regular: they are written the same whether they have a final consonant or not. You can easily remember these nine vowels by memorizing the above sentence.

Just as the consonant symbol *hɔ̌ɔ* changes a low consonant into a high one, so *ʔɔɔ* changes a low consonant into a mid one. It is used only with *yɔɔ*, however, and only in the four words *yùu*, *yàak*, *yàaŋ*, and *yàa*.

Many words that are basically long get shortened by certain rhythm patterns. Thus *kaaŋkeeŋ* and *khɔ̌ɔŋ* (when it means *of*) are normally pronounced *kaŋkeeŋ* and *khɔ́ŋ*.

Practice reading and writing the following sentences.

เลี้ยวซ้ายที่สี่แยก โรงเรียนอยู่ทางขวา

เลี้ยวขวาที่ซอยหน้า โรงเรียนอยู่ทางซ้าย

หน้าต่างเสียมาหลายเดือนแล้ว

เพื่อนของน้องชายเรียนอยู่ที่ เอ ยู เอ มา

หลายปีแล้ว

บทที่ ๓๗

๓๗.๑ คำศัพท์

สุริวงศ์	เคย
ถนนสุริวงศ์	ปวด
ออฟฟิต	หัว
	ปวดหัว
ที่หลัง	
	แม่ครัว
เสื้อ (ชั้น) ใน	
กางเกง (ชั้น) ใน	สวน
เธอ	ตื่น

๓๗.๒ โครงสร้างของประโยค

กินข้าวก่อน	ไม่เคยพูดกับเขา
กินกาแฟที่หลัง	ไม่เคยไปหาหมอ
ทำงานก่อน	ไม่เคยปวดหัว
ไปดูหนังที่หลัง	
	ฉันเคยอยู่ที่ซอยหก
ปวดหัว	ฉันเคยทำงานที่นั่น
ปวดฟัน	ฉันเคยไปเมืองจีน
ปวดหลัง	
ปวดหู	

เคยไปอังกฤษไหม
เคยกินแกงเผ็ดไหม
เคยลืมเอาหนังสือมาไหม

LESSON 37

37.1 Vocabulary and expansions.

suriwoŋ	Suriwong.
thanǒn suriwoŋ	Suriwong Road.
ʔɔpfít	Office
thii lǎŋ	Afterwards, later.
sɨa (chán) nay	Undershirt.
kaŋkeeŋ (chán) nay	Underpants.
thəə	You (to an intimate or inferior).
khəəy	To have ever, used to.
pùat	To ache.
hǔa	Head.
pùat hǔa	To have a headache.
mɛ̂ɛ khrua	A cook (female).
sǔan	A garden or orchard.
tɨɨn	To wake up.

37.2 Patterns.

kin khâaw kɔ̀ɔn.	Eat first.
kin kaafɛɛ thii lǎŋ.	Drink coffee afterwards.
tham ŋaan kɔ̀ɔn.	Work first.
pay duu nǎŋ thii lǎŋ.	Go to a movie later.
pùat hǔa.	To have a headache.
pùat fan.	To have a toothache.
pùat lǎŋ.	To have a backache.
pùat hǔu.	To have an earache.
khəəy pay ʔaŋkrìt máy.	Have you ever been to England?
khəəy kin kɛɛŋ phèt máy.	Have you ever eaten hot curry?
khəəy lɨɨm ʔaw naŋsɨɨ maa máy.	Have you ever forgotten to bring your book?
mây khəəy phûut kàp kháw.	I've never spoken to him.
mây khəəy pay hǎa mɔ̌ɔ.	I've never been to see a doctor.
mây khəəy pùat hǔa.	I've never had a headache.
chán khəəy yùu thîi sɔɔy hòk.	I used to live on Soi 6.
chán khəəy tham ŋaan thîi nân.	I used to work there.
chán khəəy pay mɨaŋ ciin.	I've been to China.

217

๓๗.๓ บทสนทนา

ก. มาหาใครคะ

ข. ผมอยากพบคุณหมอครับ
อยู่ไหมฮะ

ก. ยังไม่มาทำงานเลยฮะ

ข. ไปไหนทราบไหมฮะ

ก. เอารถไปแก้ฮะ

ข. จะมาทำงานเมื่อไหร่ฮะ

ก. ไม่แน่ฮะ, คุณจะคอยไหมฮะ

ข. ผมคอยไม่ได้ฮะ มีธุระ
บ้านคุณหมออยู่ที่ไหนฮะ
ผมจะไปหาเขาที่บ้าน

ก. รู้จักแบงค์อเมริกาไหมฮะ

ข. รู้จักฮะ อยู่ที่ถนนสุริวงศ์

ก. ถูกแล้วฮะ ไปตามถนนสุริวงศ์
เลยแบงค์อเมริกาไปหน่อย
แล้วเลี้ยวซ้าย
บ้านคุณหมออยู่ทางขวาฮะ
ที่หน้าบ้านมีปั๊มน้ำมัน

ข. บ้านเลขที่เท่าไหร่ฮะ

ก. เลขที่ ๑๔๓/๒ ฮะ

ข. ถ้าไม่พบคุณหมอที่บ้าน จะกลับ
มาที่นี่อีกนะฮะ

ก. ค่ะ, ขอโทษ คุณชื่ออะไรฮะ

ข. ชื่อประภาสครับ ช่วยบอกหมอ
นะว่าผมอยากพบมาก นะฮะ

ก. ค่ะ แล้วดิฉันจะบอกให้

37.3 Dialog.

A. maa hǎa khray khá.

Who are you looking for?

B. phǒm yàak phóp khun mɔ̌ɔ khráp.
yùu máy há?.

I want to see the doctor.
Is he in?

A. yaŋ mây maa tham ŋaan ləəy hâ.

He hasn't come to work yet.

B. pay nǎy, sâap máy há?.

Do you know where he has gone?

A. ʔaw rót pay kɛ̂ɛ hâ.

He has taken his car to be repaired.

B. ca maa tham ŋaan mûarày há?.

When will he come to work?

A. mây nɛ̂ɛ hâ.
khun ca khɔɔy máy há.

I'm not sure.
Will you wait?

B. phǒm khɔɔy mây dây há?.
mii thúrá?.
bâan khun mɔ̌ɔ yùu thîi nǎy há?.
phǒm ca pay hǎa kháw thîi bâan.

I can't wait.
I've got something to do.
Where is the doctor's house?
I'll go see him at his home.

A. rúucàk bɛ́ŋ ʔameerikaa máy há.

Do you know the Bank of America?

B. rúucàk há?.
yùu thîi thanǒn suriwoŋ.

Yes.
It's on Suriwong Road

A. thùuk lɛ́ɛw hâ.
pay taam thanǒn suriwoŋ.
ləəy bɛ́ŋ ʔameerikaa pay nɔ̀y,
lɛ́ɛw líaw sáay.
bâan khun mɔ̌ɔ yùu thaaŋ khwǎa hâ.
thîi nâa bâan mii pám námman.

That's right.
Go along Suriwong Road.
Go a little past the Bank of America,
and then turn left.
The doctor's house is on the right.
There's a gas pump in front of the house.

B. bâan lêek thîi thâwrày há?.

What's the house number?

A. lêek thîi 143 tháp 2 hâ.

Number 143 slash 2.

B. thâa mây phóp khun mɔ̌ɔ thîi bâan,
ca klàp maa thîi nîi ʔìik ná há?.

If I don't see the doctor at his home,
I'll come back here again.

A. khâ.
khɔ̌ɔ thôot, khun chûu ʔaray há.

O.K.
Excuse me, what's your name?

B. chûu praphâat khráp.
chûay bɔ̀ɔk mɔ̌ɔ ná wâa
phǒm yàak phóp mâak ná há?.

My name is Prapart.
Please tell the doctor
I want to see him very much.

A. khâ. lɛ́ɛw dichán ca bɔ̀ɔk hây.

Yes, I'll tell him.

219

๓๗.๔ แบบฝึกหัดการฟังและการออกเสียงสูงต่ำ

ก.

ถั่วงอก   ช้างเผือก   ถือตัว   เมียหลวง   น่ารัก

ข.

เขาชื่อประชุม
   ประชุมหรือ ฉันก็ชื่อประชุม

เขาชื่อประพัทธ์
   ประพัทธ์หรือ ฉันก็ชื่อประพัทธ์

เขาชื่อประสงค์
   ประสงค์หรือ ฉันก็ชื่อประสงค์

เขาชื่อประเสริฐ
   ประเสริฐหรือ ฉันก็ชื่อประเสริฐ

เขาชื่อประภาส
   ประภาสหรือ ฉันก็ชื่อประภาส

เขาชื่อแดง
   แดงหรือ ฉันก็ชื่อแดง

เขาชื่อแอ๊ด
   แอ๊ดหรือ ฉันก็ชื่อแอ๊ด

เขาชื่อศรี
   ศรีหรือ ฉันก็ชื่อศรี

เขาชื่อหน่อย
   หน่อยหรือ ฉันก็ชื่อหน่อย

เขาชื่อต้อย
   ต้อยหรือ ฉันก็ชื่อต้อย

37.4 Tone identification and production.

a. Identify the tones and record the number of repetitions required.

Bean sprouts.	thua ŋɔɔk	....	....
White elephant.	chaaŋ phʉak	....	....
To be haughty.	thʉʉ tua	....	....
Major wife.	mia luaŋ	....	....
Cute, loveable.	naa rak	....	....

b. Response drill.

The main purpose of this drill is to maintain tonal accuracy at high speed.

kháw chʉʉ prachum. prachum lɔ̌ə. chán kɔ̂ chʉʉ prachum.	His name is Prachum. Prachum? That's my name, too.
kháw chʉʉ praphát. praphát lɔ̌ə. chán kɔ̂ chʉʉ praphát.	His name is Prapat. Prapat? That's my name, too.
kháw chʉʉ prasɔ̌ŋ. prasɔ̌ŋ lɔ̌ə. chán kɔ̂ chʉʉ prasɔ̌ŋ.	His name is Prasong. Prasong? That's my name, too.
kháw chʉʉ prasə̀ət. prasə̀ət lɔ̌ə. chán kɔ̂ chʉʉ prasə̀ət.	His name is Prasert. Prasert? That's my name, too.
kháw chʉʉ praphâat. praphâat lɔ̌ə. chán kɔ̂ chʉʉ praphâat.	His name is Prapart. Prapart? That's my name, too.
kháw chʉʉ dɛɛŋ. dɛɛŋ lɔ̌ə. chán kɔ̂ chʉʉ dɛɛŋ.	Her name is Daeng. Daeng? That's my name, too.
kháw chʉʉ ʔéɛt. ʔéɛt lɔ̌ə. chán kɔ̂ chʉʉ ʔéɛt.	Her name is At. At? That's my name, too.
kháw chʉʉ sǐi. sǐi lɔ̌ə. chán kɔ̂ chʉʉ sǐi.	Her name is Sri. Sri? That's my name, too.
kháw chʉʉ nɔ̀y. nɔ̀y lɔ̌ə. chán kɔ̂ chʉʉ nɔ̀y.	Her name is Noy. Noy? That's my name, too.
kháw chʉʉ tôy. tôy lɔ̌ə. chán kɔ̂ chʉʉ tôy.	Her name is Toy. Toy? That's my name, too.

221

๓๗.๕ แบบฝึกหัดการสลับเสียงสูงต่ำ

ก.

อย่าลืมบอกนะแอ๊ด   (แดง)   อย่าลืมทักนะศรี   (บอก)

อย่าลืมบอกนะแดง   (ทัก)   อย่าลืมบอกนะศรี   (ต้อย)

อย่าลืมทักนะแดง   (แอ๊ด)   อย่าลืมบอกนะต้อย   (หน่อย)

อย่าลืมทักนะแอ๊ด   (เตือน)   อย่าลืมบอกนะหน่อย   (ทัก)

อย่าลืมเตือนนะแอ๊ด   (พูด)   อย่าลืมทักนะหน่อย   (เตือน)

อย่าลืมพูดนะแอ๊ด   (ถาม)   อย่าลืมเตือนนะหน่อย   (พูด)

อย่าลืมถามนะแอ๊ด   (แดง)   อย่าลืมพูดนะหน่อย   (ต้อย)

อย่าลืมถามนะแดง   (พูด)   อย่าลืมพูดนะต้อย   (ศรี)

อย่าลืมพูดนะแดง   (เตือน)   อย่าลืมพูดนะศรี   (ถาม)

อย่าลืมเตือนนะแดง   (ศรี)   อย่าลืมถามนะศรี   (ต้อย)

อย่าลืมเตือนนะศรี   (ต้อย)   อย่าลืมถามนะต้อย   (หน่อย)

อย่าลืมเตือนนะต้อย   (ทัก)   อย่าลืมถามนะหน่อย

อย่าลืมทักนะต้อย   (ศรี)

๓๗.๖ แบบฝึกหัดการออกเสียงสระและพยัญชนะ

ก.

อูอุย   อัวอวย   โอออย   ออออย   อาอาย   เออเอย   เอือเอือย

ข.

ด่าแดงทำไม   ด่าต้อยทำไม

   ไม่ได้ด่าแดง ด่าต้อย   ไม่ได้ด่าต้อย ด่าแดง

ตีแดงทำไม   ตีต้อยทำไม

   ไม่ได้ตีแดง ตีต้อย   ไม่ได้ตีต้อย ตีแดง

37.5 Tone manipulation.

a. Substitution drill.

yàa lɯɯm bɔ̀ɔk ná, ʔɛ́ɛt. (dɛɛŋ)	Don't forget to tell him, At.
yàa lɯɯm bɔ̀ɔk ná, dɛɛŋ. (thák)	Don't forget to tell him, Daeng.
yàa lɯɯm thák ná, dɛɛŋ. (ʔɛ́ɛt)	Don't forget to say hello, Daeng.
yàa lɯɯm thák ná, ʔɛ́ɛt. (tɯan)	Don't forget to say hello, At.
yàa lɯɯm tɯan ná, ʔɛ́ɛt. (phûut)	Don't forget to remind me, At.
yàa lɯɯm phûut ná, ʔɛ́ɛt. (thǎam)	Don't forget to say something, At.
yàa lɯɯm thǎam ná, ʔɛ́ɛt. (dɛɛŋ)	Don't forget to ask, At.
yàa lɯɯm thǎam ná, dɛɛŋ. (phûut)	Don't forget to ask, Daeng.
yàa lɯɯm phûut ná, dɛɛŋ. (tɯan)	Don't forget to say something, Daeng.
yàa lɯɯm tɯan ná, dɛɛŋ. (sǐi)	Don't forget to remind me, Daeng.
yàa lɯɯm tɯan ná, sǐi. (tôy)	Don't forget to remind me, Sri.
yàa lɯɯm tɯan ná, tôy. (thák)	Don't forget to remind me, Toy.
yàa lɯɯm thák ná, tôy. (sǐi)	Don't forget to say hello, Toy.
yàa lɯɯm thák ná, sǐi. (bɔ̀ɔk)	Don't forget to say hello, Sri.
yàa lɯɯm bɔ̀ɔk ná, sǐi. (tôy)	Don't forget to tell him, Sri.
yàa lɯɯm bɔ̀ɔk ná, tôy. (nɔ̀y)	Don't forget to tell him, Toy.
yàa lɯɯm bɔ̀ɔk ná, nɔ̀y. (thák)	Don't forget to tell him, Noy.
yàa lɯɯm thák ná, nɔ̀y. (tɯan)	Don't forget to say hello, Noy.
yàa lɯɯm tɯan ná, nɔ̀y. (phûut)	Don't forget to remind me, Noy.
yàa lɯɯm phûut ná, nɔ̀y. (tôy)	Don't forget to say something, Noy.
yàa lɯɯm phûut ná, tôy. (sǐi)	Don't forget to say something, Toy.
yàa lɯɯm phûut ná, sǐi. (thǎam)	Don't forget to say something, Sri.
yàa lɯɯm thǎam ná, sǐi. (tôy)	Don't forget to ask, Sri.
yàa lɯɯm thǎam ná, tôy. (nɔ̀y)	Don't forget to ask, Toy.
yàa lɯɯm thǎam ná, nɔ̀y.	Don't forget to ask, Noy.

37.6 Vowel and consonant drills.

a. Vowels with final y.

ʔuu ʔuy   ʔua ʔuay   ʔoo ʔooy   ʔɔɔ ʔɔɔy   ʔaa ʔaay   ʔəə ʔəəy   ʔɯa ʔɯay

b. Response drill. (t and d).

dàa dɛɛŋ thammay.	Why did you swear at Daeng?
mây dây dàa dɛɛŋ. dàa tôy.	I didn't swear at Daeng. I swore at Toy.
tii dɛɛŋ thammay.	Why did you beat Daeng?
mây dây tii dɛɛŋ. tii tôy.	I didn't beat Daeng. I beat Toy.
dàa tôy thammay.	Why did you swear at Toy?
mây dây dàa tôy. dàa dɛɛŋ.	I didn't swear at Toy. I swore at Daeng.
tii tôy thammay.	Why did you beat Toy?
mây dây tii tôy. tii dɛɛŋ.	I didn't beat Toy. I beat Daeng.

๓๗.๗ แบบฝึกหัดไวยากรณ์

ก.

คุณทำเองหรือ
  เปล่า, มีคนทำให้

คุณซื้อเองหรือ
  เปล่า, มีคนซื้อให้

คุณขับเองหรือ
  เปล่า, มีคนขับให้

คุณแก้เองหรือ
  เปล่า, มีคนแก้ให้

คุณสั่งเองหรือ
  เปล่า, มีคนสั่งให้

ข.

ดำอยู่ที่ออฟฟิต และแดงคอยข้างนอก
คนไหนดำ
  คนที่อยู่ที่ออฟฟิต
คนไหนแดง
  คนที่คอยข้างนอก

ดำเลี้ยวขวา และแดงเลี้ยวซ้าย
คนไหนดำ
  คนที่เลี้ยวขวา
คนไหนแดง
  คนที่เลี้ยวซ้าย

ดำไปก่อน และแดงไปทีหลัง
คนไหนดำ
  คนที่ไปก่อน
คนไหนแดง
  คนที่ไปทีหลัง

ดำกินอาหารไทย และแดงกินอาหารฝรั่ง
คนไหนดำ
  คนที่กินอาหารไทย
คนไหนแดง
  คนที่กินอาหารฝรั่ง

ดำไปไปรษณีย์ และแดงไปธนาคาร
คนไหนดำ
  คนที่ไปไปรษณีย์
คนไหนแดง
  คนที่ไปธนาคาร

37.7 Grammar drills.

a. Response drill.

khun tham ?een lɔ̌ə.
  plàaw. mii khon tham hây.

     You did it yourself, did you?
      No. Someone did it for me.

khun khàp ?een lɔ̌ə.
  plàaw. mii khon khàp hây.

     Do you drive yourself?
      No. Someone drives for me.

khun sàŋ ?een lɔ̌ə.
  plàaw. mii khon sàŋ hây.

     I suppose you ordered it yourself?
      No. Someone ordered it for me.

khun sɨ́ɨ ?een lɔ̌ə.
  plàaw. mii khon sɨ́ɨ hây.

     You bought it yourself?
      No. Someone bought it for me.

khun kɛ̂ɛ ?een lɔ̌ə.
  plàaw. mii khon kɛ̂ɛ hây.

     Did you fix it yourself?
      No. Someone fixed it for me.

b. Response drill.

dam yùu thîi ?ɔpfít,
lɛ́? deeŋ khɔɔy khâŋ nɔ̂ɔk.
khon nǎy dam.
  khon thîi yùu thîi ?ɔpfít.
khon nǎy deeŋ.
  khon thîi khɔɔy khâŋ nɔ̂ɔk.

     Black is in the office,
     and Red is waiting outside.
     Which one is Black?
      The one in the office.
     Which is Red?
      The one waiting outside.

dam pay kɔ̀ɔn,
lɛ́? deeŋ pay thii lǎŋ.
khon nǎy dam.
  khon thîi pay kɔ̀ɔn.
khon nǎy deeŋ.
  khon thîi pay thii lǎŋ.

     Black went first,
     and Red went later.
     Which one was Black?
      The one who went first.
     Which was Red?
      The one who went later.

dam pay praysanii,
lɛ́? deeŋ pay thanaakhaan.
khon nǎy dam.
  khon thîi pay praysanii.
khon nǎy deeŋ.
  khon thîi pay thanaakhaan.

     Black went to the post office,
     and Red went to the bank.
     Which one was Black?
      The one who went to the post office.
     Which was Red?
      The one who went to the bank.

dam líaw khwǎa,
lɛ́? deeŋ liaw sáay.
khon nǎy dam.
  khon thîi líaw khwǎa.
khon nǎy deeŋ.
  khon thîi líaw sáay.

     Black turned right,
     and Red turned left.
     Which one was Black?
      The one who turned right.
     Which was Red?
      The one who turned left.

dam kin ?aahǎan thay,
lɛ́? deeŋ kin ?aahǎan faràŋ.
khon nǎy dam.
  khon thîi kin ?aahǎan thay.
khon nǎy deeŋ.
  khon thîi kin ?aahǎan faràŋ.

     Black ate Thai food,
     and Red ate Farang food.
     Which one was Black?
      The one who ate Thai food.
     Which was Red?
      The one who ate Farang food.

ค.

ศรีสั่งแกงเผ็ด
  ต้อยก็สั่งแกงเผ็ดเหมือนกัน

ต้อยไปตลาด
  ศรีก็ไปตลาดเหมือนกัน

ศรีกำลังกินเบียร์
  ต้อยก็กำลังกินเบียร์เหมือนกัน

ต้อยต้องไปหาหมอ
  ศรีก็ต้องไปหาหมอเหมือนกัน

ศรีเรียนภาษาอังกฤษ
  ต้อยก็เรียนภาษาอังกฤษเหมือนกัน

ต้อยทำงานทุกวัน
  ศรีก็ทำงานทุกวันเหมือนกัน

ศรีขับรถเป็น
  ต้อยก็ขับรถเป็นเหมือนกัน

ต้อยไม่ชอบทำงาน
  ศรีก็ไม่ชอบทำงานเหมือนกัน

๓๗.๘ **เดือน**

  มิถุนายน
  ตุลาคม

c. Response drill.

sǐi sàŋ kɛɛŋ phèt.
  tɔ̂y kɔ̂ sàŋ kɛɛŋ phèt mɯ́ankan.

Sri ordered hot curry.
  Toy ordered hot curry, too.

tɔ̂y pay talàat.
  sǐi kɔ̂ pay talàat mɯ́ankan.

Toy went to the market.
  Sri went to the market, too.

sǐi kamlaŋ kin bia.
  tɔ̂y kɔ̂ kamlaŋ kin bia mɯ́ankan.

Sri is drinking beer.
  Toy is drinking beer, too.

tɔ̂y tɔ̂ŋ pay hǎa mɔ̌ɔ.
  sǐi kɔ̂ tɔ̂ŋ pay hǎa mɔ̌ɔ mɯ́ankan.

Toy has to go see a doctor.
  Sri has to go see a doctor, too.

sǐi rian phasǎa ʔaŋkrìt.
  tɔ̂y kɔ̂ rian phasǎa ʔaŋkrìt mɯ́ankan.

Sri is studying English.
  Toy is studying English, too.

tɔ̂y tham ŋaan thúk wan.
  sǐi kɔ̂ tham ŋaan thúk wan mɯ́ankan.

Toy works every day.
  Sri works every day, too.

sǐi khàp rót pen.
  tɔ̂y kɔ̂ khàp rót pen mɯ́ankan.

Sri knows how to drive a car.
  Toy knows how to drive a car, too.

tɔ̂y mây chɔ̂ɔp tham ŋaan.
  sǐi kɔ̂ mây chɔ̂ɔp tham ŋaan mɯ́ankan.

Toy doesn't like to work.
  Sri doesn't like to work, either.

37.8 Months.

The two remaining months of the year are given below. The student should practice them in class until he can say them rapidly without the slightest hesitation.

míthunaayon	June.
tulaakhom	October.

Practice translating the following English month names into Thai for increased speed.

July.	August.	September.	June.
October.	April.	March.	July.
February.	May.	October.	August.
June.	October.	May.	September.
March.	January.	June.	December.
September.	June.	November.	October.
May.	July.	August.	April.

37.9 Conversation.

Follow the form of the dialog on page 185 to buy any of the following items: shirts, trousers, shoes, undershirts, shorts, soap, toothpaste, books. Make appropriate modifications. For example, in place of *nǎa pay nɔ̀y*, you might say something like 'it's too big', 'the sleeves are too long', or after asking the price, 'it's too expensive'.

227

๓๗.๑๐ การเขียน

เธอเคยเดิน   ลืมชื้อ   ปวดหัว

เธอลืมซื้อเนยด้วย

เธอลืมเปิดหน้าต่างครัวด้วย

แม่ครัวชื่อเพลิน

ลูกแม่ครัวชื่อหมวย

เพลินยืนอยู่ที่ครัว

หมวยเดินอยู่ที่สวน

เพลินเคยตื่นก่อนหมวย

37.10 Writing. (The three irregular long vowels.)

เธอเคยเดิน ลืมชื่อ ปวดหัว

thəə khəəy dəən   lɯɯm chɯ̂ɯ   pùat hŭa
You used to walk.   I forgot your name.   I've got a headache.

There is an irregular low consonant symbol for each of the low consonants with an *h* (ph, th, ch, and kh). These symbols occur in words borrowed from Sanskrit (bh, dh, jh, and gh respectively). The irregular low *th* is used in the word *thəə*.

Practice reading and writing the following sentences.

เธอลืมซื้อเนยด้วย

เธอลืมเปิดหน้าต่างครัวด้วย

แม่ครัวชื่อเพลิน

ลูกแม่ครัวชื่อหมวย

เพลินยืนอยู่ที่ครัว

หมวยเดินอยู่ที่สวน

เพลินเคยตื่นก่อนหมวย

บทที่ ๓๘

๓๘.๑ คำศัพท์

เป็น	ถู้
เป็นอะไร	พื้น
เป็นอะไรไป	ถูพื้น
ไข้	กาง
หวัด	มุ้ง
	กางมุ้ง
โรค	หุง
	หุงข้าว
บ้า	ถ่าน
แถว	
แถวน	สามี
ชวน	ภรรยา
รีด	เก่า
รีดเสื้อ	ธรรมดา

๓๘.๒ โครงสร้างของประโยค

เป็นไข้	ทำยังไงดี
เป็นหวัด	ไปไหนดี
เป็นโรค	นั่งที่ไหนดี
เป็นบ้า	

LESSON 38

38.1 Vocabulary and expansions.

pen	To have or be in some unnatural condition.
pen ʔaray	What's the matter with you?
pen ʔaray pay	*pay*, like *maa* and *yùu* (see 26.1) is used to add secondary meanings to the main verb. Here it suggests 'departing from the normal'.
khây	A fever.
wàt	A cold.
rôok	A disease.
bâa	Crazy.
thɛ̌w	A row.
thɛ̌w níi	Around here.
chuan	To invite.
rîit	To press, iron.
rîit sûa	To iron a shirt.
thǔu	To scrub.
phɯ́ɯn	Floor.
thǔu phɯ́ɯn	To scrub the floor.
kaaŋ	To spread out, hang out.
múŋ	Mosquito net.
kaaŋ múŋ	To put up a mosquito net.
hǔŋ	To cook (especially rice).
hǔŋ khâaw	To cook rice.
thàan	Charcoal.
sǎamii	Husband.
phanrayaa	Wife.
kàw	To be old (opposite of *new* – not *young*).
thammadaa	Usual, common.

38.2 Patterns.

pen khây.	To have a fever.
pen wàt.	To have a cold.
pen rôok.	To have a disease.
pen bâa.	To be crazy.
tham yaŋŋay dii.	What would it be good to do? What should I do?
pay nǎy dii.	Where would it be good to go? Where should I go?
nâŋ thîi nǎy dii.	Where would it be good to sit? Where shall we sit?

231

๓๘.๓ บทสนทนา

ก. ไปไหนครับ คุณปรีชา

ข. อ้อ สวัสดีครับคุณสุจินต์
เป็นยังไงบ้าง ไม่ได้พบกันเลย

ก. สบายดีฮะ สองสามวันก่อน
ผมพบเพื่อนคุณที่สถานีรถไฟ

ข. ใครฮะ

ก. เขาทำงานอยู่กับคุณแต่ผมลืมชื่อเขา
เขาบอกว่าคุณไม่ได้ไปทำงานหลาย
วันแล้ว เป็นอะไรไปฮะ

ข. ไม่สบายนิดหน่อย

ก. เวลานี้สบายดีแล้วหรือฮะ

ข. สบายดีแล้วฮะ
คุณจะไปทำงานหรือฮะ

ก. เปล่าฮะ ที่ทำงานปิดวันหนึ่ง
ผมจะไปหาอะไรทาน
ไปด้วยกันไหมฮะ

ข. ขอบคุณมากฮะ
ผมหิวแล้วเหมือนกัน

ก. จะไปทานที่ร้านไหนดี

ข. ทานอาหารฝรั่งเป็นไหมฮะ

ก. เป็นฮะ ผมอยากทานมานานแล้ว

ข. ถ้ายังงั้นไปทานอาหารฝรั่งกัน

ก. แถวนี้มีร้านอาหารดี ๆ บ้างไหมฮะ

ข. มีอยู่ที่สี่แยกโน่นร้านหนึ่ง

38.3 Dialog.

A. pay nǎy khráp, khun priichaa.

   B. ʔɔ̌ɔ, sawàtdiᵋ khráp, khun sucin.
pen yaŋŋay bâaŋ.
mây dây phóp kan ləəy.

A. sabaay dii háʔ.
sɔ̌ɔŋ sǎam wan kɔ̀ɔn
phǒm phóp phûan khun
thîi sathǎanii rót fay.

   B. khray háʔ.

A. kháw tham ŋaan yùu ka khun.
tɛ̀ɛ phǒm lʉʉm chʉʉ kháw.
kháw bɔ̀ɔk wâa khun mây dây pay
tham ŋaan lǎay wan lɛ́ɛw.
pen ʔaray pay háʔ.

   B. mây sabaay nítnɔ̀y.

A. weelaa níi sabaay dii lɛ́ɛw lɔ̌ə háʔ.

   B. sabaay dii lɛ́ɛw háʔ.
khun ca pay tham ŋaan lɔ̌ə háʔ.

A. plàaw háʔ.
thîi tham ŋaan pìt wan nʉŋ.
phǒm ca pay hǎa ʔaray thaan.
pay dûaykan máy háʔ.

   B. khɔ̀ɔpkhun mâak háʔ.
phǒm hǐw lɛ́ɛw mʉankan.

A. ca pay thaan thîi ráan nǎy dii.

   B. thaan ʔaahǎan faràŋ pen máy háʔ.

A. pen háʔ.
phǒm yàak thaan maa naan lɛ́ɛw.

   B. thâa yaŋŋán pay thaan ʔaahǎan
faràŋ kan.

A. thɛ̌w níi mii ráan ʔaahǎan didii
bâaŋ máy háʔ.

   B. mii yùu thîi sìiyɛ̂ɛk nôon
ráan nʉŋ.

Where are you going, Preecha?

Oh, hello, Sujin.
How are you?
We haven't seen each other at all.

I'm fine.
A couple of days ago
I met a friend of yours
at the railroad station.

Who?

He works with you.
But I've forgotten his name.
He told me you hadn't gone
to work for several days.
What was wrong?

I wasn't feeling very well.

Are you all right now?

Yes.
Are you on your way to work?

No.
My office is closed for a day.
I'm going to get something to eat.
Do you want to go eat with me?

Thank you very much.
I'm hungry, too.

Where's a good place to go?

Can you eat Farang food?

Yes.
I've wanted to have some for a
long time.

Well then let's go and have some
Farang food.

Are there any good restaurants
around here?

There's one on the corner
over there.

233

๓๘.๔ แบบฝึกหัดการฟังและการออกเสียงสูงต่ำ

ก.

    แตกต่าง   เครื่องหมาย   หอพัก   รับรอง   ชมพู่

ข.

ชวนศรีไปดูหนัง
    ไปดูหนังไหม, ศรี

ชวนเอ๊ดไปดูหนัง
    ไปดูหนังไหม, เอ๊ด

ชวนแดงไปดูหนัง
    ไปดูหนังไหม, แดง

ชวนหน่อยไปดูหนัง
    ไปดูหนังไหม, หน่อย

ชวนต้อยไปดูหนัง
    ไปดูหนังไหม, ต้อย

ชวนประสงค์ไปดูหนัง
    ไปดูหนังไหม, ประสงค์

ชวนประพัทธ์ไปดูหนัง
    ไปดูหนังไหม, ประพัทธ์

ชวนประชุมไปดูหนัง
    ไปดูหนังไหม, ประชุม

ชวนประเสริฐไปดูหนัง
    ไปดูหนังไหม, ประเสริฐ

ชวนประภาสไปดูหนัง
    ไปดูหนังไหม, ประภาส

38.4 Tone identification and production.

a. Identify the tones and record the number of repetitions required.

To differ.	tɛɛk taaŋ	....	....
Symbol.	khrʉaŋ maay	....	....
Dormitory.	hɔɔ phak	....	....
To guarantee.	raprɔɔŋ	....	....
Rose apple.	chomphuu	....	....

b. Response drill.

The main purpose of this drill is to maintain tonal accuracy at high speed.

chuan sǐi pay duu nǎŋ. pay duu nǎŋ máy, sǐi.	Invite Sri to the show. Do you want to go to the show, Sri?
chuan ʔéɛt pay duu nǎŋ. pay duu nǎŋ máy, ʔéɛt.	Invite At to the show. Do you want to go to the show, At?
chuan dɛɛŋ pay duu nǎŋ. pay duu nǎŋ máy, dɛɛŋ.	Invite Daeng to the show. Do you want to go to the show, Daeng?
chuan nɔ̀y pay duu nǎŋ. pay duu nǎŋ máy, nɔ̀y.	Invite Noy to the show. Do you want to go to the show, Noy?
chuan tôy pay duu nǎŋ. pay duu nǎŋ máy, tôy.	Invite Toy to the show. Do you want to go to the show, Toy?
chuan prasǒŋ pay duu nǎŋ. pay duu nǎŋ máy, prasǒŋ.	Invite Prasong to the show. Do you want to go to the show, Prasong?
chuan praphát pay duu nǎŋ. pay duu nǎŋ máy, praphát.	Invite Prapat to the show. Do you want to go to the show, Prapat?
chuan prachum pay duu nǎŋ. pay duu nǎŋ máy, prachum.	Invite Prachum to the show. Do you want to go to the show, Prachum?
chuan prasɔ̀ət pay duu nǎŋ. pay duu nǎŋ máy, prasɔ̀ət.	Invite Prasert to the show. Do you want to go to the show, Prasert?
chuan praphâat pay duu nǎŋ. pay duu nǎŋ máy, praphâat.	Invite Prapart to the show. Do you want to go to the show, Prapart?

๓๘.๕ แบบฝึกหัดการสลับเสียงสูงต่ำ

ก.

ช่วยทำแกงให้หน่อย, ต้อย
    แกงหรือฮะ ทำแล้วฮ่ะ

ช่วยสั่งไข่ให้หน่อย, ต้อย
    ไข่หรือฮะ สั่งแล้วฮ่ะ

ช่วยรีดเสื้อให้หน่อย, ต้อย
    เสื้อหรือฮะ รีดแล้วฮ่ะ

ช่วยซ้อหมูให้หน่อย, ต้อย
    หมูหรือฮะ ซ้อแล้วฮ่ะ

ช่วยถูพื้นให้หน่อย, ต้อย
    พื้นหรือฮะ ถูแล้วฮ่ะ

ช่วยกางมุ้งให้หน่อย, ต้อย
    มุ้งหรือฮะ กางแล้วฮ่ะ

ช่วยปิดไฟให้หน่อย, ต้อย
    ไฟหรือฮะ ปิดแล้วฮ่ะ

ช่วยทอดหมูให้หน่อย, ต้อย
    หมูหรือฮะ ทอดแล้วฮ่ะ

ช่วยซื้อถ่านให้หน่อย, ต้อย
    ถ่านหรือฮะ ซื้อแล้วฮ่ะ

ช่วยหุงข้าวให้หน่อย, ต้อย
    ข้าวหรือฮะ หุงแล้วฮ่ะ

๓๘.๖ แบบฝึกหัดการออกเสียงสระและพยัญชนะ

ก.

ใครยึมปึน
    บัดยึมปึน

ปัดยึมปึนใคร
    บัดยึมปึนชั่น

บัดยึมปึนชั่น
    ชั่นก็ยึมปึนบัด

ชั่นยึมปึนบัด
    ปัดก็ยึมปึนชั่น

ข.

    กะเพื่อน   ปะถุง   กะควาย
    กับเพื่อน   บัดถุง   กักควาย

38.5 Tone manipulation.

a. Response drill.

chûay tham kɛɛŋ hây nɔ̀y, tôy.
    kɛɛŋ lɔ̌ə há. tham lɛ́ɛw hâ.

Please fix the curry for me, Toy.
    The curry? I've already fixed it.

chûay sàŋ khày hây nɔ̀y, tôy.
    khày lɔ̌ə há. sàŋ lɛ́ɛw hâ.

Please order some eggs for me, Toy.
    Eggs? I've already ordered some.

chûay rîit sûa hây nɔ̀y, tôy.
    sûa lɔ̌ə há. rîit lɛ́ɛw hâ.

Please iron my shirt for me, Toy.
    Your shirt? I've already ironed it.

chûay sʉ́ʉ mǔu hây nɔ̀y, tôy.
    mǔu lɔ̌ə há. sʉ́ʉ lɛ́ɛw hâ.

Please buy some pork for me, Toy.
    Pork? I've already bought some.

chûay thǔu phʉ́ʉn hây nɔ̀y, tôy.
    phʉ́ʉn lɔ̌ə há. thǔu lɛ́ɛw hâ.

Please scrub the floor for me, Toy.
    The floor? I've already scrubbed it.

chûay kaaŋ múŋ hây nɔ̀y, tôy.
    múŋ lɔ̌ə há. kaaŋ lɛ́ɛw hâ.

Please put up the mosquito net for me, Toy.
    The mosquito net? I've already put it up.

chûay pìt fay hây nɔ̀y, tôy.
    fay lɔ̌ə há. pìt lɛ́ɛw hâ.

Please turn the light off for me, Toy.
    The light? I've already turned it off.

chûay thɔ̂ɔt mǔu hây nɔ̀y, tôy.
    mǔu lɔ̌ə há. thɔ̂ɔt lɛ́ɛw hâ.

Please fry the pork for me, Toy.
    The pork? I've already fried it.

chûay sʉ́ʉ thàan hây nɔ̀y, tôy.
    thàan lɔ̌ə há. sʉ́ʉ lɛ́ɛw hâ.

Please buy some charcoal for me, Toy.
    Charcoal? I've already bought some.

chûay hǔŋ khâaw hây nɔ̀y, tôy.
    khâaw lɔ̌ə há. hǔŋ lɛ́ɛw hâ.

Please cook the rice for me, Toy.
    The rice? I've already cooked it.

38.6 Vowel and consonant drills.

a. Response drill.

    This is exactly the same as 19.6.

It should be done now at greater speed.

khray yʉ́ʉm pʉʉn.
    pʉ́ʉt yʉ́ʉm pʉʉn.

Who borrowed the gun?
    Puet borrowed the gun.

pʉ́ʉt yʉ́ʉm pʉʉn khray.
    pʉ́ʉt yʉ́ʉm pʉʉn chʉ̂ʉn.

Whose gun did Puet borrow?
    Puet borrowed Chuen's gun.

pʉ́ʉt yʉ́ʉm pʉʉn chʉ̂ʉn.
    chʉ̂ʉn kɔ̂ yʉ́ʉm pʉʉn pʉ́ʉt.

Puet borrowed Chuen's gun.
    Chuen borrowed Puet's gun, too.

chʉ̂ʉn yʉ́ʉm pʉʉn pʉ́ʉt.
    pʉ́ʉt kɔ̂ yʉ́ʉm pʉʉn chʉ̂ʉn.

Chuen borrowed Puet's gun.
    Puet borrowed Chuen's gun, too.

b. Final ?-p, ?-t, and ?-k contrast drills.

kà? phʉ̂an	pà? thǔŋ	kà? khwaay
kàp phʉ̂an	pàt thǔŋ	kàk khwaay

237

๓๘.๗ แบบฝึกหัดไวยากรณ์

ก.

จะทำยังไง
    ไม่รู้จะทำยังไงดี

จะไปไหน
    ไม่รู้จะไปไหนดี

จะนั่งที่ไหน
    ไม่รู้จะนั่งที่ไหนดี

จะบอกใคร
    ไม่รู้จะบอกใครดี

จะไปเมื่อไหร่
    ไม่รู้จะไปเมื่อไหร่ดี

จะขายเท่าไหร่
    ไม่รู้จะขายเท่าไหร่ดี

จะซื้อที่ร้านไหน
    ไม่รู้จะซื้อที่ร้านไหนดี

ข.

คุณพ่อชอบดูหนัง (แม่)
    คุณแม่ก็ชอบดูหนังเหมือนกัน

คุณปู่ไปธนาคาร (ไปรษณีย์)
    เขาไปไปรษณีย์ด้วย

คุณป้าไปหาหมอ (ลุง)
    คุณลุงก็ไปหาหมอเหมือนกัน

คุณหมอสั่งข้าวผัด (น้ำมะนาว)
    เขาสั่งน้ำมะนาวด้วย

นายกลับบ้านแล้ว (แหม่ม)
    แหม่มก็กลับบ้านแล้วเหมือนกัน

ลูกเรียนภาษาจีน (อังกฤษ)
    เขาเรียนภาษาอังกฤษด้วย

พี่ขับรถเป็น (น้อง)
    น้องก็ขับรถเป็นเหมือนกัน

หลานเรียนตอนเช้า (ตอนบ่าย)
    เขาเรียนตอนบ่ายด้วย

สามีไปเที่ยวไม่ได้ (ภรรยา)
    ภรรยาก็ไปเที่ยวไม่ได้เหมือนกัน

38.7 Grammar drills.

a. Response drill.

ca tham yaŋŋay.
  mây rúu ca tham yaŋŋay dii.

What are you going to do?
  I don't know what to do.

ca pay nǎy.
  mây rúu ca pay nǎy dii.

Where are you going to go?
  I don't know where to go.

ca nâŋ thîi nǎy.
  mây rúu ca nâŋ thîi nǎy dii.

Where are you going to sit?
  I don't know where to sit.

ca bɔ̀ɔk khray.
  mây rúu ca bɔ̀ɔk khray dii.

Who are you going to tell?
  I don't know who to tell.

ca pay mɨarày.
  mây rúu ca pay mɨarày dii.

When are you going to go?
  I don't know when to go.

ca khǎay thâwrày.
  mây rúu ca khǎay thâwrày dii.

How much are you going to sell it for?
  I don't know how much to sell it for.

ca sɨ́ɨ thîi ráan nǎy.
  mây rúu ca sɨ́ɨ thîi ráan nǎy dii.

Which store are you going to buy it at?
  I don't know which store to buy it at.

b. Response drill.

khun phɔ̂ɔ chɔ̂ɔp duu nǎŋ. (mɛ̂ɛ)
  khun mɛ̂ɛ kɔ̂ chɔ̂ɔp duu nǎŋ mɨankan.

Father likes to see shows. (Mother)
  Mother likes to see shows, too.

khun pùu pay thanaakhaan.
(praysanii)
  kháw pay praysanii dûay.

Grandfather went to the bank.
(post office)
  He went to the post office, too.

khun pâa pay hǎa mɔ̌ɔ. (luŋ)
  khun luŋ kɔ̂ pay hǎa mɔ̌ɔ mɨankan.

Auntie went to see a doctor. (Uncle)
  Uncle went to see a doctor, too.

khun mɔ̌ɔ sàŋ khâaw phàt.
(nám manaaw)
  kháw sàŋ nám manaaw dûay.

The doctor ordered fried rice.
(limeade)
  He ordered limeade, too.

naay klàp bâan lɛ́ɛw. (mɛ̀m)
  mɛ̀m kɔ̂ klàp bâan lɛ́ɛw mɨankan.

The master has come home. (madame)
  The madame has come home, too.

lûuk rian phasǎa ciin. (ʔaŋkrìt)
  kháw rian phasǎa ʔaŋkrìt dûay.

The child is studying Chinese. (English)
  He's studying English, too.

phîi khàp rót pen.
(nɔ́ɔŋ)
  nɔ́ɔŋ kɔ̂ khàp rót pen mɨankan.

Older brother can drive a car.
(younger brother)
  Younger brother can drive a car, too.

lǎan rian tɔɔn cháaw.
(tɔɔn bàay)
  kháw rian tɔɔn bàay dûay.

Nephew studies in the mornings.
(in the afternoons)
  He studies in the afternoons, too.

sǎamii pay thîaw mây dây.
(phanrayaa)
  phanrayaa kɔ̂ pay thîaw mây dây
  mɨankan.

The husband can't go out.
(the wife)
  The wife can't go out,
  either.

ค.

เป็นอะไร
    เปล่า, ไม่ได้เป็นอะไร

ไปไหน
    เปล่า, ไม่ได้ไปไหน

พูดกับใคร
    เปล่า, ไม่ได้พูดกับใคร

ทำอะไร
    เปล่า, ไม่ได้ทำอะไร

เปิดไฟที่ไหน
    เปล่า, ไม่ได้เปิดไฟที่ไหน

มาหาใคร
    เปล่า, ไม่ได้มาหาใคร

สั่งอะไร
    เปล่า, ไม่ได้สั่งอะไร

ถามใคร
    เปล่า, ไม่ได้ถามใคร

ง.

พี่ไปดูหนัง
    เขาชอบหนังที่เขาไปดูหรือเปล่า

สามีกำลังอ่านหนังสือ
    เขาชอบหนังสือที่เขากำลังอ่าน
    หรือเปล่า

คุณแม่ทานโอเลี้ยง
    เขาชอบโอเลี้ยงที่เขาทานหรือเปล่า

คุณลุงไปหาหมอ
    เขาชอบหมอที่เขาไปหาหรือเปล่า

คุณพ่อกำลังกินเบียร์
    เขาชอบเบียร์ที่เขากำลังกินหรือ
    เปล่า

ภรรยาซื้อรถยนต์
    เขาชอบรถยนต์ที่เขาซื้อหรือเปล่า

ลูกไปโรงเรียนทุกวัน
    เขาชอบโรงเรียนที่เขาไปทุกวัน
    หรือเปล่า

c. Response drill.

pen ?aray.
    plàaw. mây dây pen ?aray.

pay nǎy.
    plàaw. mây dây pay nǎy.

phûut kàp khray.
    plàaw. mây dây phûut kàp khray.

tham ?aray.
    plàaw. mây dây tham ?aray.

pə̀ət fay thîi nǎy.
    plàaw. mây dây pə̀ət fay thîi nǎy.

maa hǎa khray.
    plàaw. mây dây maa hǎa khray.

sàŋ ?aray.
    plàaw. mây dây sàŋ ?aray.

thǎam khray.
    plàaw. mây dây thǎam khray.

What's the matter?
Nothing's the matter.

Where did you go?
I didn't go anywhere.

Who did you talk to?
I didn't talk to anybody.

What did you do?
I didn't do anything.

Where did you turn a light on?
I didn't turn a light on anywhere.

Who have you come to see?
I haven't come to see anybody.

What did you order?
I didn't order anything.

Who did you ask?
I didn't ask anybody.

d. Response drill.

phîi pay duu nǎŋ.
    kháw chɔ̂ɔp nǎŋ thîi kháw pay duu
    rɨ́ plàaw.

sǎamii kamlaŋ ?àan naŋsɨ̆ɨ.
    kháw chɔ̂ɔp naŋsɨ̆ɨ thîi kháw kamlaŋ
    ?àan rɨ́ plàaw.

khun mɛ̂ɛ thaan ?oolíaŋ.
    kháw chɔ̂ɔp ?oolíaŋ thîi kháw thaan
    rɨ́ plàaw.

khun luŋ pay hǎa mɔ̆ɔ.
    kháw chɔ̂ɔp mɔ̆ɔ thîi kháw pay hǎa
    rɨ́ plàaw.

khun phɔ̂ɔ kamlaŋ kin bia.
    kháw chɔ̂ɔp bia thîi kháw kamlaŋ
    kin rɨ́ plàaw.

phanrayaa sɨ́ɨ rót yon.
    kháw chɔ̂ɔp rót yon thîi kháw sɨ́ɨ
    rɨ́ plàaw.

lûuk pay rooŋrian thúk wan.
    kháw chɔ̂ɔp rooŋrian thîi kháw pay
    thúk wan rɨ́ plàaw.

Older sister went to a show.
Did she like the show she went to?

The husband is reading a book.
Does he like the book he's reading?

Mother drank iced coffee.
Did she like the iced coffee she drank?

Uncle went to see a doctor.
Did he like the doctor he went to see?

Father is drinking some beer.
Does he like the beer he's drinking?

The wife bought a car.
Does she like the car she bought?

The daughter goes to school every day.
Does she like the school she goes
to every day?

๓๘.๔ วัน

วันที่หนึ่งเดือนมกราคมปีสองพันห้าร้อยสิบเอ็ด

๓๘.๕ การสนทนาโต้ตอบ

(เมื่อวันเสาร์ที่แล้วคุณสุจินต์ ซื้อโต๊ะทำงานใหม่ตัวหนึ่งเพราะว่าตัวเก่าเล็กไป วันเสาร์หน้าเขาจะซื้อเก้าอี้ทำงานสองตัว นะฮะ)

คุณสุจินต์ซื้อโต๊ะแล้วหรือยังฮะ	ซื้อแล้วฮะ
เขาซื้อเก้าอี้แล้วหรือยังฮะ	ยังฮะ
ใครซื้อฮะ	คุณสุจินต์ฮะ
ซื้ออะไรฮะ	ซื้อโต๊ะฮะ
โต๊ะอะไรฮะ	โต๊ะทำงานฮะ
กี่ตัวฮะ	ตัวเดียวฮะ
ซื้อเมื่อไหร่ฮะ	เมื่อวันเสาร์ที่แล้วฮะ
ซื้อทำไมฮะ	เพราะว่าโต๊ะตัวเก่าเล็กไปฮะ
โต๊ะตัวไหนใหญ่กว่าฮะ	ตัวใหม่ฮะ
ตัวไหนเล็กกว่าฮะ	ตัวเก่าฮะ
โต๊ะตัวใหม่เล็กกว่าตัวเก่าใช่ไหมฮะ	ไม่ใช่ฮะ, ตัวใหม่ใหญ่กว่าตัวเก่า
โต๊ะตัวเก่าเล็กกว่าตัวใหม่ใช่ไหมฮะ	ใช่ฮะ
โต๊ะตัวใหม่ใหญ่กว่าตัวเก่าใช่ไหมฮะ	ใช่ฮะ
โต๊ะตัวเก่าใหญ่กว่าตัวใหม่ใช่ไหมฮะ	ไม่ใช่ฮะ, ตัวเก่าเล็กกว่าตัวใหม่
วันเสาร์หน้าคุณสุจินต์จะซื้ออะไรฮะ	เก้าอี้ฮะ
เก้าอี้อะไรฮะ	เก้าอี้ทำงานฮะ
กี่ตัวฮะ	สองตัวฮะ
เมื่อวันเสาร์ที่แล้วคุณสุจินต์ซื้อเก้าอี้ ใช่ไหมฮะ	ไม่ใช่ฮะ, เขาซื้อโต๊ะ
โต๊ะกินข้าวใช่ไหมฮะ	ไม่ใช่ฮะ, โต๊ะทำงาน
สองตัวใช่ไหมฮะ	ไม่ใช่ฮะ, ตัวเดียว
ตัวเก่าใหญ่ไปใช่ไหมฮะ	ไม่ใช่ฮะ, เล็กไป
วันเสาร์หน้าเขาจะซื้อโต๊ะใช่ไหมฮะ	ไม่ใช่ฮะ, เขาจะซื้อเก้าอี้
เก้าอี้ธรรมดาใช่ไหมฮะ	ไม่ใช่ฮะ, เก้าอี้ทำงาน
ตัวเดียวใช่ไหมฮะ	ไม่ใช่ฮะ, สองตัว
เขาจะซื้อวันจันทร์หน้าใช่ไหมฮะ	ไม่ใช่ฮะ, วันเสาร์หน้า
จะซื้อโต๊ะกับเก้าอี้ใช่ไหมฮะ	ไม่ใช่ฮะ, จะซื้อเก้าอี้อย่างเดียว เขาซื้อโต๊ะแล้วฮะ

38.8 Dates.

1 January 2511 wan thîi nừŋ dựan mókkaraakhom pii sɔ̌ɔŋ phan hâa rɔ́ɔy sìp èt.

Practice reading the following dates for increased speed.

5	December	2470	12	August	2475	23	October	2453
22	February	1732	5	March	1953	10	May	1857
24	June	2475	6	April	2325	8	September	2497
4	July	1776	11	November	1918	12	October	1492
14	October	1066	14	July	1789	28	January	1925

38.9 Conversation.

(mừa wan sǎw thîi lɛ́ɛw khun sucin sựự tɔ́ʔ tham ŋaan mày tua nừŋ phrɔ́ʔ wâa tua kàw
lék pay. wan sǎw nâa kháw ca sựự kâwʔîi tham ŋaan sɔ̌ɔŋ tua. ná há.)

khun sucin sựự tɔ́ʔ lɛ́ɛw rú yaŋ há.
kháw sựự kâwʔîi lɛ́ɛw rú yaŋ há.
khray sựự há.
sựự ʔaray há.
tɔ́ʔ ʔaray há.
kìi tua há.
sựự mừaràay há.
sựự thammay há.
tɔ́ʔ tua nǎy yày kwàa há.
tua nǎy lék kwàa há.
tɔ́ʔ tua mày lék kwàa tua kàw chây máy há.
tɔ́ʔ tua kàw lék kwàa tua mày chây máy há.
tɔ́ʔ tua mày yày kwàa tua kàw chây máy há.
tɔ́ʔ tua kàw yày kwàa tua mày chây máy há.
wan sǎw nâa khun sucin ca sựự ʔaray há.
kâwʔîi ʔaray há.
kìi tua há.
mừa wan sǎw thîi lɛ́ɛw khun sucin sựự kâwʔîi
  chây máy há.
tɔ́ʔ kin khâaw chây máy há.
sɔ̌ɔŋ tua chây máy há.
tua kàw yày pay chây máy há.
wan sǎw nâa kháw ca sựự tɔ́ʔ chây máy há.
kâwʔîi thammadaa chây máy há.
tua diaw chây máy há.
kháw ca sựự wan can nâa chây máy há.
ca sựự tɔ́ʔ ka kâwʔîi chây máy há.

sựự lɛ́ɛw há.
yaŋ há.
khun sucin há.
sựự tɔ́ʔ há.
tɔ́ʔ tham ŋaan há.
tua diaw há.
mừa wan sǎw thîi lɛ́ɛw há.
phrɔ́ʔ wâa tɔ́ʔ tua kàw lék pay há.
tua mày há.
tua kàw há.
mây chây há.   tua mày yày kwàa tua kàw.
chây há.
chây há.
mây chây há.   tua kàw lék kwàa tua mày.
kâwʔîi há.
kâwʔîi tham ŋaan há.
sɔ̌ɔŋ tua há.

mây chây há.   kháw sựự tɔ́ʔ.
mây chây há.   tɔ́ʔ tham ŋaan.
mây chây há.   tua diaw.
mây chây há.   lék pay.
mây chây há.   kháw ca sựự kâwʔîi.
mây chây há.   kâwʔîi tham ŋaan.
mây chây há.   sɔ̌ɔŋ tua.
mây chây há.   wan sǎw nâa.
mây chây há.   ca sựự kâwʔîi yàaŋ diaw.
   kháw sựự tɔ́ʔ lɛ́ɛw há.

243

๓๘.๑๐ การเขียน

เขาจะไม่ให้ฝรั่งทำ

ใส่	อร่อย	คะ
ได้	สบาย	ล่ะ
ใกล้	เสมอ	จ้ะ
ไกล	สตางค์	อะไร
ใน	ตลาด	มะนาว
ไก่	ถนน	ประตู
เข้าใจ	สวัสดี	ราชประสงค์

38.10 Writing. (Seven ways of writing the short vowel *a*.)

เขาจะไม่ให้ฝรั่งทำ

khâw   ca   mây   hây   faràŋ   tham
They   won't   let   Farangs   do   it.

kháw is written in Thai with a rising tone, but it is almost always pronounced high.

a (or *aʔ*) at the end of a word is written as in *ca* (also pronounced *càʔ*), and the tone follows the rules of short, dead syllables (hòk, cèt, lék). At the end of a syllable that is not at the end of a word it is written with this same symbol in some words (manaaw) and with no symbol at all in others (faràŋ).

In syllables with consonant clusters, the first consonant determines the tone (note the word *klây*). Notice that words like *faràŋ*, *talàat*, and *thanŏn* are written just as if they were single syllables with consonant clusters (fràŋ, tlàat, thnŏn); and here, too, the first consonant determines the tone of the (following) syllable. But this is only true when the second consonant is a sonorant (r, l, y, w, m, n, or ŋ). Notice the word *sabaay*.

Practice reading and writing the following words. They should all be familiar.

Thai	Roman	Thai	Roman	Thai	Roman
ใส่	sày	อร่อย	ʔaròy	คะ	khá
ได้	dây	สบาย	sabaay	ละ	lâ
ใกล้	klây	เสมอ	samŏǝ	จะ	câ
ไกล	klay	สตางค์	sataaŋ	อะไร	ʔaray
ใน	nay	ตลาด	talàat	มะนาว	manaaw
ไก่	kày	ถนน	thanŏn	ประตู	pratuu
เข้าใจ	khâwcay	สวัสดี	sawàtdii	ราชประสงค์	râatprasŏŋ

245

บทที่ ๓๙

๓๙.๑ คำศัพท์

นึก	จาก
ล่ะ	กลับจากนอก
นี่	ยูซิส
ให้	เรื่อง
เขาให้ทำ	รู้เรื่อง
เพิ่ง	เรื่องอะไร
	หนังเรื่องอะไร
เบิก	
เงิน	คิดถึง
เบิกเงิน	
	แต่งงาน
นอก	
เมืองนอก	
ไปนอก	

๓๙.๒ โครงสร้างของประโยค

ทำไมล่ะ	ไม่รู้นี่
ใครล่ะ	เขาให้ทำนี่
อะไรล่ะ	
เมื่อไหร่ล่ะ	
ที่ไหนล่ะ	

LESSON 39

39.1 Vocabulary and expansions.

núk	To think.
lâ	This particle adds a slight accusation of wrong-doing to a question. 'Why *on earth* did you do it.'
nî	This particle shifts the blame away from the speaker. 'Because he told me to do it, *that's why*.'
hây	This covers the whole area of *let-have-make* in English.
kháw hây tham	He let me do it. He had me do it. He made me do it. He told me to do it. He asked me to do it.
phâŋ	Just now, just a few seconds ago.
bòək	To withdraw (money).
ŋən	Silver, money.
bòək ŋən	To withdraw money.
nôok	Outside, abroad.
mɯaŋ nôok	Foreign countries. Abroad.
pay nôok	To go abroad.
càak	From, to separate from.
klàp càak nôok	To return from abroad.
yuusít	USIS. United States Information Service.
rɯ̂aŋ	A story, a matter. A classifier for stories or happenings.
rúu rɯ̂aŋ	To know what's going on.
rɯ̂aŋ ʔaray	What's it about?
nǎŋ rɯ̂aŋ ʔaray	What's the name of the movie?
khít thɯ̌ŋ	To think about someone (used in the same situations where *to miss someone* is used in English).
tèŋŋaan	To marry, get married.

39.2 Patterns.

thammay lâ.	Why!? (Said with a rising–falling intonation.)
khray lâ.	Who!?
ʔaray lâ.	What!?
mɯ̂arày lâ.	When!?
thîi nǎy lâ.	Where!?
mây rúu nî.	I didn't know. (It's not my fault.)
kháw hây tham nî.	He made me do it. (It wasn't my idea.)

247

๓๕.๔ แบบฝึกหัดการฟังและการออกเสียงสูงต่ำ

ก.

ดอกบัว   หัวหอม   ยกย่อง   จิ้งหรีด   บรรทัด

ข.

ฉันชื่อแตน   เขาชื่อประภาส
   แตนหรือ, นึกว่าชื่อศรี   ประภาสหรือ, นึกว่าชื่อประสิทธิ์

ฉันชื่อตุ่ม   เขาชื่อประเสริฐ
   ตุ่มหรือ, นึกว่าชื่อศรี   ประเสริฐหรือ, นึกว่าชื่อประสิทธิ์

ฉันชื่อต้อย   เขาชื่อประสงค์
   ต้อยหรือ, นึกว่าชื่อศรี   ประสงค์หรือ, นึกว่าชื่อประสิทธิ์

ฉันชื่อตึ๊ก   เขาชื่อประพัทธ์
   ตึ๊กหรือ, นึกว่าชื่อศรี   ประพัทธ์หรือ, นึกว่าชื่อประสิทธิ์

ฉันชื่อตุ๋ย   เขาชื่อประชุม
   ตุ๋ยหรือ, นึกว่าชื่อศรี   ประชุมหรือ, นึกว่าชื่อประสิทธิ์

39.3 Dialogs.

The dialogs of lessons 25 and 30 were intended for comprehension only when they first appeared. Practice them now for active use.

39.4 Tone identification and production.

a. Identify the tones and record the number of repetitions required.

The lotus flower.	dɔɔk bua	....	....
Onions.	hua hɔɔm	....	....
To honor, praise.	yokyɔŋ	....	....
Crickets.	ciŋriit	....	....
A line of print.	banthat	....	....

b. Response drill.

The main purpose of this drill is to maintain tonal accuracy at high speed.

chán chûʉ tɛɛn.	My name is Taen.
tɛɛn lɔ̌ə. nʉ́k wâa chûʉ sǐi.	Taen? I thought it was Sri.
chán chûʉ tùm.	My name is Toom.
tùm lɔ̌ə. nʉ́k wàa chûʉ sǐi.	Toom? I thought it was Sri.
chán chûʉ tôy.	My name is Toy.
tôy lɔ̌ə. nʉ́k wâa chûʉ sǐi.	Toy? I thought it was Sri.
chán chûʉ tík.	My name is Tick.
tík lɔ̌ə. nʉ́k wâa chûʉ sǐi.	Tick? I thought it was Sri.
chán chûʉ tǔy.	My name is Tooy.
tǔy lɔ̌ə. nʉ́k wâa chûʉ sǐi.	Tooy? I thought it was Sri.
kháw chûʉ praphâat.	His name is Prapart.
praphâat lɔ̌ə. nʉ́k wâa chûʉ prasìt.	Prapart? I thought it was Prasit.
kháw chûʉ prasə̀ət.	His name is Prasert.
prasə̀ət lɔ̌ə. nʉ́k wâa chûʉ prasìt.	Prasert? I thought it was Prasit.
kháw chûʉ prasɔ̌ŋ.	His name is Prasong.
prasɔ̌ŋ lɔ̌ə. nʉ́k wâa chûʉ prasìt.	Prasong? I thought it was Prasit.
kháw chûʉ praphát.	His name is Prapat.
praphát lɔ̌ə. nʉ́k wâa chûʉ prasìt.	Prapat? I thought it was Prasit.
kháw chûʉ prachum.	His name is Prachum.
prachum lɔ̌ə. nʉ́k wâa chûʉ prasìt.	Prachum? I thought it was Prasit.

๓๕.๕ แบบฝึกหัดการสลับเสียงสูงต่ำ

ทำไมหุงข้าวให้เขาล่ะ
   ก็เขาให้หุงให้นี่

ทำไมทอดหมูให้เขาล่ะ
   ก็เขาให้ทอดให้นี่

ทำไมกางมุ้งให้เขาล่ะ
   ก็เขาให้กางให้นี่

ทำไมซื้อหมูให้เขาล่ะ
   ก็เขาให้ซื้อให้นี่

ทำไมสั่งไข่ให้เขาล่ะ
   ก็เขาให้สั่งให้นี่

ทำไมทำแกงให้เขาล่ะ
   ก็เขาให้ทำให้นี่

ทำไมรีดเสื้อให้เขาล่ะ
   ก็เขาให้รีดให้นี่

ทำไมถูพื้นให้เขาล่ะ
   ก็เขาให้ถูให้นี่

ทำไมปิดไฟให้เขาล่ะ
   ก็เขาให้ปิดให้นี่

ทำไมซื้อถ่านให้เขาล่ะ
   ก็เขาให้ซื้อให้นี่

๓๕.๖ แบบฝึกหัดการออกเสียงสระและพยัญชนะ

ก.

เพลินเปิดนานแล้วใช่ไหม
   ไม่ใช่, เพลินเพิ่งเปิด
เพลินตัดนานแล้วใช่ไหม
   ไม่ใช่, เพลินเพิ่งตัด

พันเบิกนานแล้วใช่ไหม
   ไม่ใช่, พันเพิ่งเบิก
พันรับนานแล้วใช่ไหม
   ไม่ใช่, พันเพิ่งรับ

ข.

นวลเหนียม	(ง่วง)	เนื่องเหนียม	(ง่วง)
นวลง่วง	(เหงี่ยม)	เนื่องง่วง	(หงวน)
เหงี่ยมง่วง	(เหนื่อย)	หงวนง่วง	(เหนื่อย)
เหงี่ยมเหนื่อย	(นวล)	หงวนเหนื่อย	(เนื่อง)
นวลเหนื่อย	(เงียบ)	เนื่องเหนื่อย	(เงียบ)
นวลเงียบ	(เหงี่ยม)	เนื่องเงียบ	(หงวน)
เหงี่ยมเงียบ	(เหนียม)	หงวนเงียบ	(เหนียม)
เหงี่ยมเหนียม	(เนื่อง)	หงวนเหนียม	

39.5 Tone manipulation.

a. Response drill.

thammay hǔŋ khâaw hây kháw lâ.
kɔ̂ kháw hây hǔŋ hây nî.

Why did you cook the rice for him?
Because he made me (had me) do it.

thammay thɔ̂ɔt mǔu hây kháw lâ.
kɔ̂ kháw hây thɔ̂ɔt hây nî.

Why did you fry the pork for him?
Because he made me do it. That's why.

thammay kaaŋ múŋ hây kháw lâ.
kɔ̂ kháw hây kaaŋ hây nî.

Why did you put up the mosquito net for him?
Because he made me do it. That's why.

thammay sɯ́ɯ mǔu hây kháw lâ.
kɔ̂ kháw hây sɯ́ɯ hây nî.

Why did you buy pork for him?
Because he made me do it. That's why.

thammay sàŋ khày hây kháw lâ.
kɔ̂ kháw hây sàŋ hây nî.

Why did you order eggs for him?
Because he made me do it. That's why.

thammay tham kɛɛŋ hây kháw lâ.
kɔ̂ kháw hây tham hây nî.

Why did you fix the curry for him?
Because he made me do it. That's why.

thammay rîit sɯ̂a hây kháw lâ.
kɔ̂ kháw hây rîit hây nî.

Why did you iron his shirt for him?
Because he made me do it. That's why.

thammay thǔu phɯ́ɯn hây kháw lâ.
kɔ̂ kháw hây thǔu hây nî.

Why did you scrub the floor for him?
Because he made me do it. That's why.

thammay pìt fay hây kháw lâ.
kɔ̂ kháw hây pìt hây nî.

Why did you turn the light off for him?
Because he made me do it. That's why.

thammay sɯ́ɯ thàan hây kháw lâ.
kɔ̂ kháw hây sɯ́ɯ hây nî.

Why did you buy charcoal for him?
Because he made me do it. That's why.

39.6 Vowel and consonant drills.

a. Response drill. (ə–a).

phlǝǝn pɔ̀ǝt naan lɛ́ɛw chây máy.
mây chây. phlǝǝn phôŋ pɔ̀ǝt.

Ploen opened it long ago, didn't she?
No. She opened it just now.

phlǝǝn tàt naan lɛ́ɛw chây máy.
mây chây. phlǝǝn phôŋ tàt.

Ploen cut it long ago, didn't she?
No. She cut it just now.

phan bɔ̀ǝk naan lɛ́ɛw chây máy.
mây chây. phan phôŋ bɔ̀ǝk.

Pun withdrew it long ago, didn't he?
No. He withdrew it just now.

phan ráp naan lɛ́ɛw chây máy.
mây chây. phan phôŋ ráp.

Pun got it long ago, didn't he?
No. He got it just now.

b. Substitution drill. (ŋ).

nuan nǐam.	(ŋûaŋ)	Nuan's shy.	nɯ̂aŋ nǐam.	(ŋûaŋ)	Nueang's shy.
nuan ŋûaŋ.	(ŋìam)	Nuan's sleepy.	nɯ̂aŋ ŋûaŋ.	(ŋǔan)	Nueang's sleepy.
ŋìam ŋûaŋ.	(nɯ̀ay)	Ngiam's sleepy.	ŋǔan ŋûaŋ.	(nɯ̀ay)	Nguan's sleepy.
ŋìam nɯ̀ay.	(nuan)	Ngiam's tired.	ŋǔan nɯ̀ay.	(nɯ̂aŋ)	Nguan's tired.
nuan nɯ̀ay.	(ŋîap)	Nuan's tired.	nɯ̂aŋ nɯ̀ay.	(ŋîap)	Nueang's tired.
nuan ŋîap.	(ŋìam)	Nuan's quiet.	nɯ̂aŋ ŋîap.	(ŋǔan)	Nueang's quiet.
ŋìam ŋîap.	(nǐam)	Ngiam's quiet.	ŋǔan ŋîap.	(nǐam)	Nguan's quiet.
ŋìam nǐam.	(nɯ̂aŋ)	Ngiam's shy.	ŋǔan nǐam.		Nguan's shy.

๓๕.๗ แบบฝึกหัดไวยากรณ์

ก.

คุณพ่อไปเชียงใหม่แล้วหรือยัง
  ไปแล้วไปเมื่อวานนี้
แล้วคุณแม่ล่ะ, ไปแล้วหรือยัง
  ยัง, เขาจะไปพรุ่งนี้

ลูกสาวกลับจากนอกแล้วหรือยัง
  กลับแล้ว, กลับเมื่อวานนี้
แล้วลูกชายล่ะ, กลับแล้วหรือยัง
  ยัง, เขาจะกลับพรุ่งนี้

ไปยูซอมแล้วหรือยัง
  ไปแล้ว, ไปเมื่อวานนี้
แล้วยูซิสล่ะ,, ไปแล้วหรือยัง
  ยัง, ฉันจะไปพรุ่งนี้

พี่ชายซื้อรถแล้วหรือยัง
  ซื้อแล้ว, ซื้อเมื่อวานนี้
แล้วพี่สาวล่ะ, ซื้อแล้วหรือยัง
  ยัง, เขาจะซื้อพรุ่งนี้

บอกคุณลุงแล้วหรือยัง
  บอกแล้ว, บอกเมื่อวานนี้
แล้วคุณป้าล่ะ, บอกเขาแล้วหรือยัง
  ยัง, ฉันจะบอกพรุ่งนี้

น้องสาวทำงานเสร็จแล้วหรือยัง
  เสร็จแล้ว, ทำเสร็จเมื่อวานนี้
แล้วน้องชายล่ะ, ทำเสร็จแล้วหรือยัง
  ยัง, เขาจะทำพรุ่งนี้

ข.

ประเสริฐช่วยประสงค์ นะฮะ
คนไหนประเสริฐ
  คนที่ช่วยประสงค์
คนไหนประสงค์
  คนที่ประเสริฐช่วย

ประภาสบอกประชุม นะฮะ
คนไหนประชุม
  คนที่ประภาสบอก
คนไหนประภาส
  คนที่บอกประชุม

ต้อยถามต๋อย นะฮะ
คนไหนต๋อย
  คนที่ถามต๋อย
คนไหนต้อย
  คนที่ต๋อยถาม

39.7 Grammar drills.

a. Response drill.

khun phɔ̂ɔ pay chiaŋmày lɛ́ɛw rɨ́ yaŋ.	Has your father been to Chiang Mai yet?
pay lɛ́ɛw. pay mɨ̂a waan níi.	Yes. He went there yesterday.
lɛ́ɛw khun mɛ̂ɛ lâ. pay lɛ́ɛw rɨ́ yaŋ.	And your mother? Has she gone yet?
yaŋ. kháw ca pay phrûŋ níi.	No. She's going tomorrow.
lûuk sǎaw klàp càak nɔ̂ɔk lɛ́ɛw rɨ́ yaŋ.	Has your daughter returned from abroad yet?
klàp lɛ́ɛw. klàp mɨ̂a waan níi.	Yes. She got back yesterday.
lɛ́ɛw lûuk chaay lâ. klàp lɛ́ɛw rɨ́ yaŋ.	And your son? Has he come back yet?
yaŋ. kháw ca klàp phrûŋ níi.	No. He'll return tomorrow.
pay yuusɔ̌m lɛ́ɛw rɨ́ yaŋ.	Have you been to USOM yet?
pay lɛ́ɛw. pay mɨ̂a waan níi.	Yes. I went there yesterday.
lɛ́ɛw yuusít lâ. pay lɛ́ɛw rɨ́ yaŋ.	And USIS? Have you been there yet?
yaŋ. chán ca pay phrûŋ níi.	No. I'm going there tomorrow.
phîi chaay sɨ́ɨ rót lɛ́ɛw rɨ́ yaŋ.	Has your older brother bought a car yet?
sɨ́ɨ lɛ́ɛw. sɨ́ɨ mɨ̂a waan níi.	Yes. He bought one yesterday.
lɛ́ɛw phîi sǎaw lâ. sɨ́ɨ lɛ́ɛw rɨ́ yaŋ.	And your older sister? Has she?
yaŋ. kháw ca sɨ́ɨ phrûŋ níi.	No. She's buying one tomorrow.
bɔ̀ɔk khun luŋ lɛ́ɛw rɨ́ yaŋ.	Have you told Uncle yet?
bɔ̀ɔk lɛ́ɛw. bɔ̀ɔk mɨ̂a waan níi.	Yes. I told him yesterday.
lɛ́ɛw khun pâa lâ. bɔ̀ɔk kháw lɛ́ɛw rɨ́ yaŋ.	And Auntie? Have you told her yet?
yaŋ. chán ca bɔ̀ɔk phrûŋ níi.	No. I'll tell her tomorrow.
nɔ́ɔŋ sǎaw tham ŋaan sèt lɛ́ɛw rɨ́ yaŋ.	Has your younger sister finished the work yet?
sèt lɛ́ɛw. tham sèt mɨ̂a waan níi.	Yes. She finished it yesterday.
lɛ́ɛw nɔ́ɔŋ chaay lâ.	And how about your younger brother?
tham sèt lɛ́ɛw rɨ́ yaŋ.	Has he finished it yet?
yaŋ. kháw ca tham phrûŋ níi.	No. He'll finish it tomorrow.

b. Response drill.

prasə̀ət chûay prasǒŋ, ná há.	Prasert helped Prasong.
khon nǎy prasə̀ət.	Which one is Prasert?
khon thîi chûay prasǒŋ.	The one who helped Prasong.
khon nǎy prasǒŋ.	Which one is Prasong?
khon thîi prasə̀ət chûay.	The one who Prasert helped.
praphâat bɔ̀ɔk prachum. ná há.	Prapart told Prachum.
khon nǎy prachum.	Which one is Prachum?
khon thîi praphâat bɔ̀ɔk.	The one who Prapart told.
khon nǎy praphâat.	Which one is Prapart?
khon thîi bɔ̀ɔk prachum.	The one who told Prachum.
tɔ̂y thǎam tɔ̌y. ná há.	Toy Fall asked Toy Rise.
khon nǎy tɔ̂y.	Which one is Toy Fall?
khon thîi thǎam tɔ̌y.	The one who asked Toy Rise.
khon nǎy tɔ̌y.	Which one is Toy Rise?
khon thîi tɔ̂y thǎam.	The one who Toy Fall asked.

ค.

เด็กผู้ชายไปดูหนัง
   เขาชอบหรือเปล่า
ใคร
   เด็กที่ไปดูหนัง
ชอบอะไร
   หนังที่เขาไปดู
ฮึม, เด็กที่ไปดูหนัง
ชอบหนังที่เขาไปดู
   เด็กที่ไปดูหนังชื่ออะไร
ชื่อแดง
   และหนังที่เขาไปดูเรื่องอะไร
เรื่องไซโค
   แล้วเด็กที่ไปดูหนัง
   ชอบหนังที่เขาไปดูใช่ไหม
ใช่, แดงชอบไซโค

เด็กผู้หญิงอ่านหนังสือ
   เขาชอบหรือเปล่า
ใคร
   เด็กที่อ่านหนังสือ
ชอบอะไร
   หนังสือที่เขาอ่าน
ฮึม, เด็กที่อ่านหนังสือ
ชอบหนังสือที่เขาอ่าน
   เด็กที่อ่านหนังสือชื่ออะไร
ชื่อแดง
   และหนังสือที่เขาอ่านเรื่องอะไร
เรื่องผู้ดี
   แล้วเด็กที่อ่านหนังสือ
   ชอบหนังสือที่เขาอ่านใช่ไหม
ใช่, แดงชอบผู้ดี

c. Response drill.

dèk phûu chaay pay duu năŋ.
  kháw chôɔp rɨ́ plàaw.
khray.
  dèk thîi pay duu năŋ.
chôɔp ʔaray.
  năŋ thîi kháw pay duu.
hm̂m. dèk thîi pay duu năŋ
chôɔp năŋ thîi kháw pay duu.
  dèk thîi pay duu năŋ
  chɨ̂ɨ ʔaray.
chɨ̂ɨ dɛɛŋ.
  lɛ́ʔ năŋ thîi kháw pay duu rɨ̂aŋ ʔaray.
rɨ̂aŋ *saykhoo.*
  lɛ́ɛw dèk thîi pay duu năŋ
  chôɔp năŋ thîi kháw pay duu chây máy.
chây. dɛɛŋ chôɔp *saykhoo.*

The little boy went to a show.
  Did he like it?
Who?
  The boy who went to a show.
Like what?
  The show he went to.
Yes. The boy who went to a show
liked the show he went to.
  What was the name of the boy
  who went to a show?
Daeng.
  And what was the show he went to?
Psycho.
  And the boy who went to a show
  liked the show he went to. Right?
Yes. Daeng liked *Psycho.*

dèk phûu yĭŋ ʔàan naŋsɨ̌ɨ.
  kháw chôɔp rɨ́ plàaw.
khray.
  dèk thîi ʔàan naŋsɨ̌ɨ.
chôɔp ʔaray.
  naŋsɨ̌ɨ thîi kháw ʔàan.
hm̂m. dèk thîi ʔàan naŋsɨ̌ɨ
chôɔp naŋsɨ̌ɨ thîi kháw ʔàan.
  dèk thîi ʔàan naŋsɨ̌ɨ
  chɨ̂ɨ ʔaray.
chɨ̂ɨ dɛɛŋ.
  lɛ́ʔ naŋsɨ̌ɨ thîi kháw ʔàan rɨ̂aŋ ʔaray.
rɨ̂aŋ *phûu dii*
  lɛ́ɛw dèk thîi ʔàan naŋsɨ̌ɨ
  chôɔp naŋsɨ̌ɨ thîi kháw ʔàan chây máy.
chây. dɛɛŋ chôɔp *phûu dii.*

The little girl read a book.
  Did she like it?
Who?
  The girl who read a book.
Like what?
  The book she read.
Yes. The girl who read a book
liked the book she read.
  What was the name of the girl
  who read a book?
Daeng.
  And what was the book she read?
Good People.
  And the girl who read a book
  liked the book she read. Right?
Yes. Daeng liked *Good People.*

39.8 Days and months.

Write the English names of the months and days of the week on cards. Go through them giving the Thai names as fast as you can. Shuffle them and go through them again. Continue practicing until you can do it in under 30 seconds.

255

๓๕.๑๐ การเขียน

กางเกงของเพื่อนแดงอยู่ที่โรงเรียน

เธอเคยเดิน   ลืมชื่อ   ปวดหัว

เขาจะไม่ให้ฝรั่งทำ   คิดถึงเด็กทุกคน

เด็กเก่งต้องทำเอง

39.9 Conversation.

The teacher should read the narrative of lesson 30 to the students and ask them the questions.

39.10 Writing.   Summary of vowels.

Examples of the twelve long vowel sounds appear in the following sentences.

กางเกงของเพื่อนแดงอยู่ที่โรงเรียน

เธอเคยเดิน   ลืมชื่อ   ปวดหัว

And here are examples of six of the nine short vowels.

เขาจะไม่ให้ฝรั่งทำ   คิดถึงเด็กทุกคน

The *e–ee* distinction can be shown only when there is no tonal marker: the vowel shortener never appears together with a tonal marker. But this leads to very few possible ambiguities since almost all of the words with tonal markers are short.

เด็กเก่งต้องทำเอง

dèk kèŋ tôŋ tham ʔeeŋ
Clever children must do it themselves.

With only one common exception (khɛ̌ŋ, which is written with the vowel shortener), the length distinction for the vowels ɛ, ɔ, and ə is not shown in the Thai system of writing. This will offer no problem in writing words that you already know.   But when you see these vowels in unfamiliar words written in Thai writing, you will not know whether they are long or short.   With the following guide, however, you will be right most of the time.

In words with no final consonant, long.   tɛ̀ɛ, plɛɛ, khɔ̌ɔ phɔɔ, thəə.

In words with a final but no tone marker, long. dɛɛŋ, khɛ̌ɛn, pɛ̀ɛt, nɔɔn, sɔ̌ɔŋ, thɔ̀ɔt, dəən, pə̀ət. But notice: hɛm, thɔ̌y, ŋən.

In words with a final consonant and *mǎy thoo*, long. hɛ̂ɛn, lɛ́ɛw, kɔ̂ɔn, rɔ́ɔn. But notice: hɔ̂ŋ, tôŋ.

In words with a final consonant and *mǎy ʔèek*, short. tɛ̀ŋŋaan, ʔarɔ̀y, phâŋ. But notice: kɔ̀ɔn.

The three vowel clusters (ia, ɯa, and ua) almost never occur short.

257

บทที่ ๔๐

ตัวเขาเอง   นอกจาก   ย่า   แก   สะใภ้   แก่   อ่อน

คุณประสิทธิ์แต่งงานแล้วแต่เขายังอยู่ที่บ้านพ่อแม่เขา เขามีพี่น้องสี่คน มีพี่ชาย พี่สาว ตัวเขาเองแล้วก็น้องสาวคนหนึ่ง คุณประสิทธิ์กับภรรยาเขามีลูกคนเดียวเป็นผู้ชาย ชื่อแดง พี่น้องของประสิทธิ์ยังไม่มีใครแต่งงาน นอกจากตัวเขาเอง

ที่บ้านนั้นมีทั้งหมดแปดคน ถ้าถามคุณประสิทธิ์ว่ามีใครบ้าง เขาจะบอกว่านอกจากตัวเขาเอง มีพ่อ แม่ พี่ชาย พี่สาว น้องสาวแล้วก็ภรรยากับลูก

ถ้าถามแดงเขาจะบอกว่านอกจากตัวเขาเองมีปู่ ย่า ลุง ป้า อาแล้วก็พ่อแม่เขา

ถ้าถามคุณพ่อของประสิทธิ์ แกจะบอกว่านอกจากตัวแกเอง มีภรรยา ลูกชายสองคน ลูกสาวสองคนแล้วก็ลูกสะใภ้กับหลาน

ถ้าถามพี่ชายของประสิทธิ์ เขาจะบอกว่านอกจากตัวเขาเอง มีพ่อ แม่ น้องสาวสองคน น้องชายคนหนึ่งแล้วก็น้องสะใภ้กับหลาน

ถ้าถามน้องสาวของประสิทธิ์เขาจะบอกว่านอกจากตัวเขาเองมีพ่อ แม่ พี่ชายสองคน พี่สาวคนหนึ่ง แล้วก็พี่สะใภ้กับหลาน

พ่อของประสิทธิ์เป็นอะไรกับแดง	เป็นปู่
แม่ของประสิทธิ์เป็นอะไรกับแดง	เป็นย่า
พี่ชายของประสิทธิ์เป็นอะไรกับแดง	เป็นลุง
แล้วพี่สาวล่ะ	เป็นป้า
ภรรยาของประสิทธิ์เป็นอะไรกับแดง	เป็นแม่
น้องสาวของประสิทธิ์เป็นอะไรกับแดง	เป็นอา
แม่ของแดงเป็นอะไรกับประสิทธิ์	เป็นภรรยา
ปู่ของแดงเป็นอะไรกับประสิทธิ์	เป็นพ่อ
แล้วย่าล่ะ	เป็นแม่

LESSON 40

(Review)

40.a Review sections 3,5,7, and 9 of lessons 36-39.

40.b Narrative.

tua kháw ʔeeŋ	He himself, she herself.
nɔ̂ɔkcàak	Outside from, besides.
yâa	Father's mother, grandmother.
kɛɛ	He, she (moɪe respectful than *kháw*).
sapháy	A female relative by marriage, female in-law.
kɛ̀ɛ	To be old (compare *kàw*, page 231).
ʔɔ̀ɔn	To be young.

khun prasìt tɛ̀ŋŋaan lɛ́ɛw, tɛ̀ɛ kháw yaŋ yùu thîi bâan phɔ̂ɔ mɛ̂ɛ kháw. kháw mii phîi nɔ́ɔŋ sìi khon. mii phîi chaay, phîi sǎaw, tua kháw ʔeeŋ, lɛ́ɛw kɔ̂ nɔ́ɔŋ sǎaw khon nɯŋ. khun prasìt kàp phanrayaa kháw mii lûuk khon diaw. pen phûu chaay. chɯ̂ɯ dɛɛŋ. phîi nɔ́ɔŋ khɔ́ŋ prasìt yaŋ mây mii khray tɛ̀ŋŋaan nɔ̂ɔk càak tua kháw ʔeeŋ.

thîi bâan nán mii tháŋmòt pɛ̀ɛt khon. thâa thǎam khun prasìt wâa mii khray bâan, kháw ca bɔ̀ɔk wâa nɔ̂ɔkcàak tua kháw ʔeeŋ mii phɔ̂ɔ, mɛ̂ɛ, phîi chaay, phîi sǎaw, nɔ́ɔŋ sǎaw, lɛ́ɛw kɔ̂ phanrayaa kàp lûuk.

thâa thǎam dɛɛŋ, kháw ca bɔ̀ɔk wâa nɔ̂ɔkcàak tua kháw ʔeeŋ mii pùu, yâa, luŋ, pâa, ʔaa, lɛ́ɛw kɔ̂ phɔ̂ɔ mɛ̂ɛ kháw.

thâa thǎam khun phɔ̂ɔ khɔ́ŋ prasìt, kɛɛ ca bɔ̀ɔk wâa nɔ̂ɔkcàak tua kɛɛ ʔeeŋ mii phanrayaa, lûuk chaay sɔ̌ɔŋ khon, lûuk sǎaw sɔ̌ɔŋ khon, lɛ́ɛw kɔ̂ lûuk sapháy kàp lǎan.

thâa thǎam phîi chaay khɔ́ŋ prasìt kháw ca bɔ̀ɔk wâa nɔ̂ɔkcàak tua kháw ʔeeŋ mii phɔ̂ɔ, mɛ̂ɛ, nɔ́ɔŋ sǎaw sɔ̌ɔŋ khon, nɔ́ɔŋ chaay khon nɯŋ, lɛ́ɛw kɔ̂ nɔ́ɔŋ sapháy kàp lǎan.

thâa thǎam nɔ́ɔŋ sǎaw khɔ́ŋ prasìt, kháw ca bɔ̀ɔk wâa nɔ̂ɔkcàak tua kháw ʔeeŋ mii phɔ̂ɔ, mɛ̂ɛ, phîi chaay sɔ̌ɔŋ khon, phîi sǎaw khon nɯŋ, lɛ́ɛw kɔ̂ phîi sapháy kàp lǎan.

After reading and listening to the following questions and answers for comprehension, try answering them without looking.

phɔ̂ɔ khɔ́ŋ prasìt pen ʔaray kàp dɛɛŋ.	pen pùu.
mɛ̂ɛ khɔ́ŋ prasìt pen ʔaray kàp dɛɛŋ.	pen yâa.
phîi chaay khɔ́ŋ prasìt pen ʔaray kàp dɛɛŋ.	pen luŋ.
lɛ́ɛw phîi sǎaw lâ.	pen pâa.
phanrayaa khɔ́ŋ prasìt pen ʔaray kàp dɛɛŋ.	pen mɛ̂ɛ.
nɔ́ɔŋ sǎaw khɔ́ŋ prasìt pen ʔaray kàp dɛɛŋ.	pen ʔaa.
mɛ̂ɛ khɔ́ŋ dɛɛŋ pen ʔaray kàp prasìt.	pen phanrayaa.
pùu khɔ́ŋ dɛɛŋ pen ʔaray kàp prasìt.	pen phɔ̂ɔ.
lɛ́ɛw yâa lâ.	pen mɛ̂ɛ.

(More.)

259

ลุงของแดงเป็นอะไรกับประสิทธิ์	เป็นพี่ชาย
แล้วป้าล่ะ	เป็นพี่สาว
อาของแดงเป็นอะไรกับประสิทธิ์	เป็นน้อง
แดงเป็นอะไรกับพ่อของเขา	เป็นลูก
แดงเป็นอะไรกับแม่ของเขา	เป็นลูก
แดงเป็นอะไรกับปู่ของเขา	เป็นหลาน
แดงเป็นอะไรกับย่าของเขา	เป็นหลาน
แดงเป็นอะไรกับลุงของเขา	เป็นหลาน
ประสิทธิ์เป็นอะไรกับภรรยาของเขา	เป็นสามี
ประสิทธิ์เป็นอะไรกับปู่ของแดง	เป็นลูก
ประสิทธิ์เป็นอะไรกับลุงของแดง	เป็นน้อง
ประสิทธิ์เป็นอะไรกับอาของแดง	เป็นพี่
ประสิทธิ์เป็นอะไรกับแม่ของแดง	เป็นสามี

พ่อของประสิทธิ์แก่กว่าลุงของแดงใช่ไหม	ใช่
แม่ของประสิทธิ์แก่กว่าป้าของแดงใช่ไหม	ใช่
น้องของประสิทธิ์แก่กว่าลุงของแดงใช่ไหม	ไม่ใช่
ลุงของแดงแก่กว่าพ่อของประสิทธิ์ใช่ไหม	ไม่ใช่
ป้าของแดงแก่กว่าอาของแดงใช่ไหม	ใช่
อาของแดงอ่อนกว่าลุงของแดงใช่ไหม	ใช่
ป้าของแดงอ่อนกว่าอาของแดงใช่ไหม	ไม่ใช่
ป้าของแดงอ่อนกว่าปู่ของแดงใช่ไหม	ใช่
ย่าของแดงอ่อนกว่าป้าของแดงใช่ไหม	ไม่ใช่
ลุงของแดงอ่อนกว่าย่าของแดงใช่ไหม	ใช่
อาของแดงแก่กว่าหรืออ่อนกว่าพี่ของประสิทธิ์	อ่อนกว่า
น้องของประสิทธิ์แก่กว่าหรืออ่อนกว่าป้าของแดง	อ่อนกว่า
ลุงของแดงแก่กว่าหรืออ่อนกว่าอาของแดง	แก่กว่า
ลุงของแดงกับอาของแดงใครแก่กว่ากัน	ลุงแก่กว่า
อาของแดงกับป้าของแดงใครแก่กว่ากัน	ป้าแก่กว่า
พ่อของแดงกับอาของแดงใครอ่อนกว่ากัน	อาอ่อนกว่า

260

luŋ khɔ́ŋ dɛɛŋ pen ʔaray kàp prasìt.   pen phîi chaay.
léɛw pâa lâ.   pen phîi sǎaw.
ʔaa khɔ́ŋ dɛɛŋ pen ʔaray kàp prasìt.   pen nɔ́ɔŋ.
dɛɛŋ pen ʔaray kàp phɔ̂ɔ khɔ́ŋ kháw.   pen lûuk.
dɛɛŋ pen ʔaray kàp mɛ̂ɛ khɔ́ŋ kháw.   pen lûuk.
dɛɛŋ pen ʔaray kàp pùu khɔ́ŋ kháw.   pen lǎan.
dɛɛŋ pen ʔaray kàp yâa khɔ́ŋ kháw.   pen lǎan.
dɛɛŋ pen ʔaray kàp luŋ khɔ́ŋ kháw.   pen lǎan.
prasìt pen ʔaray kàp phanrayaa khɔ́ŋ kháw.   pen sǎamii.
prasìt pen ʔaray kàp pùu khɔ́ŋ dɛɛŋ.   pen lûuk.
prasìt pen ʔaray kàp luŋ khɔ́ŋ dɛɛŋ.   pen nɔ́ɔŋ.
prasìt pen ʔaray kàp ʔaa khɔ́ŋ dɛɛŋ.   pen phîi.
prasìt pen ʔaray kàp mɛ̂ɛ khɔ́ŋ dɛɛŋ.   pen sǎamii.

phɔ̂ɔ khɔ́ŋ prasìt kɛ̀ɛ kwàa luŋ khɔ́ŋ dɛɛŋ chây máy.   chây.
mɛ̂ɛ khɔ́ŋ prasìt kɛ̀ɛ kwàa pâa khɔ́ŋ dɛɛŋ chây máy.   chây.
nɔ́ɔŋ khɔ́ŋ prasìt kɛ̀ɛ kwàa luŋ khɔ́ŋ dɛɛŋ chây máy.   mây chây.
luŋ khɔ́ŋ dɛɛŋ kɛ̀ɛ kwàa phɔ̂ɔ khɔ́ŋ prasìt chây máy.   mây chây.
pâa khɔ́ŋ dɛɛŋ kɛ̀ɛ kwàa ʔaa khɔ́ŋ dɛɛŋ chây máy.   chây.
ʔaa khɔ́ŋ dɛɛŋ ʔɔ̀ɔn kwàa luŋ khɔ́ŋ dɛɛŋ chây máy.   chây.
pâa khɔ́ŋ dɛɛŋ ʔɔ̀ɔn kwàa ʔaa khɔ́ŋ dɛɛŋ chây máy.   mây chây.
pâa khɔ́ŋ dɛɛŋ ʔɔ̀ɔn kwàa pùu khɔ́ŋ dɛɛŋ chây máy.   chây.
yâa khɔ́ŋ dɛɛŋ ʔɔ̀ɔn kwàa pâa khɔ́ŋ dɛɛŋ chây máy.   mây chây.
luŋ khɔ́ŋ dɛɛŋ ʔɔ̀ɔn kwàa yâa khɔ́ŋ dɛɛŋ chây máy.   chây.
ʔaa khɔ́ŋ dɛɛŋ kɛ̀ɛ kwàa rɨ́ ʔɔ̀ɔn kwàa phîi khɔ́ŋ prasìt.   ʔɔ̀ɔn kwàa.
nɔ́ɔŋ khɔ́ŋ prasìt kɛ̀ɛ kwàa rɨ́ ʔɔ̀ɔn kwàa pâa khɔ́ŋ dɛɛŋ.   ʔɔ̀ɔn kwàa.
luŋ khɔ́ŋ dɛɛŋ kɛ̀ɛ kwàa rɨ́ ʔɔ̀ɔn kwàa ʔaa khɔ́ŋ dɛɛŋ.   kɛ̀ɛ kwàa.
luŋ khɔ́ŋ dɛɛŋ kàp ʔaa khɔ́ŋ dɛɛŋ khray kɛ̀ɛ kwàa kan.   luŋ kɛ̀ɛ kwàa.
ʔaa khɔ́ŋ dɛɛŋ kàp pâa khɔ́ŋ dɛɛŋ khray kɛ̀ɛ kwàa kan.   pâa kɛ̀ɛ kwàa.
phɔ̂ɔ khɔ́ŋ dɛɛŋ kàp ʔaa khɔ́ŋ dɛɛŋ khray ʔɔ̀ɔn kwàa kan.   ʔaa ʔɔ̀ɔn kwàa.

(More.)

คุณประสิทธิ์มีพี่น้องกี่คน	สี่คน
เขามีพี่กี่คน	สองคน
เขามีน้องกี่คน	คนเดียว
คุณประสิทธิ์แต่งงานแล้วหรือยัง	แต่งงานแล้ว
เขามีลูกกี่คน	คนเดียว
แดงแต่งงานแล้วหรือยัง	ยัง
เขามีพี่น้องกี่คน	มีเขาคนเดียว
พี่ชายคุณประสิทธิ์แต่งงานแล้วหรือยัง	ยัง
เขามีพี่น้องกี่คน	สี่คน
ปู่ของแดงมีลูกกี่คน	สี่คน
มีหลานกี่คน	คนเดียว
คุณประสิทธิ์มีลูกชายกี่คน	คนเดียว
เขามีลูกสาวกี่คน	ไม่มีเลย
ย่าของแดงมีลูกสะใภ้กี่คน	คนเดียว
เป็นภรรยาของใคร	ของคุณประสิทธิ์
ก่อนประสิทธิ์แต่งงาน ที่บ้านเขามีคนอยู่กี่คน	หกคน
แล้วเดี๋ยวนี้มีกี่คน	แปดคน
คุณประสิทธิ์มีพี่สะใภ้กี่คน	ไม่มีเลย
ภรรยาของคุณประสิทธิ์มีลูกกี่คน	คนเดียว
ผู้หญิงหรือผู้ชาย	ผู้ชาย
เขามีพี่น้องกี่คน	ไม่ทราบ

262

khun prasìt mii phîi nɔ́ɔŋ kìi khon.

kháw mii phîi kìi khon.

kháw mii nɔ́ɔŋ kìi khon.

khun prasìt tὲŋŋaan lέεw rɯ́ yaŋ.

kháw mii lûuk kìi khon.

dεεŋ tὲŋŋaan lέεw rɯ́ yaŋ.

kháw mii phîi nɔ́ɔŋ kìi khon.

phîi chaay khun prasìt tὲŋŋaan lέεw rɯ́ yaŋ.

kháw mii phîi nɔ́ɔŋ kìi khon.

pùu khɔ́ŋ dεεŋ mii lûuk kìi khon.

mii lǎan kìi khon.

khun prasìt mii lûuk chaay kìi khon.

kháw mii lûuk sǎaw kìi khon.

yâa khɔ́ŋ dεεŋ mii lûuk sapháy kìi khon.

pen phanrayaa khɔ́ŋ khray.

kɔ̀ɔn prasìt tὲŋŋaan, thîi bâan kháw mii khon yùu kìi khon.

lέεw dǐawníi mii kìi khon.

khun prasìt mii phîi sapháy kìi khon.

phanrayaa khɔ́ŋ khun prasìt mii lûuk kìi khon.

phûu yǐŋ rɯ́ phûu chaay.

kháw mii phîi nɔ́ɔŋ kìi khon.

sìi khon.

sɔ̌ɔŋ khon.

khon diaw.

tὲŋŋaan lέεw.

khon diaw.

yaŋ.

mii kháw khon diaw.

yaŋ.

sìi khon.

sìi khon.

khon diaw.

khon diaw.

mây mii ləəy.

khon diaw.

khɔ́ŋ khun prasìt.

hòk khon.

pὲεt khon.

mây mii ləəy.

khon diaw.

phûu chaay.

mây sâap.

GLOSSARY

The following alphabetical order is followed in the glossary: ʔ a b c d e ə ɛ f h i k m n ŋ o ɔ p r s t u ʉ w y. The number immediately following each entry refers to the sectio where it is first used.

ʔaa 26.4 Father's younger sibling.

ʔaahǎan 3.3 Food.

ʔàan 13.5 To read.

ʔameerikaa 17.2 America.

ʔameerikan 9.3 American.

ʔaŋkrìt 9.2 England, English.

ʔaŋkhaan (See following entries.)

  daaw ʔaŋkhaan Mars.

  wan ʔaŋkhaan 27.8 Tuesday.

ʔaray 6.5 What? Something.

ʔarɔ̀y 23.3 To taste good.

ʔathít 26.7 Week.

  phráʔ ʔathít Sun.

  wan ʔathít 27.8 Sunday.

ʔaw 17.3 To take, to accept.

ʔâw 32.9 A word used to announce that a demonstration is ready to start. All right?

ʔeeŋ 26.3 Self.

ʔeerawan 6.3 Erawan (a hotel).

ʔee yuu ʔee 11.7 AUA. American University Alumni Association.

ʔèt 4.8 One (in 21, 31, etc.).

ʔìik 8.3 Another, one more, more.

  ʔìik thii 8.3 Again, another time.

ʔìm 23.3 To have eaten enough.

ʔooliaŋ 23.2 Black, iced coffee.

ʔooyúaʔ 23.2 Black, hot coffee.

ʔop 8.4 To roast or bake.

ʔɔ̌ɔ 19.3 Oh, I see.

ʔɔ̀ɔk 29.7 To exit, to go or come out.

ʔɔ̀ɔn 40.b To be soft, tender, young.

ʔɔpfít 37.7 Office.

ʔûan 1.5 To be fat.

ʔùtnǔn 31.4 To patronize, support.

bàa 2.6 Shoulder.

bâa 38.2 Crazy.

bâan 10.b House, home.

baaŋ 33.2 To be thin.

baaŋsɛ̌ɛn 29.4 Bang Saen (a resort beach in Chon Buri Province).

bâaŋ 17.3 Some.

bàat 7.8 Baht, ticals.

bàay 14.4 Afternoon.

banthát 39.4 A line of print.

baŋkháp 34.4 To force.

bay 22.5 Leaf. A classifier for container (dishes, glasses, etc.).

bəə 13.3 Number. (See 13.1)

bə̀ək 39.6 To withdraw (money).

bɛ́ŋ 28.3 Bank.

bia 23.3 Beer.

bìip 9.6 To squeeze.

bon 8.3 On, the upper part of.

  khâŋbon 8.3 Upstairs.

bɔ̀ɔk 18.3 To tell.

bɔ̀y 25.b Often.

burìi 14.7 Cigaret.

câ 1.2 Polite particle, confirmative. (See 1.1 and 3.1)

cá 4.2 Polite particle. (See 1.1).

càʔ, ca 11.3 Will.

càak 32.9 From, to separate from.

caam 29.6 To sneeze.

caan 12.6, 22.3 A plate.

cam 29.6 To remember.

can (See following entries.)

  phráʔ can The moon.

  wan can 17.4 Monday.

càp 12.6 To catch, grab.

cèt 3.8 Seven.

chaa 23.3 Tea.

cháa 14.3 To be slow.

chaam 21.5 A bowl.

265

cháaŋ 37.4 Elephant.

   cháaŋ phùak 37.4 White elephant.

châat 25.b Nationality.

cháaw 14.4 Morning.

chaay 7.3 Male (people only).

chǎay 18.10 To shine a light.

chát 34.3 To be clear, distinct.

chây 9.3 To be the one meant, to be so, to be a fact. That's right.

cháy 13.5 To use.

chét 12.6 To wipe.

chəən 11.3 To invite. Go ahead. Please do.

chiaŋmày 26.4 Chiang Mai (a province in northern Thailand).

chín 24.3 A piece of something.

chomphûu 38.4 Rose apple.

chɔ́ɔn 12.6 A spoon.

chɔ̂ɔp 7.4 To like.

chûamooŋ 27.3 An hour.

chuan 35.b To invite.

chûay 17.3 To help. (See 17.1)

chûak 28.7 Rope.

chɯ̂ɯ 18.3 Name, to be named.

ciin 14.2 Chinese.

cìip 29.6 To pleat; to flirt.

cîŋcòk 36.5 House lizard.

cîŋrìit 39.4 Crickets.

cìp 29.6 To sip.

còtmǎay 23.4 A letter (mail).

cɔ̀ɔt 26.3 To park, bring to a stop.

cuan 29.3 Almost, approaching, getting close to.

cɯ̀ɯt 24.7 To be tasteless.

dàa 27.6 To curse, scold, swear at.

daaw 27.9 Stars.

dâay 11.6 Thread.

dam 16.6 Black.

dan 31.4 To push.

dây 8.3 Can, to be able.

dây 18.1, 24.5 To get.

dèk 7.1 Child (the age term: boy or girl).

dəən 6.3 To walk.

dɛɛŋ 14.4 Red.

dèɛt 17.4 Sunshine, sunlight.

diaw 19.3 Single, only one, one and the same.

dǐaw 22.3 In a moment.

dǐawníi 35.6 Now.

dichán 8.2 I (woman speaking). (See 8.1)

dii 1.5 To be good.

dinsɔ̌ɔ 16.3 Pencil.

dɔ̀ɔk bua 39.4 The lotus flower.

dûay 17.3 Also, too. (See 17.1)

dûaykan 21.3 Together.

duu 32.2 To look at.

dɯan 26.7 Month.

dɯŋ 11.6 To pull.

fáa 14.4 Sky, light blue.

fan 33.3 Teeth.

faŋ 18.5 To listen to.

faràŋ 24.1 Occidental (European, American, etc.).

fay 16.3 Fire, light, electricity.

fǒn 18.10 Rain.

hâ, há 32.9 Short form of *khâ, khá*.

há? 31.3 Short from of *khráp*.

hâa 1.8 Five.

hǎa 13.3 To look for.

hâaŋ 34.3 A business firm, store.

hây 17.3 To give. (See 17.1)

hěn 7.4 To see.

hɛ̂ɛŋ 8.4 To be dry.

hǐn 22.5 Rock, stone.

hǐw 21.3 To hunger or thirst for.

   hǐw khâaw 21.1 To be hungry.

   hǐw náam 21.1 To be thirsty.

hm̂m 3.5 A confirmative. (See 3.1)

hòk 2.8 Six.

hɔ̂ŋ 3.2 Room.

   hɔ̂ŋnáam 7.3 Bathroom.

hɔ̂ŋkoŋ 15.b Hong Kong.

hɔ̌ɔ phák 38.4 Dormitory.

hɔ̌ɔm 23.2 To smell good, fragrant.

hǔa 37.10 Head.

hǔahǐn 26.4 Hua Hin (a resort beach in Prachuab Khiri Khan Province).

hǔa hɔ̌ɔm 39.4 Onions.

hǔarɔ́ʔ 32.4 To laugh.

hǔŋ 38.5 To cook (especially rice).

hǔu 16.4 Ear.

kaaŋ 38.5 To spread out, hang out.

kaafɛɛ 23.3 Coffee.

kâaw 3.8 Nine.

kâaw 14.6 A step, to step.

kamlaŋ 30.b In the process of.

   kamlaŋ ca 32.3 To be about to.

kan 6.5 The other, each other, mutually.

kanyaayon 36.8 September.

kaŋkeeŋ 27.5 Trousers.

   kaŋkeeŋ nay 37.9 Underpants.

kàp 6.9 With, and.

karákkadaakhom 36.8 July.

kàt 9.6 To bite.

kaw 28.6 To scratch lightly.

kàw 38.9 To be old (not new).

kâwʔii 19.4 Chair.

kày 7.4 Chicken.

kèŋ 15.b To be skillful or good at something.

kə̀ət 9.6 To be born.

kɛɛ 40.b He, she (respectful).

kɛ̂ɛ 40.b To be old in age.

kɛ̂ɛ 26.3 To repair, make right.

kɛ̂ɛm 16.4 Cheeks.

kɛɛŋ 13.6 Curry.

kɛ̂ɛw 13.6 Glass, a glass.

khâ 1.3 Polite particle, confirmative. (See 1.1 and 3.1)

khá 2.3 Polite particle. (See 1.1)

khǎa 34.7 Leg.

khâaŋ 4.1 A side.

khâaw 21.3 Rice.

khǎaw 14.4 White.

khǎay 11.3 To sell.

kham 19.3 Word.

khan 28.1 Classifier for cars.

khanǒm 23.1 Pastry, sweets, dessert.

khanǒmpaŋ 23.7 Bread.

khàp 26.3 To drive.

kháp 32.3 Tight.

khàw 28.4 The knees.

khâw 29.7 To enter, to go or come in.

kháw 1.9 He, she, they (people only)

khâwcay 8.3 To understand.

khày 24.3 Eggs.

   khày daaw 27.9 Fried eggs.

   khày lûak 27.9 Very soft boiled eggs.

khây 38.2 A fever.

khǎy 29.6 To unlock, to wind a clock.

khěmkhàt 33.4 A belt.

khəəy 37.2 To have ever, used to.

khɛ̌ɛn 13.6 Arm, sleeve.

khɛ̌ŋ 23.3 To be hard.

khìa 17.3 To remove or dislodge something with light stroking movements of the finger or some instrument.

khǐan 13.5 To write.

khǐaŋ 33.5 A chopping board.

khǐaw 14.4 Green.

khîi kìat 31.4 To be lazy.

khîi nǐaw 36.4 To be stingy.

khiim 33.5 Pliers.

khít 26.9 To figure, think.

   khít thǔŋ 39.10 To think about someone (used in the same situations where *to miss someone* is used in English).

khon 2.9 Person, people.

khón khwáa 26.4 To research.

khoorâat 27.4 Korat (a city in northeast Thailand).

khɔɔ sɔ̌ɔ 14.8 The Christian era.

khɔ̌ɔ 2.3 To ask for.

   khɔ̌ɔ thôot 2.3 Excuse me, I'm sorry.

khɔ̌ɔnkɛ̀n 21.4 Khon Kaen (a province in northeast Thailand).

khɔ̌ɔŋ 22.2 Things.

khɔ̌ɔŋ, khɔ̌ŋ, khɔ́ŋ 36.2 Of (possessive).

khɔ̌ɔpcay 25.c Thanks (used with intimates or social inferiors).

khɔ̌ɔpkhun 3.3 Thanks.

khɔɔy 26.3 To wait for.

khráp 1.3 Polite particle, confirmative. (See 1.1 and 3.1)

khray 7.9 Who?

khrók 33.5 A mortar.

khrua 13.4 Kitchen.

khruu 34.4 Teacher.

khrûaŋ mǎay 38.4 Symbol.

khrûŋ 21.8 Half.

khùan 13.6 To scratch (painfully).

khùat 21.5 A bottle.

khúk khàw 28.4 To kneel.

khun 4.3 A respectful title, you. (See 4.1 and 6.1)

khùt 29.6 To dig.

khûu 31.3 A pair (classifier).

khùut 29.6 To scrape off.

khûn 29.1 To ascend, to go or come up. To increase.

khɯɯn 31.8 Night.

khwǎa 4.2 Right (hand or side).

khwaay 6.5 Water buffalo.

kìi 14.6 How many?

kiloo (kram) 28.7 Kilogram.

kiloo (méet) 28.7 Kilometer.

kin 11.4 To eat.

klaaŋ 24.3 Center, middle.

klaaŋ wan 24.3 Midday.

klàp 12.3 To return.

klàp rót 27.3 To turn the car around.

klay 28.7 To be far.

klây 11.3 To be near.

klɯa 23.7 Salt.

koon nùat 32.4 To shave.

kɔ̂ 14.6 Also, too.

kɔ̀ɔn 11.3 Before, first.

kɔ̂ɔn 33.3 A lump. Classifier for things in lumps.

kradàat 16.3 Paper.

kruŋthêep 28.7 Bangkok.

kúaytǐaw 23.3 Noodles.

kumphaaphan 33.8 February.

kûŋ 7.4 Shrimps.

kùak 23.6 Shoes (vulgar).

kùap 29.1 Almost, approximately, being close to.

kwàa 6.5 More (than),—er (than).

lâ 4.3 A question particle. (See 4.1)

lâ 39.5 A particle. (See 39.1)

lá 34.3 Per.

láan 19.8 A million.

lǎan 11.4 Nephew, niece, grandchild.

lâaŋ 8.3 Lower.

khâŋ lâaŋ 8.3 Downstairs.

láaŋ 31.4 To wash.

lǎay 26.3 Several.

lǎŋ 4.2 The back.

lǎŋ càak 36.2 After.

lǎŋ 27.5 Classifier for houses.

lǎŋkhaa 34.4 Roof.

lêek 12.3 Number. (See 13.1)

lêek thîi 12.3 A number used as a designation. (See 13.1)

lèk 33.5 Iron.

lék 2.5 To be little.

lêm 27.5 Classifier for books.

lɔ̌ɔ 2.3 A question particle. (See 2.1)

ləəy 27.3 To be beyond.

ləəy . . . pay 27.3 To go beyond . . . .
mây . . . ləəy 4.5 Not . . . at all.

ləəy 35.6 Therefore, so.

lɛ́ʔ 15.b And.

lɛ́ɛw 4.3 And then, subsequently.

lɛ́ɛw kɔ̂ 22.3 And, and then.

lɛ́ɛw 8.3 Already. (See 8.1)

líaw 6.3 To turn.

lìik lîaŋ 34.4 To avoid.

líncìi 27.4 Litchi, lichee nuts.

lít 28.7 Liter.

lom 16.3 Wind, air.

lòm 2.4 A muddy place.

lóm 2.4 To fall over, topple.

loŋ 27.3 29.2 To descend, to go or come down. To diminish.

lɔ́ɔ   28.1   Wheel.

lɔ̀ɔt   33.3 Tube. Classifier for things in tubes.

lûak   27.9   To scald.

lǔam   32.2   To be loose.

lûat   23.4   A wire.

luŋ   11.4   Older brother of father or mother, uncle.

lûuk   7.5   Child (the relationship term: son or daughter).

lûuk   22.5   A ball of something. Classifier for 'ball' like things.

lûuk hǐn   22.5   A marble.

lǔaŋ   14.4   Yellow.

luɯm   17.3   To forget.

maa   8.1   To come.

mǎa   27.5   Dog.

mâak   3.3   Very, a lot.

máay   17.3   Wood, a stick.

man   24.1   Potatoes, yams, etc.

  man faràŋ   24.1   Potatoes.

  man thɔ̂ɔt   24.3   Fried potatoes, potato chips.

man   28.7   The fat of an animal.

manaaw   22.3   Limes.

máykhìit   17.3   Matches.

màay   11.3   To be new, anew.

mây   1.5   Not.

  mâydây...   13.5   Didn't ...

mây   3.4   To burn.

máy   1.5   A question particle. (See 1.1)

mǎy   3.4   Silk.

mêek   17.4   Clouds.

meesǎayon   34.8 April.

méet   28.7   Meter.

mét   22.5   A seed. Classifier for 'kernel' like things.

mɛ̂ɛ   17.4   Mother.

  mɛ̂ɛ khrua   37.10   A cook (female).

mɛ̂ɛ rɛɛŋ   32.4   A car jack.

mɛ̀m   36.1   Ma'am. The usual term used by servants when speaking to or about a Farang lady.

mia lǔaŋ   37.4   Major wife.

mii   7.4   To have, there is.

miinaakhom   34.8   March.

mîit   33.5   Knife.

míthunaayon   37.8   June.

mókkaraakhom   33.8   January.

mooŋ   21.8   O'clock (daytime hours).

mòt   32.3   To be all gone, to the last one.

mɔ̀ʔsǒm   28.4   To be appropriate.

mɔ̌ɔ   32.2   Doctor.

  mɔ̌ɔ nûat   36.4   Masseur, masseuse.

mɔ̌ɔn   19.4   Pillow.

muan   34.7   Classifier for cigarets.

mûaŋ   14.4   Purple.

múŋ   38.5   Mosquito net.

  múŋ lûat   23.4   A wire screen.

mǔu   7.4   Pig, pork.

mɯ̂a   24.2   When . . .

  mɯ̂arày   When?

mɯ̌ankan   22.3   Likewise.

mɯaŋ   34.3   Town, city, country.

  mɯaŋ nɔ̂ɔk   39.1   Foreign countries.

mɯɯ   16.4   Hands.

mɯ̀ɯn   16.8   Ten thousand.

mɯ̂ɯt   18.3   To be dark.

ná   7.9, 14.3   A question particle. (See 7.1, 14.1, and 19.1)

naa   1.4   Rice field.

nâa   1.4   Face.

  khâŋ nâa   4.2   In front of.

náa   4.4   Mother's younger sibling.

nǎa   1.4   To be thick.

nâa rák   37.4   Cute, loveable.

naalikaa   11.8   Watch, clock, o'clock (in the 24 hour system).

náam   7.3   Water, liquid, juice, fluid. (See nám.)

naan   26.2   To be long in time.

nâataaŋ   16.3   Window.

naathii   11.8   Minute.

nǎaw   17.4   Cold (weather).

naay   34.3   Mr., master, boss.

  naay hâaŋ   34.3   The boss of a firm. (See 34.1)

nàk 28.7 To be heavy.

námkhěŋ 23.3 Ice.

námman 28.7 Oil, gasoline.

námŋən 16.6 Blue.

nám phrík 25.b A hot sauce.

námtaan 23.7 Sugar.

nân 6.7 There.

nán 2.9 That, the one mentioned.

nâŋ 20.b To sit.

năŋ 32.2 Moving pictures.

naŋsǔu 14.3 Book.

nay 29.7 In.

năy 3.3 Where? Which?

nəəy 24.1 Butter.

   nəəy khěŋ 24.3 Cheese.

nɛ́ʔnam 29.4 To advise, introduce.

nɛ̂ɛ 24.3 To be certain.

nĭam 29.6 To be shy.

nî 39.5 A sentence particle. (See 39.1)

nîi 3.2 Here.

níi 6.3 This.

nítnɔ̀y 14.3 A little bit.

níw 16.4 Fingers, toes.

nom 23.7 Milk, cream.

nôon 3.3 Over there.

nóon 6.2 That (farther away than nán).

nɔ̂ɔk 24.3 Outside of, abroad.

   nɔ̂ɔkcàak 40.b Outside of, besides.

nɔ̂ɔmáay 33.4 Bamboo shoots.

nɔɔn 7.1 To lie down.

nɔ́ɔŋ 11.4 Younger brother or sister.

nɔ́ɔynàa 22.4 Custard apple.

nɔ̀y 14.3 A little. (See 14.1)

nǔu 4.2 Mouse. (See 4.1, 6.1, and 8.1)

nɯ́a 7.4 Meat, beef.

nɯ̀ay 34.6 To be tired.

nɯ́k 39.4 To think.

nɯ̀ŋ 2.8 One.

ŋaan 9.3 Work, party, ceremony.

ŋán 30.c Short for thâa yaŋŋán.

ŋən 33.5 Silver, money.

ŋîap 34.6 To be quiet.

ŋûaŋ nɔɔn 8.6 To be sleepy.

pàa 2.6 Jungle.

pâa 21.6 The older sister of one's Father or mother, aunt.

pǎa 9.6 Father (used mainly with foreigners).

pàak 16.4 Mouth.

pàaknáam 24.4 Paknam (a town at the mouth of the Chao Phya River).

pàkkaa (pàakkaa) 27.4 Pen.

pám 29.3 Pump.

   pám námman 29.3 A gas pump, a gas station.

pàt 17.6 To brush or dust off.

pàw 9.6 To blow (with the mouth).

pay 6.3 To go.

pay 28.3 Too. 'Going' in the direction of excess.

pen 2.3, 10.b To be someone or something.

pen 26.3 To be mentally able, to know how.

pen 38.3 To have or be in some unnatural condition.

pépsîi 21.4 Pepsi Cola.

pèt 27.9 Duck.

pɔ̀ət 17.6 To open, turn on.

pɛ̀ɛt 3.8 Eight.

phaa 32.3 To take someone somewhere.

phàa 2.6 To split, cut open.

phâa 9.6 Cloth.

phàan 33.3 To pass a fixed object.

phǒnyoothin 17.8 Paholyothin (a road).

phanrayaa 38.7 Wife.

phàk kàat 9.6 Lettuce.

phamâa 14.2 Burmese.

phan 13.8 A thousand.

phárɯhàt (See following entries.)

   daaw phárɯhàt Jupiter.

   wan phárɯhàt 27.8 Thursday.

phasǎa 14.3 Language.

phàt 22.3 To stir fry.

phát 16.3 To blow (as the wind).

phátlom 16.3 Electric fan.

phǎw 29.4, 31.4 To burn something.

  phǎw sòp 29.4 To cremate a corpse.

phèt 24.7 To be hot (peppery).

phôŋ (phûŋ) 18.6 Just a minute ago.

phɛ́ʔ 8.4 A goat.

phɛ́ɛ 26.6 To lose to someone (as in a game).

phɛɛŋ 28.3 Expensive.

phɛ̀n 22.5 A sheet of something. A classifier for 'sheet' like things.

phîi 9.6 Older brother or sister.

phǐw nǎŋ 27.4 Skin.

phlɔɔncìt 9.2 Ploenchit (a road).

phǒm (phóm) 8.2 I (man speaking). (See 8.1)

phǒm 3.2 Hair (head only).

phǒnlamáay 24.3 Fruit.

phóp 11.3 To see, meet, find.

phɔɔ 23.3 Enough.

  phɔɔ cháy dây 31.3 Good enough to use, passable.

phɔɔ 32.9 As soon as.

phɔɔ sɔ́ɔ 14.8 The Buddhist era.

phɔ̂ɔ 7.5 Father.

phɔ̌ɔm 1.5 To be thin.

phrík 23.1 Peppers, chilies.

  phrík thay 23.7 Pepper.

phrɔ́ʔ 23.2 To sound good.

phrɔ́ʔ 27.3 Because.

phrûŋ níi 28.8 Tomorrow.

phrʉ́tsacikaayon 33.8 November.

phrʉ́tsaphaakhom 34.8 May.

phút (See following entries.)

  daaw phút Mercury.

  wan phút 17.4 Wednesday.

phûu 7.3 Person.

  phûu chaay 7.3 Boy, man.

  phûu yǐŋ 7.3 Girl, woman.

phuukhǎw 33.4 Mountains.

phûut 8.3 To speak.

phʉ̂an 30.b Friend.

phʉ́ʉn 38.5 Floor.

pii 30.b Year.

pìi 9.6 A wind instrument, horn.

pîŋ 27.9 To toast.

pìt 19.3 To close, turn off.

plaa 7.4 Fish.

plàaw 11.3 Empty. No.

plɛɛ 24.3 To mean, to translate.

pòkkatìʔ 27.9 Normally, ordinarily.

pɔ̌ɔn 26.6 To feed someone.

pratuu 16.3 Door.

praysanii 28.3 Post office.

prɛɛŋ 33.4 A brush, to brush.

prìap thîap 22.4 To compare.

pùat 37.10 To ache.

puu 27.9 Crab.

pùu 9.6 Father's father, grandfather.

pʉʉn 19.6 Gun.

ráan 3.3 Shop, store.

râatdamrìʔ 11.2 Rajdamri (a road).

râatprasǒŋ 11.3 Rajprasong (an intersection).

raaw 28.3 Approximately.

raaykaan 26.9 A list of items.

rakhaa 31.3 Price, cost.

ráksǎa 34.4 To take care of, treat.

ráp 26.3 To receive, to pick up someone.

rápprathaan 21.1 To eat (formal).

ráprɔɔŋ 38.4 To guarantee.

raw 24.3 We, I, you.

ray 2.3 Short from of ʔaray.

rew 21.3 Fast.

rîak 14.3 To call.

rian 11.3 To study.

rîap rɔ́ɔy 29.4 In good order.

rîit 38.5 To press, iron.

rôok 38.2 A disease.

rooŋrian 11.3 School.

rooŋrɛɛm 4.3 Hotel.

rópkuan 33.4 To bother.

rót 26.3 Any wheeled vehicle.

  rót fay 27.2 Train.

  rót mee 27.2 Bus.

271

rót yon 26.1 Automobile.

rɔŋtháaw 31.3 Shoes.

rɔɔ 22.3 To wait for.

rɔ́ɔn 2.5 To be hot.

rɔ́ɔŋhâay 32.4 To cry.

rɔ́ɔy 12.8 A hundred.

rúu 13.3 To know (a subject). (See 13.1)

rúucàk 6.3 To know a person, place, or thing. To be acquainted with. (See 13.1)

rŭɯ (rú) 7.9 Or.

rɯ̂aŋ 39.7 A story, a matter. Classifier for stories or happenings.

rɯɯn (See following entry.)

   marɯɯn níi 29.8 The day after tomorrow.

sǎaladɛɛŋ 11.2 Saladaeng (an intersection).

sǎam 1.8 Three.

sǎamlɔ́ɔ 28.3 Samlor, tricycle taxi.

sǎamii 38.7 Husband.

sâaŋ 29.6 To build.

sâap 13.3 To know (information). (See 13.1)

sǎathɔɔn 22.4 Sathorn (a road).

sǎaw 19.9 Young woman, unmarried woman.
saay 22.5 Sand.

sàay 29.6 To move back and forth.

sáay 4.3 Left (hand or side).

sǎay 14.4 Late morning.

sabaay 2.3 To be comfortable, feel nice.

sabùu 33.3 Soap.

sák 31.3 At least, or so.

salàt 27.9 Salad.

samɔ̌ɔ 30.b Always.

sân 3.5 To be short (in length).

sanǎam 17.4 Yard, field, court.

sàŋ 11.4 To order, leave a message.

sapháy 40.b A female in-law.

sapɔ̀ɔt khláp 32.9 Sports Club.

sataaŋ 26.1 One hundredth part of a baht. Money.

sathǎanii 27.3 Station.

sathǎanthûut 9.3 Embassy.

sǎw (See following entries.)

   daaw sǎw Saturn.

wan sǎw 17.4 Saturday.

sawàtdii 1.3 Greetings, hello, goodbye.

sày 7.4 To put in or on.

sên 22.5 A line. Classifier for 'string' like things.

sèt 22.3 To finish, be finished.

sɛ̌ɛn 18.8 A hundred thousand.

sɛɛnwít 24.3 Sandwich.

sɛ̂ɛt 14.4 Orange (the color).

sî 34.4 A sentence particle requesting an action. (See 34.1)

sí 18.3 A sentence particle requesting an action. (See 18.1)

sǐa 26.3 To be spoiled, out of order.

sìi 2.8 Four.

siiyɛ̂ɛk 6.3 Intersection (four forks).

sǐi 14.4 Color.

sǐi 33.3 To rub, scrub.

   sǐi fan 31.4 To brush the teeth.

sǐŋhǎakhom 36.8 August.

sìp 3.8 Ten.

sôm 26.4 Oranges, tangerines, grapefruits.

   sôm ʔoo 26.4 Pomelo.

sòŋ 17.3 To send. (See 17.1)

sǒŋkhlǎa 24.4 Songkhla (a province in southern Thailand).

soodaa 23.4 Soda water.

sòp 29.4 A corpse.

sɔɔŋ 34.7 An envelope. A pack of cigarets.

sɔ̌ɔŋ 1.8 Two.

sɔɔy 12.3 Soi, lane.

sûam 7.1 Toilet.

sǔan 37.10 A garden, orchard, or park.

sǔan lum 32.9 Lumpini Park.

sùk (See following entries.)

   daaw sùk Venus.

   wan sùk 17.4 Friday.

sùkhǎa 7.1 Toilet (formal).

sùkhǔmwít 12.3 Sukhumvit (a road).

súp 24.3 Soup.

suriwoŋ 37.3 Suriwong (a road).

sùt 34.3 The end, extreme, utmost.

sǔun　12.3　Zero.

sǔuŋ　2.5　To be tall.

sùup　33.4　To draw on, pump, smoke.

sùa　19.4　Mat.

sûa　31.2　Upper garment, shirt, blouse, coat, sweater.

sûa chɔ́ət　27.4　A dress shirt.

sûa nay　37.9　Undershirt.

sûa phâa　32.3　Clothing.

sùksǎa　32.4　To educate.

súɯ　7.4　To buy.

suɯn　(See following entry.)

　mûa wan suɯn níi　29.8　The day before yesterday.

taa　11.6　Eyes.

taam　22.3　To follow.

talàat　4.3　Market.

tamnɛ̀ŋ　36.4　Rank, position.

tamrùat　27.3　Police.

taŋ　26.9　The usual pronunciation of *sataaŋ*.

tâŋ　29.6　To set up.

taŋhàak　36.5　On the contrary.

tàt　3.2　To cut.

tênram　24.4　To dance (western style).

tɛ̀ɛ　15.b　But.

tɛ̀ɛk tàaŋ　38.4　To differ.

tɛ̀ŋŋaan　39.1　To marry, get married.

thâa　18.3　If.

thâa yaŋŋán　22.3　In that case.

thǎam　18.3　To ask.

thaan　21.3　Short for *rápprathaan*. To eat.

thàan　38.5　Charcoal.

thaaŋ　4.3　Way, path.

tháaw　31.3　Feet.

thàay rûup　29.4　To photograph.

thák　21.4　To greet, say hello to.

tham　9.3　To do, make.

　tham dûay　33.5　To be made of.

　tham ŋaan　9.3　To work.

thammadaa　38.9　Usual, common.

thammay　21.3　Why?

thanaakhaan　28.2　Bank.

thanwaakhom　33.8　December.

tháŋ　25.b　All of.

　tháŋ sɔ̌ɔŋ　25.b　Both.

　tháŋmòt　25.c　Altogether.

thǎŋ　21.5　A bucket.

tháp　12.3　To lay on top of.

thâwnán　15.b　Only.

thâwrày　12.3　How much? How many?

thay　14.2　Thai.

thəə　37.10　You (to an intimate or inferior)

thəəm　2.6　Term.

thɛɛŋ　27.6　To stab.

thɛ́ksîi　27.3　Taxi.

thɛ̌w　38.3　A row.

thîaŋ　14.4　Noon.

thîaw　22.2　To go form place to place.

thii　8.3　A time.

　thii lǎŋ　37.2　Afterwards, later.

thîi　3.3　At.

thîi　17.3　A place.

　thîi khìa burìi　17.3　Ash tray.

thîi　12.3　Precedes cardinal numbers to form ordinals. -th.

thîi　36.7　The relative pronoun. Who, that, which.

thîisùt　34.3　The most, extremely.

thíŋ　11.6　To throw away.

thoo　24.3　Short form of *thoorasàp*.

thoorasàp　13.3　Telephone, to telephone.

thôot　2.3　Punishment.

thɔɔn　29.3　To give change to.

thɔɔŋ　18.4　Gold.

thɔ̂ɔt　11.4　To fry (in large pieces).

thɔ̌y　26.3　To back up.

thùa ŋɔ̂ɔk　37.4　Bean sprouts.

thûay　23.7　A cup.

thúk　36.9　Every.

thûm　23.8　O'clock (used only with hours from evening to midnight).

thǔŋ　34.3　A sack, bag.

thǔŋtháaw　34.3　Stockings.

thúráʔ　32.3　An item of business, an errand.

thuu　(See following entry.)

273

plaa thuu 8.4 A fish resembling a herring or a mackerel.

thǔu 38.5 To scrub.

thùuk 16.3 To be correct. (See 16.2)

thùuk 28.1 To be cheap.

thɤ̆ŋ 6.3 To arrive at, reach.

thɤ̆ɤ tua 37.4 To be haughty.

tia 2.5 To be short (in height).

tiaŋ 19.4 Bed.

tii 1.6 To beat, hit.

tóʔ 20.b Table.

tòkloŋ 22.3 To come to an agreement, decide.

tôm 24.3 To boil something.

   tôm yam 27.9 A hot, sour soup.

tôn hèet 34.4 The cause of something.

tôn máay 22.4 Tree.

tɔ̂ŋ 18.3 To have to, must.

tɔ̂ŋkaan 19.3 To want, need.

tɔ̀ɔ rakhaa 35.b To bargain.

tɔɔn 14.4 A section or period.

   tɔɔn yen 14.4 Evening.

tɔ̀ɔp thɛɛn 36.4 To pay back.

troŋ 4.3 To be straight.

tua 27.5 Body. Classifier for animals, chairs, tables, and articles of clothing.

   tua kháw ʔeeŋ 40.b He himself, she herself.

tulaakhom 37.8 October.

tûu 27.3 Cupboard, closet.

   tûu yaam tamrùat 27.3 A police box.

tɯan 21.4 To remind, warn.

tɯ̀ɯn 37.10 To wake up.

wâa 14.3 A quotation signal. (See 14.1)

waan (See following entry.)

   mɯ̂a waan níi 28.8 Yesterday.

wǎan 8.4 To be sweet.

wâaŋ 21.3 To be unoccupied, free.

waay ʔem sii ʔee 30.b YMCA.

wan 17.4 Day.

wàt 38.2 A cold.

wǎy 26.1 To be physically able, to be up to.

weelaa 21.3 Time.

wîatnaam 14.2 Vietnam.

wǐi 33.4 A comb, to comb.

wítthayú? 9.3 Radio, wireless.

woŋwian 11.2 A traffic circle.

wua 6.5 Cattle, cow, bull.

yaa 27.5 Medicine.

yàa 30.c The negative imperative. Don't!

yâa 40.b Father's mother, grandmother.

yàak 18.3 To want.

yaam 27.3 A guard, watchman.

yàaŋ 18.3 Kind, sort, variety.

   yàaŋray, yaŋray, yaŋŋay, ŋay 18.3 In what way? How?

yaaw 3.5 To be long.

yáay 29.6 To relocate.

yaŋ 21.3 Still, yet.

yày 2.5 To be big.

yen 2.5 To be cold (of things), cool (of weather).

yɔ́ʔyɛ́ʔ 31.4 Plenty.

yɛ̂ɛk 6.3 To fork, separate.

yîam 28.4 To visit.

yîi 6.8 Two (only in the twenties).

yîihɔ̂ɔ 33.4 A brand, trademark, or make.

yím 34.3 To smile.

yǐŋ 7.3 Female (people only).

yókwén 36.4 To except.

yókyɔ̂ŋ 39.4 To honor, praise.

yuŋ 36.5 Mosquito.

yùu 3.3 To be some place.

yuusít 39.7 USIS. United States Information Service.

yuusɔ̂m 30.b USOM. United States Operations Mission.

yɯɯm 19.6 To borrow, lend.

yɯɯn 26.3 To stand.